So you really want

LATIN
PREP

BOOK 3

Theo Zinn M.A. (Oxon.)

Series Editor: Nicholas Oulton M.A. (Oxon.)

www.galorepark.co.uk

Independent Schools
Examinations Board

GALORE PARK

Published by ISEB Publications, and imprint of
Galore Park Publishing Ltd,
PO Box 96, Cranbrook TN17 4WS
www.galorepark.co.uk

Illustrations by Ian Douglass
Cover design by GKA Design, London WC2
Printed by The Bath Press

ISBN 10 1 902984 36 6
ISBN 13 978 1 902984 36 0

First published 2005

Also available:
Latin Prep Book 1   1902984153
Latin Prep Book 1 Answer Book   1902984161
Latin Prep Book 2   1902984412
Latin Prep Book 2 Answer Book   1902984420
Latin Prep Book 3 Answer Book   1902984439

Available in the series:
English
French
Spanish
Maths
Science

Contents

Chapter 1

Chapter 2

Chapter 3

Chapter 4

Chapter 5

Chapter 6

Chapter 7

Chapter 8

Chapter 9

Chapter 10

Vocabularies

Acknowledgements

Once again I am exceedingly grateful to Peter and Jackie Fennymore for the unfailing help they have given me in getting not only this book, but all three *Latin Preps* together, and I thank Rupert Fennymore again for his IT wizardry. I am immensely grateful as ever to Peter Brown, of Trinity College, Oxford for always rising to the occasion in helping me meticulously to solve as accurately as possible the most abstruse problems. I am also tremendously grateful to Nicholas Oulton for his customary kindness, patience and common sense which have helped to prune this last volume so creatively and to Bill Inge of Ashfold School who read the proofs with such care and attention to detail. Finally, my special thanks are due to Stephen Anderson of Winchester College for his many valuable and illuminating comments and suggestions. I need hardly say that all mistakes and infelicities in this volume are entirely my own.

Preface

I must admit that this tome is perhaps a trifle long-winded. I plead in defence the following: whereas I thought originally that, for example, indirect statement could be dealt with adequately in one or two well chosen sentences, no sooner had I embarked upon it than I saw how wrong I had been. Then again, there are so many things I thought I knew, which, on checking, raised unexpected complications. Take for example the forms and quantities of Greek names in their Latin versions – if you want a few sleepless nights! All I can do now is beg forebearance wherever my conclusions differ from those of any of my readers.

It is a great but sad relief to have brought this work to an end. I hope that those who read it will realise that Latin, if approached calmly, need not be impossibly difficult. And I hope that many of my readers will choose to take Latin as one of their subjects in the public exams that will soon be upon them, and that they will find themselves able to translate from and into Latin with ever greater confidence and pleasure.

I am especially thankful to those whose kindly comments on *Latin Prep* 1 and *Latin Prep* 2 have been relayed to me. They have contributed greatly to keeping me at it with *Latin Prep* 3 and I hope that they will like this volume too.

TLZ, September 2005

Chapter 1

Salvē, salvē, salvē

Greetings! Here we are again. Three times lucky! And indeed, we are truly lucky this third time round. There is such a wealth of wonderful things about to be spread before you in this volume, that I really envy you. So, let's start straight off with the relative pronoun quī, meaning 'who' or 'which'. We have often met quī in our stories and this is how it goes in full in the singular:

quī, quae, quod

quī, quae, quod = 'who, which'		
Singular		
	Masculine	**Feminine**	**Neuter**
Nominative	quī	quae	quod
Accusative	quem	quam	quod
Genitive	cuius	cuius	cuius
Dative	cui	cui	cui
Ablative	quō	quā	quō

Notes:
(i)   quī has no vocative.
(ii)   cuius was originally cuiius, both 'i's being consonantal, pronounced like 'y-y' in y-yes; it should still be pronounced this way; the 'u' before them is not long by nature and should not be pronounced as such (see *Latin Prep* 2, p.22 on huius).
(iii) The 'ui' of cui is a diphthong.
(iv)   Even as 'with me' (in my company) is mēcum, so 'with whom' or 'with which' is quōcum, quācum, quōcum.

What is a relative (other than an uncle or an aunt, etc.)? The relative is a pronoun; it picks up a noun in a clause, and creates a new subordinate clause of its own, telling us something new about that noun. This subordinate clause has, of course, a verb of its own. The noun picked up by the relative pronoun is called its 'antecedent', from the Latin, meaning 'that which comes before' (in sense). Thus:

   mīles, quī cum senibus pugnat, crūdēlis est.
   The soldier, who is fighting with the old men, is cruel.

The quī picks up the mīles out of the clause mīles crūdēlis est and tells us more about the mīles in its own relative clause, which here is tucked into the main clause (as it regularly is). This may sound more complicated than it need be, but for some reason people keep getting relative clauses wrong and this is why I think they should be mastered from the start.

So here comes a…

Solemn Rule

The relative pronoun must agree with its antecedent in its gender and its number, but not necessarily in its case.

Take, for example, the following sentence:

> mīles, quem vidētis, crūdēlis est.
> The soldier, whom you see, is cruel.

The quem agrees with mīles in being masculine, singular, but whereas mīles is nominative, quem is accusative. This is because quem is the object of the verb in the subordinate clause which it has created.

Again:

> puerum, cui dōna dedī, laudāvī.
> I praised the boy, to whom I gave gifts.

puerum is governed by laudāvī and cui is governed by dedī.

A relative clause, looking for its antecedent

Beware!

Unless the Latin antecedent is a living being, we must translate its relative by 'which', whatever its gender may be. For example:

> urbs, quam vidētis, pulchra est.
> The city, <u>which</u> you see, is beautiful.

> ventus, quī mūrum dēlēvit, saevus erat.
> The wind, <u>which</u> destroyed the wall, was savage.

Conversely, be <u>very</u> careful to translate the English word 'which' into the right gender in Latin. For example:

> The voice, which we hear, is the master's.
> vōx, <u>quam</u> audīmus, dominī est.

> The book, which I have read, is very good.
> liber, <u>quem</u> lēgī, optimus est.

Whom

I am a devoted supporter of the word 'whom', which is a rare survivor of the massacre of cases which has taken place in our language. It is used as the accusative singular and plural of 'who', i.e. 'the boy/boys <u>whom</u> I saw', and after prepositions, i.e. 'by whom', 'with whom', etc. Long may 'whom' continue to survive!

Exercise 1.1

Make up five English sentences, in each of which the relative pronoun appears in a different case! Note that you will have to translate these into Latin (see below).

Exercise 1.2

Translate your sentences from Exercise 1.1 into Latin:
Here are some useful new nouns:

annus, -ī, m. = year	opus, operis, n. = work, task*
custōs, custōdis, c. = guard	gēns, gentis, f. = race, nation, clan, family
labor, -ōris, m. = work, labour	somnus, -ī, m. = sleep

*i.e. something achieved by work; e.g. Beethoven's 5th Symphony, opus 67, is his 67th important work.

Exercise 1.3

Translate into English:

1. homō, quī fessus est, somnum cupit.
2. hoc opus, quod scrīpsistī, pulcherrimum est.
3. locus, in quō ambulāmus, sacer est.
4. custōs, cui gladium dedī, dormit.
5. urbem vidētis quam omnēs laudant.
6. mulierī, cuius fīlia pulchra est, multī dōna dedērunt.
7. puerum, quem pūnīvit magister, nōn amō.
8. hoc dōnum puellae dā quae multōs librōs lēgit.
9. vīdistīne iuvenem cuius pater in illō oppidō habitat?
10. mulierem cui pecūniam dedī laudāvī.

Exercise 1.4

Translate into Latin:

1. I do not like work which is difficult.
2. They live in a town which all men love.
3. Is there really a race which is more famous than ours?
4. Sulpicia is a woman whom all men praise.
5. We watched the guard to whom we had given food.
6. Where is the boy whose sister we saw yesterday?
7. Slaves do not love a master who drinks much wine.
8. I saw the old man whom the citizens feared.
9. The leader whose forces are present in the city will soon depart.
10. The sailor to whom we gave food and wine is sleeping.

Two voices are there

No, we're still sane (nearly), and haven't side-stepped by mistake into a Wordsworth sonnet. We're still dealing with things which are just as exciting, namely the weird and wonderful workings of verbs. You may not have realised it, but, until this very moment, we have only been handling verbs in their **active** voice. The word 'active' comes from a Latin verb, one of whose meanings is 'to do'. Active verbs are those which are doing something. But now, with much blowing of horns and trumpets, we are turning to the **passive** voice. 'Passive' comes from another Latin verb, which means 'suffering' or just 'having something done to one'. This is how the voices work:

(i)   mīles senem vulnerat.
       The soldier is wounding the old man.

Here, vulnerat is **active**, telling us what the
soldier is **doing**.

(ii)   senex vulnerātur.
       The old man is being wounded.

In this sentence, vulnerātur is **passive**, telling us
what the old man is **having done to him**.

amor and moneor

This is how the present passive of amō and
moneō goes:

Present passive of amō (1st conjugation)

1st person singular	amor	I am being loved
2nd person singular	amāris	you (sing.) are being loved
3rd person singular	amātur	he, she, it is being loved
1st person plural	amāmur	we are being loved
2nd person plural	amāminī	you (pl.) are being loved
3rd person plural	amantur	they are being loved

Present passive of moneō (2nd conjugation)

1st person singular	moneor	I am being warned, advised
2nd person singular	monēris	you (sing.) are being warned, advised
3rd person singular	monētur	he, she, it is being warned, advised
1st person plural	monēmur	we are being warned, advised
2nd person plural	monēminī	you (pl.) are being warned, advised
3rd person plural	monentur	they are being warned, advised

We can translate the passive by 'I am being loved' or 'I am loved' etc., depending on
the context.

I must admit that I love amāminī and monēminī.

Pronouncing -or

A note on '-or'. This should not be pronounced like English 'or', but as a short 'o' followed by the consonant 'r'. Similarly, '-ur' is not pronounced as in English 'fur', but as a short 'u' followed by consonantal 'r' (see *Latin Prep* 1, p.6).

Exercise 1.5

Write out in full the present passive of:

1. laudō
2. vocō
3. dēleō
4. teneō

5. aedificō
6. necō
7. videō
8. terreō

Translating 'by'

After a passive verb, 'by' is expressed by the ablative:

> The citizens are being killed **by arrows**.
> cīvēs **sagittīs** necantur.

<u>But</u>, when the noun in the ablative is a living being, it must be preceded by ā (ab before a vowel or an 'h'):

> The soldiers are being praised **by the inhabitants**.
> mīlitēs **ab incolīs** laudantur.

Exercise 1.6

Translate into English:

1. ā magistrō laudāmur.
2. nōnne ā rēge monēminī?
3. ab amīcō servāris.
4. ā dominō līberāminī.
5. cīvēs ā mīlitibus terrentur.
6. gladiī ab hostibus tenentur.
7. hastīs vulneror.
8. sagittīsne vulnerāminī?
9. nōnne puerī et puellae ā magistrō laudantur?
10. festīnāte, ancillae; ā rēgīnā vocāmur.

Exercise 1.7

Translate into Latin:

1. Swords are being held by you (pl.).
2. You (pl.) are being wounded by spears.
3. I am being praised by the teachers.
4. You (sing.) are being advised by your parents.
5. We are being set free by our masters.
6. Are you (pl.) really frightened by savage winds?
7. These cities are being occupied by slaves.
8. Many gifts are being given to us.
9. This city is being saved by a wall.
10. We are being watched by the old man.

Exercise 1.8

Translate into English:

1. miserī agricolae ā crūdēlibus nautīs terrentur.
2. magnus mūrus ab incolīs aedificātur.
3. illud oppidum ab hostibus oppugnātur.
4. magnum opus ā Quīntō, poētā, parātur.
5. quid ā puerō, quī in viā stat, portātur?
6. haec ancilla, quam vidēs, saepe ā rēgīnā vocātur.
7. aurum in templum ā servīs movētur.
8. puer, cuius soror ab omnibus laudātur, semper ā magistrō monētur.
9. puella, cui ā mātre pulchrum dōnum datur[1], laetissima est.
10. ventus, quō hic mūrus dēlētur, saevus est.

[1] Note that the 'a' of datur remains stubbornly short.

Exercise 1.9

Translate into Latin:

1. Why is a sword being held by this boy?
2. The town is being occupied by enemies.
3. The girl, whom her parents love, is being praised by the teachers.
4. Many citizens are being wounded by spears and swords.
5. The farmer, who was working in this field, is being greeted by his friend.
6. This slave, whose courage is well known, is being freed by his master.
7. The island, in which we used to live, is being destroyed by the sea.
8. The girl, with whom he was walking, is being watched by her sister.
9. The city, which we used to love, is being attacked by many sailors.
10. The wall, which you (pl.) see, is being built by these boys.

Exercise 1.10

And now for a story.

Read the following passage carefully and answer the questions on it:

The Story of Aeneas (1): Sinon Deceives the Trojans

1 Aenēās, <u>Veneris</u> fīlius, <u>hērōs</u> <u>Troiānus</u> erat, quī frūstrā urbem suam dēfendēbat. Graecī eam <u>per</u> decem annōs oppugnābant; sed tandem discessērunt. equum tamen <u>ligneum</u>, quī

5 maximus erat, <u>relīquērunt</u>; hominem quoque <u>relīquērunt</u> nōmine Sinōnem, quem <u>Troiānī</u> cēpērunt et ad rēgem Priamum dūxērunt. tum Sinōn haec verba dīxit: 'Graecus sum quī <u>invīsus</u> eram Graecīs; eī amīcum meum occīderant et

10 mē occīdere cupiēbant; eōs tamen effūgī.' rogāvit rēx Priamus Sinōnem: 'hic equus quem Graecī in <u>lītore</u> <u>relīquērunt</u>, quid <u>significat</u>?' respondit Sinōn: '<u>sī</u> eum <u>violābitis</u>, miserrimī eritis; dūcite igitur eum tūtum in urbem vestram;

15 nam sīc fēlīcissimī eritis.'

Venus, Veneris, f. = Venus, the
 goddess of love
hērōs, hērōis, m. = hero
Troiānus, -a, -um = Trojan
per (here) = throughout
ligneus, -a, -um = wooden
relinquō, -ere, relīquī, relictum
 = I leave (trans.)
invīsus, -a, -um = hateful
lītus, -oris, n. = sea-shore
significō, -āre, -āvī, -ātum =
 I mean, signify
sī = if
violō, -āre, -āvī, -ātum = I violate

1. Answer the following questions:
    (a) In line 1, who was Aeneas?
    (b) In lines 2-3, for how long had the Greeks been attacking Troy?
    (c) In lines 4-5, what did the Greeks leave behind after departing?
    (d) In lines 5-6, what else did they leave behind?
    (e) In lines 6-7, what did the Trojans do to Sinon after capturing him?
    (f) In line 7, who was Priam?
    (g) In lines 9-10, what did Sinon say the Greeks had done to his friend and wanted to do to him?
    (h) In lines 11-12, what did Priam ask Sinon?
    (i) In lines 13-14, what did Sinon advise the Trojans not to do to the horse?
    (j) In lines 14-15, what did he encourage them to do with it?

2. Translate the passage horsily.

3. Answer the following questions:
    (a) In line 2, to what noun does eam refer?
    (b) In line 3, what is the case of annōs and why is it in this case?
    (c) In line 4, in what case is quī and why is it in this case?
    (d) In line 5, what do you know about the use and meaning of quoque?
    (e) In line 6, in what case is quem and why is it in this case?
    (f) In line 7, how does the word Priamum relate to the word rēgem?
    (g) In line 9, what is the tense of occīderant?
    (h) In line 10, if, instead of 'I escaped', we wanted to say 'I shall escape', to what would we have to change effūgī?
    (i) In line 11, explain the case, number and gender of quem.
    (j) In line 15, what is the comparative of fēlīcissimus in all three genders?

quī, quae, quae

Let us now turn to the plural of quī, which goes as follows:

quī, quae, quae = 'who, which'		
Plural		
	Masculine	**Feminine**	**Neuter**
Nominative	quī	quae	quae
Accusative	quōs	quās	quae
Genitive	quōrum	quārum	quōrum
Dative	quibus	quibus	quibus
Ablative	quibus	quibus	quibus

Notes:
(i)   'With whom', 'with which', is quibuscum.
(ii) quīs is sometimes found for quibus.

Exercise 1.11

Translate into English:

1. mīlitēs, quōs vidētis, urbem oppugnant.
2. agricolās, quī in agrō labōrant, laudāmus.
3. puerī, quibuscum in oppidum ambulāvī, fessī sunt.
4. puellae, quārum mātrēs adsunt, laetae sunt.
5. servī, quibus dominus nihil dat, miserrimī sunt.
6. agricolās, ā quibus hic mūrus aedificātur, omnēs laudant.
7. urbēs, in quibus multī cīvēs habitant, magnae sunt.
8. incolae, quōs magnopere laudō, bonī et sapientēs sunt.
9. mūrī quibus servāmur altī sunt.
10. patrēs, quōrum fīliī bene labōrant, laetī sunt.

Exercise 1.12

Translate into Latin:

1. These boys are the sons of a citizen who is very brave.
2. The girls, who are singing in the temple, are very good.
3. Do not praise the soldiers by whom the inhabitants are being wounded.
4. We fear the savage winds, by which our walls are being destroyed.
5. The wars which are long are the worst.
6. Are not the girls whom we see Aulus' sisters?
7. The swords, which you (pl.) are holding, belong to[1] the soldiers.
8. The street, which is near the temple, is new.
9. Slaves to whom masters give money are happy.
10. The journey which we have made was difficult.

[1] Say 'are of'.

regor and audior

And now for the present passive of the 3rd and 4th conjugations:

Present passive of regō (3rd conjugation)		
1st person singular	regor	I am being ruled
2nd person singular	regeris	you (sing.) are being ruled
3rd person singular	regitur	he, she, it is being ruled
1st person plural	regimur	we are being ruled
2nd person plural	regiminī	you (pl.) are being ruled
3rd person plural	reguntur	they are being ruled

This, being 3rd (the awkward!) conjugation, is a little tricky; regor is fair enough, being regō + 'r' (with a short 'o'), and reguntur is easy, being regunt + 'ur'. regeris is a beast, and just has to be learnt; the other three parts add the usual passive endings to regi-.

Present passive of audiō (4th conjugation)

1st person singular	audior	I am being heard
2ndperson singular	audīris	you (sing.) are being heard
3rd person singular	audītur	he, she, it is being heard
1st person plural	audīmur	we are being heard
2nd person plural	audīminī	you (pl.) are being heard
3rd person plural	audiuntur	they are being heard

This is really well-behaved and gives us exactly what we would expect from the present active.

Exercise 1.13

Write out in full, as regor and audior are written out, the present passive of:

1. mittō
2. scrībō
3. pūniō
4. pōnō
5. inveniō
6. dēfendō

Exercise 1.14

Translate into English:

1. haec urbs ā fortibus cīvibus dēfenditur.
2. multum vīnum ā mīlitibus bibitur.
3. incolae in urbem dūcuntur.
4. num ab hostibus vincimur?
5. ā bonō et sapientī rēge regiminī.
6. urbēs mūrīs dēfenduntur.
7. num ā magistrō pūnīminī?
8. nōnne in urbem ā duce mitteris?
9. in agrōs ab agricolīs dūcor.
10. in proeliō multī gladiīs occīduntur.

Exercise 1.15

Translate into Latin:

1. The slaves are being led back into the town.
2. The soldiers are being killed by spears.
3. Beautiful gifts are being chosen by these women.
4. Many books are being written by this poet.
5. The big city is being defended by big walls.
6. What is being eaten by those little boys?
7. Gold is being found in the field.
8. We are being ruled by a wise queen.
9. Are you (pl.) really being led by youths?
10. Why are you (sing.) being punished by the teacher?

Note the difference, in English, between 'is being eaten' (expressing what is happening now) and 'is eaten' (expressing a state or a *general* fact). For example, 'this is eaten by the natives' expresses a general fact; 'he is loved by his mother' expresses a state or condition. 'His mother is being eaten by the natives', on the other hand, expresses the grisly reality of what is happening now, at this moment. In Latin this distinction does not exist: cōnsūmitur means 'it is eaten' or 'it is being eaten', depending on our old friend, the context.

We turn now to a very useful word indeed:

ipse, ipsa, ipsum

ipse, ipsa, ipsum = 'self'			
Singular			
	Masculine	**Feminine**	**Neuter**
Nominative	ipse	ipsa	ipsum
Accusative	ipsum	ipsam	ipsum
Genitive	ipsīus	ipsīus	ipsīus
Dative	ipsī	ipsī	ipsī
Ablative	ipsō	ipsā	ipsō

ipse means 'self'. It can be attached to a noun:

> rēgem ipsum vīdī.
> I saw the king himself.

> ipsī puellae dōnum dedī.
> I gave a gift to the girl herself.

It can also be attached to the **person** of a verb, thus:

ipse vēnit.
He himself came.

ipsa veniet.
She herself will come.

N.B. The second 'ī' of ipsīus is sometimes short.

Exercise 1.16

Attach the right form of ipse to the following words: e.g. urbem <u>ipsam</u>; with verbs, currit (fem. i.e. she runs) becomes <u>ipsa</u> currit = she herself runs.

1.   mulierem
2.   bellum (nom.)
3.   amīcī (gen.)
4.   colligitur (neut.)
5.   lūdō (fem.)

6.   puerīs
7.   magistrum
8.   audīris (fem.)
9.   dūcit (masc.)
10.   moneor (masc.)

videor

Here's a nice little thing:

videor literally means 'I am being seen' and comes to mean 'I seem' or 'I appear'. For example:

hostēs appropinquāre videntur.
The enemy seem (appear) to be approaching.

Note that videor is regularly followed by an infinitive.

Exercise 1.17

Translate into English:

1. ipse cibum cupere vidētur.
2. fēmina ipsa gladium tenet.
3. ipse in oppidum ībō.
4. hoc dōnum puellae ipsī dā!
5. hī puerī rēgis ipsīus fīliī sunt.
6. ipsa veniet.
7. bellum ipsum longissimum est.
8. rēgīnam ipsam vīdimus.
9. hic servus ā dominō ipsō vocātur.
10. dux ipse ā cīvibus amātur.

Exercise 1.18

Translate into Latin:

1. The wall itself defended the city.
2. They are being wounded by the soldier himself.
3. I gave a beautiful gift to the queen herself.
4. The king himself will rule those inhabitants.
5. The maid-servants are being called by the queen herself.
6. Give (pl.) these gifts to the boy himself.
7. The daughters of the woman herself are very beautiful.
8. We love the leader himself.
9. I myself (fem.) have not read this book.
10. He saw his wife herself.

capior

And let's round off our presents passive with:

Present passive of capiō (mixed conjugation)		
1st person singular	capior	I am being taken
2nd person singular	caperis	you (sing.) are being taken
3rd person singular	capitur	he, she, it is being taken
1st person plural	capimur	we are being taken
2nd person plural	capiminī	you (pl.) are being taken
3rd person plural	capiuntur	they are being taken

The 2nd person singular caperis is rather nasty, but the rest is pretty tame.

Exercise 1.19

Translate into English:

1. hae urbēs ā malīs hominibus capiuntur.
2. pulchrum dōnum ā puellā accipitur.
3. nōnne ab hostibus cōnspiciminī?
4. ā saevīs iuvenibus capimur.
5. in mare ā crūdēlibus cīvibus iacior.
6. 'ō aurum!' dīxit senex; 'ā mē magnopere cuperis.'
7. haec mulier ā mīlitibus capitur.
8. cūr ab hīs cīvibus capiminī?
9. hostēs subitō ā nōbīs cōnspiciuntur.
10. sagittae multae ad nōs iaciuntur.

Exercise 1.20

Translate into Latin:

1. Why is this girl being captured?
2. I am being caught sight of by the enemy.
3. These gifts are being desired both by the boys and by the girls.
4. They are being thrown into that river.
5. You (pl.) are being captured by the wicked men.
6. 'O money!' says the master; 'you are being received by good slaves.'*
7. What is desired by all men?
8. Many arrows are being thrown at the citizens.
9. Isn't the old man being caught sight of by us?
10. Why is much gold being received by you (pl.)?

*Let no one say that we don't come up with entertaining sentences!

Vast rule

Vast rule, to be totally and utterly remembered:

There is **NO** present passive of faciō.

End of vast rule.

Exercise 1.21

Here is the continuation of the story of Aeneas. This episode is written in the historic present tense.

The story of Aeneas (2): The fall of Troy

1   Troiānī equum <u>ligneum</u> in urbem dūcunt.
laetissimī sunt et dormiunt. dormit <u>Aenēās</u> et īn
somnō <u>Hector</u>, quī fīlius erat <u>Priamī</u> et dux ipse
Troiānōrum, vidētur eī adesse; sed mortuus est;
5   nam eum necāvit <u>Achillēs</u>. dīcere tamen vidētur
<u>Hector</u> haec verba: 'Aenēā, deae fīlī; tē fugere
iubeō; nam Graecī mīlitēs in equō <u>latēbant</u>, quī
nunc exiērunt; et urbs nostra ab eīs dēlētur. tū
eam servāre nōn poteris; nōlī igitur cum
10   hostibus pugnāre, sed deōrum nostrōrum
<u>imāginēs</u> cape et cum comitibus eās circum
maria multa portā; tandem dīs nostrīs patriam
novam inveniēs.' <u>Hector</u> <u>abīre</u> vidētur, sed
<u>Aenēās</u> <u>āmēns</u> in proelium ruit.

ligneus, -a, -um = wooden
Aenēās, -ae, m. = Aeneas (the vocative Aēnēā is a Greek form)
Hector, -is, m. = Hector (Priam's eldest son)
Priamus, -ī, m. = Priam (king of Troy)
Achillēs, -is, m. = Achilles (the greatest of the Greek heroes at Troy)
lateō, -ēre, latuī, no supine = I lie hid
imāgō, imāginis, f. (here) = statue
āmēns, āmentis = mindless, mad
abēo, -īre, -iī, -itum, = I go away

1.   Answer the following questions:
   (a) In line 2, why were the Trojans so happy? (See story on p.8)
   (b) In lines 3-4, what had Hector been in addition to being the son of Priam?
   (c) In lines 3-4, was Hector really present?
   (d) In line 4, what makes the answer to (c) more certain than ever?

(e) In lines 6-7, what did Hector tell Aeneas to do?

(f) In lines 7-9, what reason does Hector give for telling Aeneas to do this?

(g) In lines 9-10, what does Hector tell Aeneas not to do?

(h) In lines 10-11, what did Hector tell Aeneas to take?

(i) In line 11, did Hector tell Aeneas to go alone? Which words help you to answer this? Translate them.

(j) In lines 13-14, did Aeneas obey Hector's instructions? Explain your answer.

2. Translate the passage dreamily.

3. Answer the following questions:

(a) In line 2, if, instead of 'are sleeping' we wanted to say 'will sleep', what would we have to write instead of dormiunt?

(b) In line 4, what part of its verb is adesse? Translate it and mention and translate all other such parts in the passage.

(c) In line 5, what would necāvit be in the present passive?

(d) In line 6, what is the case of fīlī?

(e) In line 7, what is the case of quī? Translate it.

(f) In line 8, give the principal parts and meaning of the verb from which exiērunt comes.

(g) In line 9, what part of what verb is poteris? What does it mean?

(h) In line 9, what does igitur mean? What should we remember about it, when using it?

(i) In line 12, what is the case of maria here? How do you know this?

(j) In line 13, put inveniēs into the pluperfect.

This story is told in the *Aeneid*, the great epic poem by P. Vergilius Marō (70-19 BC), whom we call Virgil.

Exercise 1.22

Of what English words do the following Latin words remind you? Explain the connexion between the Latin words and the English words you have chosen.

1. annus
2. somnus (if you can't sleep, what are you suffering from?)
3. custōs
4. hōra (not too difficult, I hope)
5. labor (this isn't too challenging, either)

amābar

Believe it or not, there's still something pretty big to come in here, but it's really a gentle giant, because it happens to be ridiculously easy. It is the imperfect passive. The endings are the same for all conjugations. So here it is from amō:

Imperfect passive of amō (1st conjugation)

1st person singular	amābar	I was being loved
2nd person singular	amābāris	you (sing.) were being loved
3rd person singular	amābātur	he, she, it was being loved
1st person plural	amābāmur	we were being loved
2nd person plural	amābāminī	you (pl.) were being loved
3rd person plural	amābantur	they were being loved

From moneō, regō, audiō, and capiō we have monēbar, regēbar, audiēbar and capiēbar etc.

N.B. The '-ar' in amābar should not be pronounced as in English 'far' but as a short 'a' followed by consonantal 'r'.

Another vast rule

Here comes another vast rule. Forget it at your peril!

There is **NO** imperfect passive of faciō!

End of another vast rule.

Exercise 1.23

Translate into English:

1. vīnum ā mīlitibus bibēbātur.
2. puerī malī pūniēbantur.
3. sagittīs vulnerābar.
4. ā crūdēlī rēge regēbāminī.
5. nōnne ā magistrō monēbāris?
6. aurum ā nautīs capiēbātur.
7. num ab hostibus vincēbāmur?
8. quid hīc movēbātur?
9. illud oppidum ab hostibus oppugnābātur.
10. sagittae in urbem iaciēbantur.

Exercise 1.24

Translate into Latin:

1. Spears were being thrown into the temple.
2. The food was being eaten by the boys.
3. You (sing.) were being carried by the slaves.
4. We were being led by the best leader.
5. You (pl.) were being wounded by spears.
6. We were not being overcome by the enemy.
7. I was being warned by my father.
8. A few inhabitants were being captured by the soldiers.
9. A large ship was being moved by the sailors.
10. The boys and girls were being heard by the teacher.

Exercise 1.25

Translate into Latin:

1. Good maid-servants love the beautiful queen.
2. The brave leaders were leading the tired soldiers.
3. The bad young man was wounding the wretched old man with[1] a sword.
4. All the girls listen to the wise teacher.
5. The little boys saw the strong sailors.
6. The enemy were attacking the town with[1] arrows.
7. We called the noble citizens.
8. You (sing.) have eaten my food.
9. You (pl.) have eaten our food.
10. I am reading a huge book.

[1] Use the ablative alone, omitting 'with'. Note that cum (+ abl.) is used when 'with' means 'together with'. When 'with' means 'by means of', use the ablative alone.

Vocabulary 1

As in *Latin Prep* Books 1 and 2, we shall end each chapter with a list of new words. Make sure you collect these words chapter by chapter and engrave them on your heart.

Vocabulary 1
annus, -ī, m. = year
tēlum, -ī, n. = missile, weapon, spear
hōra, -ae, f. = hour
prīnceps, prīncipis, m. = chief, prince, emperor
ipse, ipsa, ipsum = self
superbus, -a, -um = proud
crēdō, -ere, crēdidī, crēditum (+ dat.) = I believe
petō, -ere, petīvī, petītum = I seek
relinquō, -ere, relīquī, relictum = I leave (trans.)

And now, who's spoiling for Chapter Two?

Chapter 2

ipsī, ipsae, ipsa

Let's start with the plural of ipse:

ipsī, ipsae, ipsa = 'selves'			
Plural			
	Masculine	**Feminine**	**Neuter**
Nominative	ipsī	ipsae	ipsa
Accusative	ipsōs	ipsās	ipsa
Genitive	ipsōrum	ipsārum	ipsōrum
Dative	ipsīs	ipsīs	ipsīs
Ablative	ipsīs	ipsīs	ipsīs

Exercise 2.1

Add the form of ipse which would be required when it is attached to the following nouns:

1. rēgum
2. rēgīnae (gen.)
3. amīcōs
4. proelia (nom.)
5. dominī (gen.)
6. urbs
7. ducī
8. ancillīs (dat.)
9. magistrī (nom.)
10. bellum (acc.)

Moods – indicative, imperative, subjunctive

And here is something supremely and stupendously exciting. It is about a feature of Latin verbs, which lies at the very heart of the language, whereas in modern English it is hardly ever talked of at all. We discovered recently that there are two voices in Latin, only one of which we had been using. And now we shall discover that there are three moods in Latin, and that we have only been using two of them, namely the indicative mood and the imperative.

1. The indicative is used to express a fact. For example:

   puerī mūrum aedificant.
   The boys are building a wall.

   Here we are told something which boys are actually doing as a fact.

2. The imperative mood issues a command:

    puerī, audīte mē!
    Boys, hear me!

3. The third mood is called
    the subjunctive. The
    subjunctive, generally
    preceded by a suitable
    Latin word, is used to
    express something that is
    going on in the mind,
    such as a purpose, a fear,
    a request, a wish etc.

Indicative,   imperative,   subjunctive

Before going any further, let us see how to form a subjunctive. There are present, imperfect, perfect and pluperfect subjunctives, but we are concentrating on the imperfect subjunctive, because, you may be a little disappointed to discover, it is almost ridiculously easy to form. Here is the imperfect subjunctive of amō, and no doubt you will see for yourself how it is formed.

The imperfect subjunctive

Imperfect subjunctive of amō (1st conjugation)

1st person singular	amārem
2nd person singular	amārēs
3rd person singular	amāret
1st person plural	amārēmus
2nd person plural	amārētis
3rd person plural	amārent

Yes! You've spotted it! All you have to do is to add the suitable endings to the present infinitive – and there you are! Hey presto! It's as easy as falling off a log.
(Incidentally, I've never tried to do this, and I don't advise anyone to try it. Nor do I see why it should be all that easy.)

Note that I have not given any translation of the imperfect subjunctive. This is because it is used in so many ways that any particular translation would be misleading. We shall very soon be using the imperfect subjunctive, but meanwhile let us perfect our ability to form it.

Exercise 2.2

1. The imperfect subjunctive of moneō begins monērem. Write out the imperfect subjunctive of moneō in full.

2. Write out in full the imperfect subjunctive of:

   (a) regō   (d) ambulō   (g) pūniō
   (b) audiō   (e) iaciō   (h) rogō
   (c) capiō   (f) bibō

Purpose clauses

We have told you how to form a subjunctive, but not yet how to use it, or even what it means. Well, we are now going to do a Purpose (or Final) Clause; apologies, if this still sounds a bit like a conjuring trick. So, here goes!

In English, purpose is regularly expressed by the infinitive, frequently preceded by 'in order'. The infinitive is hardly ever used in this way in Latin, and it is considered a howler of the first order to use it to express purpose. In Latin, we use ut, followed by the subjunctive. Thus:

> He was coming to the city (in order) to see his mother.
> ut mātrem vidēret in urbem veniēbat.

Sequence of tenses

Before we begin to practise these purpose clauses, we need to learn something known as the sequence of tenses. Present, future and true perfect tenses are called **primary**. Imperfect, pluperfect and the simple past (i.e. when amāvī means 'I loved' rather than 'I have loved') are called **historic**. There is a very strict rule that, where the main verb is in a primary tense, the subjunctive following it must also be in a primary tense; and that where the main verb is in a historic tense, the subjunctive following it must also be in a historic tense.

e.g. mīlitēs, ut urbem servārent, festīnāvērunt.
    The soldiers **hurried** in order to save the city.

Note that this means 'they hurried'; it does <u>not</u> mean 'they have hurried'.

The true perfect is not historic, because its prime function is to tell us about something which is the case *now*, albeit as a result of something past.

e.g. 'I have read *Hamlet*' means that I am **now** a person who read *Hamlet* at some point in the past.

Didn't I tell you that we are entering deep waters?

nē

The negative of ut is nē = 'in order not to'; this follows exactly the same rules as ut does.

e.g.   mulierēs, nē mortuōs vidērent, discessērunt.
      The women departed in order not to see the dead.

It is sometimes translated by 'lest':

e.g.   The women departed lest they should see the dead.

Exercise 2.3

Translate into English:

1.   agricolae, ut equōs līberārent, in agrōs cucurrerant.
2.   in urbem, nē sōlus essem[1], vēnī.
3.   ut hostēs effugerēmus, ex urbe quam celerrimē exiimus.
4.   puellae semper, ut sapientēs essent, magistrum audiēbant.
5.   mūrōs, ut oppidum dēfenderent, aedificāvērunt.
6.   urbem, ut eam occupārētis, sagittīs oppugnābātis.
7.   nōnne hunc librum, nē miser essēs, lēgistī?
8.   per mare, ut ad īnsulam advenīrent, nāvigāvērunt.
9.   puerī, ut magna et valida corpora habērent, bonum cibum cōnsūmēbant.
10. mīlitēs, nē multum vīnum biberent, statim dormīverant.

[1]The imperfect subjunctive of sum is essem, coming dutifully from the infinitive esse.

Exercise 2.4

Translate into Latin:

1.   We hurried to the river in order to see the ships.
2.   The boys ate much food in order to be strong.
3.   Did you (sing.) stand near the teacher in order to hear him?
4.   The enemy were attacking the city in order to frighten the citizens.
5.   That young man was going to the mountains in order to find gold.
6.   The old men stayed in the city lest they should be in danger.
7.   Who went into the fields in order to build the wall?
8.   We were working for a long time in order to make a gift for you.
9.   The women remained in the temple in order not to fight.
10. Did you (pl.) hurry to the field in order to watch the battle?

Exercise 2.5

Read the following passage carefully, and answer the questions on it:

The story of Aeneas (3): Aeneas comes to his senses

1   Aenēās id, quod Hector eum facere iusserat,
     nōn faciēbat, sed prō patriā frūstrā pugnābat
     et, ut eam servāret, <u>terribilia</u> perīcula <u>āmēns</u>
     <u>subībat</u>; <u>paene</u> mortuus erat; sed tandem
5   māter eum ipsa discēdere iussit; et ipse patrem
     in <u>tergō</u> portāvit et in <u>collō</u> <u>imāginēs</u> deōrum et
     dextrā fīlium tenēbat et ad mare effūgit; ibi in
     <u>lītore</u> comitēs, virōs, mulierēs, puerōs, puellās
     invēnit et cum eīs montēs petīvit et ibi iter
10   longissimum parāvit; nam ut novam patriam
     invenīret <u>procul</u> nāvigāre <u>dēbuit</u>.

terribilis, -e = terrible
āmēns, āmentis = mindless, mad
subeō, subīre, subiī, subitum = I undergo
paene = almost
tergum, -ī, n. = back
collum, -ī, n. = neck
imāgō, imāginis, f. (here) = small statue
dextra, -ae, f. = right hand
lītus, -oris, n. = sea-shore
procul = far
dēbeō, -ēre, -uī, -itum = I must, have to

1.   Answer the following questions:

    (a) id...iusserat (line 1); what had this been (see page 16)?
    (b) In line 2, why was Aeneas' activity frūstrā (see page 16)?
    (c) In lines 3-4, why was it wrong for Aeneas to risk his life (see page 16)?
    (d) ipse...portāvit (line 5-6); what do we learn about Aeneas' father from these words?
    (e) Look at line 7. What do we learn about the geography of Troy from this line?
    (f) And what do we learn from line 9?
    (g) In line 9, petīvit literally means, 'he sought'. Suggest a better translation for it here.
    (h) In lines 10-11, why did Aeneas have to sail? (See p.16)

2.   Translate the passage geographically.

3.   Answer the following questions:
    (a) In line 1, what tense of what verb is iusserat? Give its principal parts and meaning.
    (b) faciēbat (line 2); if, instead of 'he was doing' we had wanted to say 'he will do', to what would we have had to change faciēbat?
    (c) Mention all the prepositions in the passage together with their nouns or pronouns and translate them.
    (d) In line 5, what part of its verb is discēdere? Give its principal parts and meaning.
    (e) In line 6, what is the case and number of deōrum? From what noun does it come?
    (f) In line 8, how do virōs...puellās relate to comitēs?
    (g) In line 11, what part of what verb is invenīret?
    (h) In line 11, why would it be wrong to translate dēbuit 'he has had to' here?

In the passage we have just done, we can see why Virgil, held by most to be the greatest of the Roman poets, in his *Aeneid*, calls Aeneas outstanding for his piety. Unfortunately, the English word 'piety' has suffered from its association with a certain type of Victorian hypocrisy, which involved being good on Sunday but far from good during the rest of the week. The adjective pius in Latin has no such overtones. It means 'truly good'. The noun pietās has not only produced our word 'piety' but also 'pity'. Certainly, pity or compassion was a very prominent part of Aeneas' character.

Let us leave Aeneas here for the time being.

More about place

Let's turn now to something completely different, namely the subject of 'place'.
We have already touched on this subject, but now we shall tackle it head on.

When we talk about 'place', we generally talk about 'to' a place, or 'in', 'on' or 'from' a place.

(i)   To express 'to' a place the accusative case is used, nearly always preceded by the prepositions ad or in; (in + accusative strictly means 'into'; ad + accusative means 'to' but not necessarily 'into'.)

    ad mūrum vēnit.
    He came to the wall

    in urbem vēnit.
    He came into the city.

Note, though, that ad + accusative quite often means 'at'.

(ii)   To express 'in' or 'on' a place the ablative is used, generally preceded by in:
    mīlitēs in oppidō pugnant.
    The soldiers are fighting in the town.

cīvēs in mūrō stant.
The citizens are standing on the wall.

(iii) To express 'from' a place, the ablative is used, generally preceded by ex/ē, ā
(āb before a vowel or an 'h'), or dē. Thus:

senēs ex[1] templō discessērunt.
The old men departed from the temple.

nautae ab īnsulā nāvigābant.
The sailors were sailing from the island.

puerī dē monte cucurrērunt.
The boys ran down from the mountain.

[1]Note that ex/ē really means 'out of', while ā/ab merely means 'away from'. We have
certainly mentioned these prepositions and the cases that follow them in *Latin Prep*
Books 1 and 2. What we should concentrate on here is the basic meanings of the
accusative and ablative cases; for example, the accusative (among other things)
involves 'motion to' which often comes to mean 'against'. The ablative takes its name
from a verb meaning 'to take away *from*', but in the process of time some old cases
disappeared into it without trace, and it came to express all their different meanings.
And so it became an amalgam of unconnected meanings, and is the most Latin of cases!

N.B. In English 'to' generally does duty for in *and* for ad. We do not usually say 'I went
<u>into</u> the town', unless 'into' needs to be particularly stressed. Similarly, we do not usually
distinguish between 'out of' and 'away from', unless a particular stress is required.
Generally a simple 'from' will suffice. When translating into Latin, we should choose our
prepositions carefully, being guided by our old friend, common-sense. If the English is
totally ambiguous, then we are free to interpret it as we wish and to translate accordingly.

Exercise 2.6

Translate into English:

1.   puerī ex agrīs discessērunt.
2.   nōs omnēs in urbem festīnāmus.
3.   multī mēcum ab īnsulā nāvigābunt.
4.   saevī ventī dē caelō vēnērunt.
5.   amīcī nostrī in templō cantant.
6.   puellae, cūr in viā lūditis?
7.   mulierēs ad flūmen currēbant.
8.   cīvēs, in mūrō stetistis.
9.   ad oppidum ambulābunt.
10.   crās ad montēs ībō.

Exercise 2.7

Translate into Latin:

1. Why are you hurrying to the town?
2. Tomorrow, these boys will sing in the temple.
3. The horses have run down from the mountain.
4. We were going from the wall of the city to the fields.
5. The girls walked from the town to the sea.
6. The farmers are working in the fields.
7. Why are the little boys standing on the wall?
8. Did you (pl.) come to the city yesterday?
9. He will go to the temple tomorrow.
10. The soldiers will soon depart from the city.

A very, very solemn rule!

At all costs take the following totally to heart. You cannot, in Latin, describe a noun by a prepositional phrase. At first sight this does not sound so very important. In fact it just sounds rather boringly obscure; so let me explain what it means!

'In the moon' is a prepositional phrase; we talk about 'the man in the moon', using this phrase to describe the man. Which man are we talking about? We are talking about the man *in the moon*. Even assuming that we knew the Latin for 'moon' (lūna, lūnae, f.), we could not say:

> We are watching the man in the moon.

for it would constitute a howler of the first order plus!

Instead of the above, we should write:

> We are watching the man *who is* in the moon.
> hominem, quī in lūnā est, spectāmus.

End of very, very solemn rule!

Exercise 2.8

Translate into Latin:

1. The boys, who are playing in the field, can see the women in the town.
2. The girls in the temple are watching the walls.
3. The men in the ships received better gifts than those who remained on land.
4. They did not believe the citizens in the street.
5. We love all the words in the book.
6. The slaves in the island love their master.
7. Why do you (sing.) praise the old men in the city?
8. Were you (pl.) really being wounded by the young men on the wall?

Here are a few useful new words:

adeō, adīre, adiī, aditum = I approach[1]
cōgō, -ere, coēgī, coāctum = I force[2]
custōdiō, -īre, -īvī, -ītum = I guard
pellō, -ere, pepulī, pulsum = I drive
nec/neque = neither, nor, and ... not
lentē = slowly

[1] adeō is yet another compound of eō, meaning literally 'I go to'.
[2] cōgō is used thus:

eum discēdere coēgī.
I forced him to depart.

Participles

And now, here's something entirely new, namely participles. Participles are verbal adjectives; there are lots of these in English, but in Latin there are only three:

(i) The present participle (active)

(ii) The past participle (passive)

(iii) The future participle (active)

For the moment we shall deal only with the present participle.

The present participle of amō is amāns, and it declines like ingēns; it means 'loving'.

Another pitfall!

You may have noticed by now that all this holding forth by me is made necessary more by English oddities and ambiguities than by Latin ones. And here English is at it again. The English verbal form ending in '-ing' has two completely different meanings:

It can be a participle:

> He walked to the river, singing.
> I heard him singing.

In these examples the word 'singing' tells us something about him; it describes him as *doing* something.

Or it can be a verbal noun:

> Singing is most enjoyable.
> He loves singing.

In these examples 'singing' is a verbal noun expressing an act, namely (here) the act of singing. This has nothing whatever to do with participles.

To return to amāns, this form is produced in the 1st, 2nd and 3rd conjugations by chopping off the '-re' of the infinitive and replacing it by '-ns'. In the mixed (3½) and 4th conjugations, the 'i' of the present tense is retained, producing, for example, audiēns and capiēns.

	Singular			Plural		
	M.	F.	N.	M.	F.	N.
Nom.	amāns	amāns	amāns	amantēs	amantēs	amantia
Acc.	amantem	amantem	amāns	amantēs	amantēs	amantia

How to use the present participles

There is nothing very mysterious about this. Simply remember that a participle is an adjective and all will be well.

> He walked to the town singing.
> ad oppidum cantāns ambulāvit.

> I heard him singing.
> eum cantantem audīvī.

Exercise 2.9

Translate into English:

1. multōs mīlitēs ab urbe discēdentēs vīdī.
2. puer ille caelum spectāns laetus est.
3. hoc templum in agrō stāns intrāte.
4. quis cīvēs ad urbem currentēs custōdit?
5. in mūrō stābat omnēs, quī inībant, exīre cōgēns.
6. mihi mala verba dīxit rīdēns.
7. incolās illōs multum vīnum bibentēs nōn laudō.
8. cīvēs in urbe dormientēs tūtī nōn erant.
9. ducem multa bene facientem amāmus.
10. hominēs pessimī aurum nostrum omne capientēs rīdēbant.

N.B. We can often best translate a participle by a clause. Thus in Q.3 above, stāns = 'which stands'.

Exercise 2.10

Translate into Latin.

1. We see the old man carrying food.
2. Quintus, the poet, lives in this city, writing many books.
3. The cruel soldiers were being watched by us wounding many inhabitants.
4. The enemy were not able to overcome the young men defending our city.
5. All men feared the Romans waging war.
6. I saw and heard the citizens drinking wine.
7. We praised the master as he gave food to his slaves.
8. I made many journeys through the mountains, seeking gold.
9. Why did you (pl.) punish him doing nothing?
10. Do you (sing.) really praise the soldiers sleeping in our city?

More purpose clauses

Here are some slightly different purpose clauses. Often, a purpose clause cannot be translated into English by 'to'. For example dōna puerīs, ut laetī essent, dedimus could not be correctly translated, 'we gave presents to the boys, to be happy'. Rather, we would have to say 'we gave presents to the boys, **in order that** they might be happy'.

Exercise 2.11

Translate into English:

1. dux mīlitēs, ut cīvēs tūtī essent, fortiter pugnāre iussit.
2. dominus servōs, ut omnēs eōs laudārent, bene labōrāre coēgit.
3. rēx cīvēs, ut sē bene gererent[1], bene rēxit.
4. puerī et puellae, ut magister vōs laudāret, bene labōrāvistis.
5. malī iuvenēs, nē dormīre possēmus, clāmābant.
6. mīlitēs, ut cīvēs laetī essent, sē bene gerēbant.
7. nē nōs hostēs vincerent, multōs mīlitēs habēre cupiēbāmus.
8. num haec, ut hostēs nōs vincerent, fēcistis?
9. nōnne parentēs fīliīs et fīliābus, ut sapientēs essent, bonum magistrum dedērunt?
10. magister puerōs nē sē male[2] gererent pūniēbat.

[1]sē gerere = to behave.
[2]male, the adverb of malus, has a short 'e'.

Exercise 2.12

Translate into Latin:

1. I gave the boy a spear in order that he might give it to the soldier.
2. The teacher used to praise the boys and girls in order that they might work well.
3. Our soldiers fought bravely in order that the enemy might flee.
4. The king remained in the city with the citizens in order that they should not be afraid.
5. They built a high wall in order that the city might be safe.
6. The queen was calling her maid-servants in a loud[1] voice in order that they might come quickly.
7. The leader ordered the soldiers to depart lest they should kill the citizens.
8. The farmers gave the horses much food in order that they might have strong bodies.
9. The young men fought bravely lest the enemy should capture the women.
10. The Romans sent help to their allies, in order that they might fight bravely.

[1]For 'loud' say 'big'.

Yet more about place

Here are some very important additional things about place. Let's start with (yes, you've guessed it) **another solemn rule:**

> When one is dealing with towns and small islands (by name), prepositions of place are omitted.

Thus:

He came to Rome.
Rōmam vēnit.

Note the absence of ad or in before Rōmam.

Similarly 'to Corinth' (Corinthus, -ī, f.), is simply Corinthum; 'to Athens' (Athēnae, -ārum, f. pl.) is Athēnās; 'to Carthage' (Carthāgō, Carthāginis, f.) is Carthāginem.

'From' is also straighforward enough. We simply use the ablative alone without ab or ex. Thus:

Rōmā discessit.
He departed from Rome.

Corinthō festīnāvī.
I hurried from Corinth.

Carthāgine fūgit.
He fled from Carthage.

Incidentally, if the prepositions ad (+ acc.) and ā, ab (+ abl.) *are* found with towns and small islands, they should be translated 'to/from the neighbourhood of' the place in question.

The locative case

So, what's all the fuss about? It's all been pretty straighforward so far. So far! And there's the rub!

It's when we come to 'in' or 'at' that the fun starts. There was originally a locative case; this, coming from locus = 'place', tells one <u>where</u> someone or something is.

1. With singular names of the first and second declensions, the locative is represented by the genitive form. Thus:

    Rōmae = at Rome (from Rōma, -ae, f.)
    Corinthī = at Corinth (from Corinthus, -ī, f.)
    Tarentī = at Tarentum (from Tarentum, -ī, n.)

2. When dealing with singular nouns of the 3rd declension, the locative is represented by the ablative form. Thus:

Carthāgine = at Carthage (from Carthāgō, -inis, f.)

3. When we are dealing with a **plural** name of any declension, such as Athēnae (= Athens) or Puteolī (= Puteoli), the locative is represented by the ablative plural. Thus:

Athēnīs = at Athens (from Athēnae, -ārum, f. pl.)
Puteolīs = at Puteoli (from Puteolī, -ōrum, m. pl.)
Gādibus = at Gades (from Gādēs, -ium, f. pl., the present-day Cadiz)

You will immediately have noticed that these ablatives could also mean 'from'. Here, as so often, we can only be guided by the context. Remember 'common-sense'?

Exercise 2.13

Translate into English:

1. Baiīs[1] Rōmam lentē ambulābāmus.
2. multī poētae Athēnīs longōs librōs scrīpsērunt.
3. Rōmānī saepe Baiās ībant.
4. multī Puteolīs[2] habitāre cupiēbant.
5. Graecī ā Graeciā Troiam nāvigāvērunt.
6. multī Carthāgine erant quī Rōmam dēlēre cupiēbant.
7. num mēcum Gādibus longum iter faciēs Athēnās?
8. Spartae[3] fortissimī virī habitābant.
9. quis mēcum Cūmās[4] ambulābit?
10. quis mēcum Cūmīs Rōmam redībit?

[1] Baiae was a popular resort visited by wealthy Romans.
[2] So was Puteoli.
[3] Sparta was a very famous Greek city in the Peloponnese (S. Greece).
[4] Cumae was an ancient Italian city.

Exercise 2.14

Translate into Latin:

1. Once upon a time, many people lived at Byzantium[1].
2. Who will return to Troy with us from Corinth?
3. Who used to live at Cumae[2]?
4. They made a journey from Sparta to Athens.
5. Many poets used to live in Rome.
6. Nobody wishes to depart from Baiae.

7. Messengers came from Gades to Carthage.
8. I lived in London[3] for a long time.
9. Will you (pl.) go from Gades to Gela[4]?
10. They remained in Gades for a long time.

Notes:

[1] Byzantium was a Greek city, eventually part of the Roman Empire. The Emperor Constantine the Great changed its name to Cōnstantīnopolis (city of Constantine), i.e. Constantinople, and it became the centre of a great Empire. The city is now named Istanbul.

[2] The answer to this is the Sibyl, a famous prophetess.

[3] The Latin for London is Londīnium, -iī, n.

[4] Gela was a Greek city in Sicily.

Exercise 2.15

Read the following passage carefully, and answer the questions on it:

The story of Philemon and Baucis

1 erat ōlim in Phrygiā <u>regiō</u> in quā habitābant
   hominēs pessimī. hī, <u>advenās</u> fessōs, sibi
   appropinquantēs et auxilium cupientēs, ā suīs
   <u>iānuīs</u> <u>expellēbant</u>. ad hanc ōlim <u>regiōnem</u>
5 advēnērunt Iuppiter et Mercurius <u>nātūram</u> suam
   <u>dīvīnam</u> <u>tegentēs</u>, et ab omnibus <u>expellēbantur</u>:
   erant igitur īrātissimī; sed tandem ad minimum
   <u>tugurium</u> advēnērunt; ibi nec dominus erat nec
   servus, sed sōlī Philēmōn senex et uxor eius
10 Baucis, <u>aequālis</u>; ibi <u>diūtissimē</u> <u>ūnā</u> habitāverant
   et, quamquam <u>pauperrimī</u> erant, laetissimī fuērunt.

regiō, regiōnis, f. = region
advena, -ae, c. = stranger
iānua, -ae, f. = door
expellō, -ere, expulī, expulsum =
   I drive away
nātūra, -ae, f. = nature
dīvīnus, -a, -um = divine
tegō, -ere, tēxī, tēctum (here) =
   I conceal
tugurium, -iī, n. = hut
aequālis, -e = of the same age
diūtissimē = for a very long time
ūnā = together
pauperrimus, -a, -um = very poor

Notes:
(i)   Phrygia (line 1) was a country in Asia Minor.
(ii)   Iuppiter (line 5) was Jupiter, the king of the gods.
(iii)   Mercurius (Mercury) (line 5) was the Roman equivalent of the Greek Hermes, the messenger of the gods.

1.   Answer the following questions:

(a) In lines 1-2, what sort of people lived in this part of Phrygia?
(b) In lines 2-4, how did these people behave to strangers?
(c) In line 3, why did these strangers approach them?
(d) In lines 5-6, how did Jupiter and Mercury appear when they entered this region?
(e) In line 7, why were they īrātissimī?
(f) In lines 7-8, to what place did they finally come?
(g) In line 7, which word shows that Philemon and Baucis were very poor?
(h) In lines 8-10, which word tells us whether anyone except Philemon and Baucis lived in the hut?
(i) In line 10, which word shows us that Baucis, as well as Philemon, was no longer young?
(j) In line 11, did their poverty upset Philemon and Baucis? Explain your answer.

2.   Translate the passage happily.

3.   Answer the following questions:

(a) hominēs pessimī (line 2) = very bad men. What would be the Latin for (i) bad men; and (ii) worse men?
(b) Give the principal parts and meaning of cupiō (line 3).
(c) expellēbant (line 4); put this verb into the perfect tense.
(d) In line 6, what part of its verb is tegentēs? Translate it. Mention and translate any other examples of this part in this passage.
(e) igitur (line 7); translate this word and mention anything you know about its position in its clause or sentence.
(f) In line 7, how does īrātissimī relate to īrātus?
(g) In line 8, if we wished to say 'they will arrive' instead of 'they arrived', to what would we have to change advēnērunt?
(h) sōlī (line 9); what is the genitive singular of this word?
(i) In line 10, what is the tense of habitāverant?
(j) quamquam...erant (line 11); say what kind of a clause this is, and explain its meaning. (See *Latin Prep* 2, p.52)

N.B. expellō is a compound of pellō: as a compound, it regularly loses the reduplication in the perfect tense.

Exercise 2.16

Of what English words do the following Latin words remind you? Explain the connexion between the English words you have chosen and the Latin words:

1. crēdō
2. petō
3. pellō (try a compound! Nay, three compounds, if not more!)
4. relinquō
5. crās (see if you can track down the splendid English compound verb, which means 'I leave things till tomorrow'.)

Exercise 2.17

Translate into Latin:

1. The wicked soldiers were seeking the brave citizens.
2. The noble young men have saved the wretched boys.
3. We are defending the women with swords.
4. The big boys have strong bodies.
5. The cruel enemy attacked our city with arrows.
6. A high temple was being built by the noble citizens.
7. The good girls are being praised by their masters.
8. Four shields are being held by these soldiers.
9. Didn't you (sing.) make a very long journey, in order to see your sister?
10. You (pl.) were being sought by your friends.

Vocabulary 2

Vocabulary 2
adeō, -īre, adiī, aditum[1] = I approach (lit. I go to)
conveniō[2], -īre, convēnī, conventum = I meet
custōdiō, -īre, -īvī, -ītum = I guard
labor, -ōris, m. = work, labour
nox, noctis, f. = night
praemium, -iī, n. = reward
tempestās, tempestātis, f. = a storm
aut = or
intereā = meanwhile
paene = almost

[1] Compound of eō
[2] Compound of veniō. Note that cum becomes con in compounds

And there goes Chapter 2 at long last!

Chapter 3

Future Passive

Let's start this chapter with the future passive. This form is pretty well-behaved; here are the 1st and 2nd conjugations in the future passive:

Future passive of amō: amābor = 'I shall be loved'

1st person singular	amābor	I shall be loved
2nd person singular	amāberis	you (sing.) will be loved
3rd person singular	amābitur	he, she, it will be loved
1st person plural	amābimur	we shall be loved
2nd person plural	amābiminī	you (pl.) will be loved
3rd person plural	amābuntur	they will be loved

The second person singular is the only part here that attempts to be unpredictable, albeit rather half-heartedly. The other parts pose no real problem.

And here is the future passive of moneō, which behaves in the same way, changing the long 'ā' of amābor to a long 'ē':

Future passive of moneō: monēbor = 'I shall be warned, advised'

1st person singular	monēbor	I shall be warned, advised
2nd person singular	monēberis	you (sing.) will be warned, advised
3rd person singular	monēbitur	he, she, it will be warned, advised
1st person plural	monēbimur	we shall be warned, advised
2nd person plural	monēbiminī	you (pl.) will be warned, advised
3rd person plural	monēbuntur	they will be warned, advised

Exercise 3.1

Write out in full the future passive of the following verbs:

1. laudō
2. parō
3. spectō
4. dēleō
5. moveō
6. terreō

Exercise 3.2

Translate into English:

1. oppidum nostrum mox ab hostibus oppugnābitur.
2. et gladiī et hastae ā mīlitibus portābuntur.
3. num hic mūrus saevīs ventīs dēlēbitur?
4. num iuvenēs puerōs timēre vidēbuntur?
5. ā senibus spectābiminī.
6. nōnne in oppidō manēre iubēberis?
7. ō! ancillae, mox ā rēgīnā vocābimur.
8. num ā custōdibus tenēbor?
9. hīc pulcherrimum templum ā cīvibus aedificābitur.
10. illī librī ā iuvenibus movēbuntur.

Exercise 3.3

Translate into Latin:

1. Will this wall really be built by boys and girls?
2. These weapons will be moved by the young men out of the city into the field.
3. You (pl.) will soon be set free by the king.
4. All the horses will be seen by the citizens.
5. Will he really be overcome by slaves?
6. You (sing.) will be frightened by a savage storm.
7. Shall I not be praised by the master?
8. Will the old men be killed by the enemy?
9. Will he really seem to fear me?
10. The farmers will be watched by the sailors.

The fifth declension: rēs

It's a very long time since we've done any new type of noun. In fact there are five declensions of nouns, and so far we've only done three. And, as the fourth declension is rather muddling, we're going to leap right into the fifth.

rēs, rei, f. = 'thing, matter, affair'		
	Singular	**Plural**
Nominative	rēs	rēs
Vocative	rēs	rēs
Accusative	rem	rēs
Genitive	reī	rērum
Dative	reī	rēbus
Ablative	rē	rēbus

Like rēs goes diēs = 'day'; but in the genitive and dative singular it has a long 'ē', because its stem, di-, ends in a vowel, thus giving diēī in both cases.

Also, although diēs is normally masculine, it becomes feminine when it is a special or appointed day. Thus:

vēnit certa diēs.
The fixed day came.

(certus, -a, -um = 'certain'; here = 'fixed')

Like rēs also go spēs (= 'hope') and fidēs (= 'faith'). But fidēs has no plural and spēs has only a nominative and accusative in the plural. Both are feminine.

Exercise 3.4

Set out the singulars of spēs and fidēs as rēs is set out above.

Exercise 3.5

Put the correct forms of hic, haec, hoc together with the following fifth declension nouns. Give diēs its usual gender, unless otherwise asked.

1. diērum
2. spē
3. rēbus (dat.)
4. rēs (acc. pl.)
5. diēī (gen.)
6. spem
7. fideī (gen. sing)
8. diēs (nom. pl.)
9. rērum
10. diem (a special day)

rēs pūblica

One of the most famous uses of rēs, is the expression rēs pūblica, often spelt as one word, both parts of which decline:

	rēs pūblica = 'republic, state, country' (lit. 'the public thing')	
	Singular	**Plural**
Nom.	rēs pūblica	rēs pūblicae
Voc.	rēs pūblica	rēs pūblicae
Acc.	rem pūblicam	rēs pūblicās
Gen.	reī pūblicae	rērum pūblicārum
Dat.	reī pūblicae	rēbus pūblicīs
Abl.	rē pūblicā	rēbus pūblicīs

Exercise 3.6

Translate into English:

1. omnium rērum virtūs optima est.
2. sextus diēs post quīntum diem veniet.
3. huic hominī nēmō fidem habet[1].
4. multī hominēs rēs pulchrās petunt.
5. incolae, quod spem nōn habent, nōn rīdent.
6. haec diēs deō sacra est.
7. hī plūs speī quam illī habent.
8. illī hominēs, quamquam rem[2] multam habent, laetī nōn sunt.
9. multī in rē pūblicā nostrā habitāre cupiunt.
10. diēs noctibus meliōrēs sunt.

[1] fidem habeō (+ dat.) = I have faith in.
[2] rēs (here) = property.

Exercise 3.7

Translate into Latin:

1. There are many days in one year.
2. All slaves have faith in a good master.
3. These boys love many things.
4. Will you (pl.) be frightened by these matters?
5. I do not have faith in our leaders.
6. He, who is never moved by hope, is very sad.
7. The queen has collected very beautiful things.
8. The sacred day has come.
9. Who does not wish to have much property?
10. Our state is better than yours (pl.).

regar, audiar, capiar

Now we are totally familiar with fifth declension nouns, let us turn to verbs again and round off the future passive. We still have to do the 3rd, 4th and mixed (3½) conjugations, so here is the future passive of regō:

Future passive of regō: regar = 'I shall be ruled'

1st person singular	regar	I shall be ruled
2nd person singular	regēris	you (sing.) will be ruled
3rd person singular	regētur	he, she, it will be ruled
1st person plural	regēmur	we shall be ruled
2nd person plural	regēminī	you (pl.) will be ruled
3rd person plural	regentur	they will be ruled

This is perfectly straightforward, and can be worked out from the future active.

N.B. Remember that the last syllable of regar is not long. It is a short 'a' followed by a consonantal 'r'.

The future passive of the 4th conjugation is again exactly what one would expect; it is audiar and it goes like regar. Similarly, the mixed conjugation, capiō, produces capiar, which goes like audiar. Remember however this:

Immensely solemn warning

There is **NO** future passive of faciō.

Exercise 3.8

As the future passive of regō is set out above, write out the future passive tense of:

1. dūcō
2. mittō
3. pōnō

Exercise 3.9

Write out similarly the future passive tense of:

1. pūniō
2. custōdiō
3. iaciō

Exercise 3.10

Translate into English:

1. illud vīnum ā nautīs bibētur.
2. ō puerī, ā magistrō cōnspiciēminī!
3. hīs mūrīs omnēs cīvēs dēfendentur.
4. malī servī ā dominō pūnientur.
5. num hīc ā comitibus meīs relinquar?
6. mīlitēs ā mīlitibus occīdentur.
7. nōs, poētae, ā cīvibus audiēmur.
8. tūtus ad parentēs tuōs redūcēris.
9. hī senēs ā iuvenibus custōdientur.
10. illud aurum ā malīs hominibus capiētur.

Exercise 3.11

Translate into Latin:

1. This food will be eaten by the farmers.
2. Many books will be read by these girls.
3. All the bad boys will be punished by their teachers.
4. You (pl.) will be defended by the wall of the city.
5. You (sing.) will be guarded by the soldiers.
6. Arrows will be thrown into the city.
7. I shall be forced to run into the field.
8. We shall be caught sight of by the enemy.
9. What will not be taken by the enemy?
10. The soldiers will be led by their leaders.

A nice little thing

Here is a nice little thing on multus.

When multus is followed by an adjective and a noun, it is regularly joined to the adjective by et. Thus:

Many good horses =
multī **et** bonī equī

And now to continue our story about Philemon and Baucis.

Exercise 3.12

Read the following passage carefully and answer the questions on it:

Philemon and Baucis – their goodness is rewarded

1   dī ad <u>tugurium</u>, in quō habitābant Philēmōn et
    Baucis, advēnērunt; hī illōs salūtāvērunt,
    cibumque eīs dedērunt et <u>ānserem</u> ā quō
    custōdiēbantur, ut <u>advenae</u> eum cōnsūmerent,
5   capere <u>temptābant</u>; sed ille <u>celerior</u> eīs erat et ad
    deōs, auxilium petēns, fūgit. tum <u>advenae</u>
    dīxērunt: 'nōs dī sumus; nōlīte <u>ānserem</u> necāre,
    sed nōbīscum montem illum <u>ascendite</u>!' <u>inde</u>
    nihil circum <u>tugurium</u> suum vident <u>nisi</u> aquam.
10 <u>vīcīnōs</u> mortuōs <u>dēflent</u>; sed <u>tugurium</u> subitō in
    templum <u>magnificum</u> <u>vertitur</u>. dīcunt dī:
    '<u>quicquid</u> cupitis faciēmus'. 'cupimus <u>sacerdōtēs</u>
    vestrī esse,' dīcunt, 'et, <u>ut</u> <u>ūnā</u> <u>vīximus</u>, sīc <u>ūnā</u>
    perīre cupimus.' et tandem post multōs annōs
15 subitō <u>Philēmona</u> videt Baucis <u>frondentem</u> et
    <u>Baucida</u> <u>frondentem</u> videt Philēmōn: in <u>duās</u>
    pulcherrimās <u>arborēs</u> <u>vertuntur</u>, quae etiam
    hodiē <u>flōrent</u>. sīc <u>piīs</u> praemia dantur.

tugurium, -iī, n. = hut
ānser, -is, m. = goose
advena, -ae, c. = stranger
temptō, -āre, -āvī, -ātum = I try (also
    spelt tentō)
celer, celeris, celere = swift, quick
ascendō, -ere, ascendī, ascēnsum =
    I ascend
inde = from there
nisi (here) = except
vīcīnus, -ī, m. = neighbour
dēfleō, -ēre, dēflēvī, dēflētum =
    I mourn, weep for
magnificus, -a, -um = magnificent
vertō, -ere, vertī, versum = I turn
quicquid = whatever
sacerdōs, -ōtis, c. = priest, priestess
ut (+ indic.) = as
ūnā = together
vīvō, -ere, vīxī, vīctum = I live
Philēmona and Baucida are Greek
    accusatives
frondeō, -ēre, no perfect or supine =
    I burst into leaf
duās is the accusative plural feminine
    of duo
arbor, -oris, f. = tree
flōreō, -ēre, -uī, no supine = I bloom
pius, -a, -um = good

1. Answer the following questions:

   (a) In line 1, what are the names of the dī (see p.35)?
   (b) In lines 3-5, why did Philemon and Baucis chase their goose?
   (c) In line 6, why did the goose run to the gods?
   (d) In line 7, why did Philemon and Baucis stop pursuing their goose?
   (e) In line 8, what were they told to do instead?
   (f) In lines 8-9, was their hut the only dwelling they saw? Explain your answer.
   (g) In lines 13-14, what was their second request?
   (h) In lines 14-18 was this request granted? Explain your answer.
   (i) In line 18, how did Philemon and Baucis deserve the reward that they received from the gods?

2. Translate the passage hospitably.

3. Answer the following questions:

   (a) In line 1, what is the singular of dī?
   (b) In line 3, put dedērunt into the imperfect.
   (c) In line 4, what part of what verb is cōnsūmerent? Why is this part used here?
   (d) In line 5, what could we have written after celerior instead of eīs here, giving the same sense?
   (e) In line 6, what tense is fūgit here? Explain your answer.
   (f) In line 8, what part of its verb is ascendite?
   (g) In line 9, if instead of 'they see' (vident), we had wished to say 'they will see', to what would we have had to change vident?
   (h) Mention all the prepositions in this passage, and translate them together with the words they govern.
   (i) In line 12, what part of faciō is faciēmus? Could you put it into the passive? Explain your answer.
   (j) In lines 15 and 16, what part of its verb is frondentem? Give its nominative singular and meaning.

Past Participle Passive

And now – talk of rites of passage! We really are about to advance into the very, very heart and soul of the Latin language, to tackle that famous part which no pupil in the good (?) old days could ever forget – the past participle passive. Just relish the splendid alliteration of this form. It speaks for itself; horns, trumpets and drums could say no more! Contemplate those three words reverently for a minute. Right? Well, here goes!

Remember the present participle which we've done very recently, which is always **active**? There's a future participle too, which is also only active; but we shall not concern ourselves with it now.

And there's the past participle passive, which is the only passive participle, and which works as follows:

(i) Its formation:

It comes directly from the supine, changing the '-um' ending to '-us'; it then becomes an adjectival form. Thus the past participle passive of amō is amātus, -a, -um. It declines regularly like bonus.

The past participles passive of moneō, regō, audiō and capiō are:

monitus, -a, -um   rēctus, -a, -um
audītus, -a, -um   captus, -a, -um

(ii) Its meaning:

The form amātus means 'loved' or 'having been loved'. Note that, being an adjectival form, the past participle passive agrees with its noun in gender, number and case. This is how the past participle passive is used:

ducēs, ab hostibus victī, fūgērunt.
The leaders, having been conquered by the enemy, fled.

ancilla, ā rēgīnā laudāta, laeta erat.
The maid-servant, having been praised by the queen, was happy.

urbem dēlētam vīdī.
I saw the destroyed city.

territus discessī.
I departed terrified.

N.B. The past participle passive is often best translated by a clause in English.

Thus:

puerī ā magistrō laudātī dōna accēpērunt.

could mean:
The boys **who were praised** by the teacher received gifts.

Exercise 3.13

Even as amātus, -a, -um is the past participle passive of amō, give the past participles passive of the following verbs and their meanings. Thus, for no.1, you would write: laudātus, -a, -um = 'praised, having been praised'.

1. laudō
2. moveō
3. spectō
4. pūniō
5. capiō
6. dūcō
7. cōnsūmō
8. iaciō
9. videō
10. scrībō

Note: There **is** a past participle passive of faciō, namely factus, -a, -um. From this we get our word 'fact': something that has been done.

Exercise 3.14

Translate into English:

1. servus, ā dominō līberātus, fēlīx erat.
2. librum ā poētā scrīptum laudāmus.
3. hī puerī ā parentibus monitī sē bene gerunt.
4. gladiī ā mīlitibus petītī in urbe nōn erant.
5. senēs ā comitibus relictī timēbant.
6. puellās ā iuvenibus custōdītās tūtās in urbem advenientēs vīdī.
7. per oppida occupāta cum amīcō ambulābam.
8. rēx ā cīvibus factus, optimus et fortissimus erat.
9. hunc mūrum ab incolīs aedificātum vidēte!
10. illōs mīlitēs ā nōbīs superātōs nōn timeō.

Exercise 3.15

Translate into Latin, using past participles passive:

1. The enemy, defeated by the Romans, fled.
2. I love all the words which have been written by the poet.
3. We saw the wall which had been destroyed by the wicked inhabitants.
4. Having been praised, the boys departed from the temple.
5. Will the little girls who have been left by their companions be safe?
6. Who will save the woman captured by the wicked young men?
7. The arrows which were thrown into the city wounded many citizens.
8. Having been caught sight of by the enemy, the old man ran into the city.
9. Will you (pl.) read books collected by the wise (men)?
10. Having been driven into the fields, the horses will be safe.

Let us leave past participles passive here for the time being. We shall soon return to them.

Meanwhile, here are a few useful words:

> contendō, -ere, contendī, contentum = I hurry, march
> interficiō, interficere, interfēcī, interfectum = I kill[1]
> iuvō, -āre, iūvī, iūtum = I help
> animal, -ālis, n. = animal[2]

[1] interficiō is a compound of faciō. As a kind of double bluff, compounds of faciō possess all the passive forms which faciō itself does not possess.
[2] It is strange that the word for 'animal' should be neuter. However, there it is.

Time

In the last chapter we dealt with place. Let us now deal with time.

(i)   'Time at, on, or in' is expressed by the ablative. Thus:

> quīntō diē vēnit.   eō annō periit.
> He came on the fifth day.   He died in that year.
>
> tertiā hōrā discessit.
> He departed at the third hour.

(ii)   'Time within which' is also expressed by the ablative. Thus:

> paucīs diēbus servābimur.
> We shall be saved within a few days.

(iii)   'Time during, or throughout which' is expressed by the accusative; it often translates the English 'for'. Thus:

> Rōmae paucōs annōs habitāvit.
> He lived in Rome for a few years.

Sometimes per is put before the accusative of time. Thus:

> per multās hōrās in illō locō mānsimus.
> We remained in that place for many hours.

Exercise 3.16

Translate into English:

1.   illō diē Rōmā discessit.
2.   duodecim hōrās in urbe mānsimus.
3.   nostrī amīcī paucīs hōrīs advenient.
4.   illa mulier per multās hōrās cantābit.
5.   eō annō mīlitēs nostrī hostēs omnēs vīcērunt.
6.   nunc exiērunt, sed paucīs diēbus redībunt.
7.   quīnque annōs urbem nostram occupāvistis.
8.   nōnne sextō annō discēdētis?
9.   magister nōnā hōrā veniet.
10.   multōs annōs hoc oppidum habitāvī.

Exercise 3.17

Translate into Latin:

1. They will arrive in Rome within eight days.
2. We waited for five days for our friends.
3. On that day the enemy at last departed.
4. The city will be attacked within a few days.
5. The horses remained in this field for ten days.
6. The Romans occupied many cities in that year.
7. We were reading the poet's work for six hours.
8. We did not eat food for three days.
9. The enemy will return within five years.
10. The boys will arrive at the sixth hour.

volō

So now time has flown away, and we shall return to verbs, this time to a very common and very irregular verb, namely volō = 'I wish'. Mercifully, we have been able to get along with cupiō for this meaning; but we may now admit that volō is more common; and remember, it is the commonest verbs which are often the most irregular. So here is volō at its worst in the present indicative:

Present tense of volō, velle, voluī = 'I wish, want'		
1st person singular	volō	I wish, want
2nd person singular	vīs	you (sing.) wish, want
3rd person singular	vult	he, she, it wishes, wants
1st person plural	volumus	we wish, want
2nd person plural	vultis	you (pl.) wish, want
3rd person plural	volunt	they wish, want

If this isn't preposterous, what is? Still, there's nothing we can do but grin and bear it and be grateful that it is unique, in other words a one-off. And we haven't finished with it.

The future, the imperfect and the perfect of volō are so innocently regular that we could be lulled into a feeling of false security. The future is volam, like regam; the imperfect is volēbam. What could be nicer? The perfect is voluī.

However, the present infinitive is velle, which is completely unpredictable, and the imperfect subjunctive is, faithfully, vellem. The present participle is regular, i.e. volēns. It can generally be translated 'willingly'. There is no supine and no passive.

Exercise 3.18

1. Write out in full the present tense of volō in all its glory. (N.B. Repeat it to yourself day and night and night and day. And after each time add: 'the present infinitive is velle'.)
2. Write out in full the future tense of volō.
3. Write out in full the imperfect tense of volō.
4. Write out in full the perfect tense of volō.

Exercise 3.19

Translate into English:

1. 'quid vīs?' mē rogāvit: 'aurum volō,' respondī.
2. illī prō amīcīs pugnāre volunt.
3. nōnne mē hīc manēre vultis?
4. numquam ex hāc urbe discēdere volēmus.
5. bonum est iuvāre velle; sed melius est iuvāre.
6. diū parentēs meōs vidēre volēbam.
7. hōs senēs numquam volēns vulnerābō.
8. mīles, quod hostēs vulnerāre volēbat, sagittās ad eōs iēcit.
9. hic puer multās hōrās dormīre vult.
10. in nostrā urbe semper habitāre volumus.

Exercise 3.20

Translate into Latin, using volō for 'wish, want':

1. Do you (sing.) wish to remain with us for many days?
2. We want a good king and great leaders.
3. The young men wish to save the women.
4. The masters wished to set free their slaves.
5. It is not good to wish to wound men.
6. Do you (pl.) want us to depart?
7. I shall soon want to go to Rome.
8. The enemy wanted to occupy the town.
9. Who wishes to sing in the temple today?
10. I wish to read the works written by this poet.

Exercise 3.21

Of what English words do the following Latin ones remind you? Describe the connexion between the Latin words and the English words you have chosen:

1. volō
2. nox
3. tempestās
4. labor

Here's a new story, which I'm sure you all know in English:

Exercise 3.22

Read the following passage and answer the questions on it:

The wicked Peliās has disinherited Jason's father, Aeson

1　urbs in Thessaliā fuit, nōmine Iōlcus; rēx Iōlcī
　　Peliās erat; is Aesonem, quī rēx esse dēbuit,
　　exhērēdāverat. Peliās Neptūnī fīlius erat; Aesōn
　　erat Aeolidēs; et Peliās et Aesōn fīliī erant Tȳrūs.
5　Peliae dīxerant vātēs: 'tū, quod frātrem
　　exhērēdāvistī, ab Aeolidā interficiēris.' Peliās
　　igitur plūrimōs Aeolidās necāvit, sed Aesonī
　　propter mātrem pepercit; eum tamen in rēgiā
　　suā nē effugeret inclūsit; ibi uxor Aesonis fīlium
10　genuit quem Peliās statim occīdere voluit; sed
　　māter puerum furtim servātum ad Chīrōnem, ut
　　eum ēducārēt ille, mīsit. post multōs annōs,
　　vātēs iterum Peliae dīxērunt: 'hominem cavē
　　ūnam crepidam gerentem!' et posteā Neptūnō
15　sacrificāns iuvenem cōnspexit pelle pardī
　　vestītum, duābus hastīs armātum, crepidam
　　gerentem ūnam.

Peliās, -ae, m. = Pelias
dēbeō, ēre, dēbuī, dēbitum =
　I ought
esse dēbuit = should have been
exhērēdō, -āre, -āvī, -ātum =
　I disinherit
Aeolidēs, -ae, m. = a son of Aeolus
　(see below)
Tȳrō, Tȳrūs, f. = Tyro (see below)
vātēs, -is, c. = prophet, poet
parcō, -ere, pepercī, parsum (+ dat.)
　= I spare
rēgia, -ae, f. = palace
inclūdō, -ere, inclūsī, inclūsum =
　I shut in; (here) = I imprison
gignō, -ere, genuī, genitum =
　I beget, give birth to
furtim = furtively, secretly
Chīrōn, Chīrōnis, m. = Chiron (see
　below)
ēducō, -āre, -āvī, -ātum = I educate
caveō, -ēre, cāvī, cautum = I am on
　guard against
crepida, -ae, f. = sandal
sacrificō, -āre, -āvī, -ātum =
　I sacrifice
pellis, -is, f. = skin, hide
pardus, -ī, m. = leopard
vestiō, -īre, -īvī, -ītum = I clothe
duābus is the f. ablative of duo
armō, -āre, -āvī, -ātum = I arm

hominem cavē ūnam crepidam gerentem!

Notes:
(i)   Thessaly (line 1) was a large district right up in the North of Greece.
(ii)   Neptūnus, -ī, m. (line 3) was the god of the sea.
(iii)   Aeolidēs, -ae (line 4): the ending -idēs is a Greek form meaning 'son of' or 'descendant of'. These nouns are first declension in Greek, and generally take the first declension endings in Latin. Aeolus was the god of the winds.
(iv)   Tȳrō (line 4) is a Greek feminine name ending in '-ō'. Tȳrūs is its Greek genitive.
(v)   Chīrōn (line 12) was a Centaur. The Centaurs were conceived of as being half-man and half-horse, the upper part being man and the lower part being horse. Chiron, of divine origin, was kind and wise, and was a famous tutor; among his other pupils were Hercules and Achilles.

1. Answer the following questions:
    (a) In lines 3-4, what was the precise relationship between Pelias and Aeson?
    (b) In lines 5-6, what reason did the prophets give for Pelias' destined death?
    (c) In lines 6-7, why did Pelias kill so many descendants of Aeolus?
    (d) In lines 7-8, why did he spare Aeson?
    (e) In lines 8-9, what did he do with Aeson?
    (f) In line 9, why did he treat him in this way?
    (g) In lines 9-11, what did the little boy's mother save him from?
    (h) In lines 11-12, why did she send him to Chiron?
    (i) In lines 14-15, what was Pelias doing when he caught sight of a young man?
    (j) In lines 15-17, how do you think Pelias felt when he saw the young man? Why did he feel like this?

2. Translate the passage guardedly.

3. Answer the following questions:
    (a) In line 3, what tense is exhērēdāverat?
    (b) In line 4, we have et...et. How should we translate this?
    (c) quod...exhērēdāvistī (lines 5-6); comment on the position of this clause in the sentence.
    (d) In line 8, if, instead of 'spared', we had wanted to say 'will spare', to what would we have had to change pepercit?
    (e) In line 9, what word could we have written instead of uxor giving the same sense?
    (f) voluit (line 10); put this into the present tense.
    (g) In line 11, what part of its verb is servātum here? Translate it. Mention and translate any other such parts in the passage.
    (h) sacrificāns (line 15); what part of its verb is this? Translate it. Mention and translate any other such part in the passage.

Exercise 3.23

Translate into Latin:

1. The good old men are advising the brave boys.
2. We were attacking the city with arrows.
3. You (sing.) have drunk all the water.
4. The new leaders hear Roman words.
5. The noble master is setting free the good slave.
6. The journey which you (pl.) are making is difficult.
7. The animals have eaten all the food which you (sing.) gave us.
8. All the girls were being helped by all the boys.
9. The citizens were happy, watching the sky.
10. You (pl.) were being defended by the wall built near the sea.

Vocabulary 3

Vocabulary 3
cōgō, -ere, coēgī, coāctum = I force
contendō, -ere, contendī, contentum = I hurry, march
iuvō, iuvāre, iūvī, iūtum = I help
pellō, -ere, pepulī, pulsum = I drive
quī, quae, quod = who, which
diēs, -ēī, m. = day. A special or appointed day is usually feminine.
fidēs, -eī, f. = trust, faith, promise
ut (+ subj.) = in order to
nē (+ subj.) = in order not to, in order that…not, lest

Incredibly, there's still quite a lot to come. So be of good cheer!

Chapter 4

The perfect passive

Let's start by rounding off our passive tenses. We still have to do the perfect and pluperfect passive and this we can now do happily, since they involve use of our new friend, the past participle passive. The perfect or past tense passive of amō is amātus sum. This means literally 'I am having been loved', i.e. 'I have been loved' or 'I was loved'. Thus amāta est means 'she has been loved' and amātum est means 'it has been loved'.

Perfect (past) tense passive of amō

1st person singular	amātus, -a, -um sum	I have been/was loved
2nd person singular	amātus, -a, -um es	you (sing.) have been/were loved
3rd person singular	amātus, -a, -um est	he, she, it has been/was loved
1st person plural	amātī, -ae, -a sumus	we have been/were loved
2nd person plural	amātī, -ae, -a estis	you (pl.) have been/were loved
3rd person plural	amātī, -ae, -a sunt	they have been/were loved

---

Throughout, we have simply added the present tense of sum to the past participle passive of the verb with which we are dealing.

Note that the participle must be in the same gender, number and case as the subject of the verb:

e.g.   puer amātus est = the boy has been/was loved
puellae amātae sunt = the girls have been/were loved

All the other conjugations go in exactly the same way, thus giving us monitus, -a, -um sum, rēctus, -a, -um sum, audītus, -a, -um sum and captus, -a, -um sum. There *is* a perfectly (sorry) good perfect (or past) tense passive of faciō; it is factus, -a, -um sum.

Exercise 4.1

Write out in full, as above, the perfect (or past) tense passive of:

1.   parō
2.   spectō
3.   moveō
4.   cōnsūmō
5.   videō
6.   petō
7.   pūniō
8.   trādō
9.   iaciō
10.   custōdiō

Exercise 4.2

Translate into English. Give both the perfect and the past in your translation: e.g. in question 1, say 'you have been called / were called.'

1. ō ancilla, ā rēgīnā vocāta es.
2. haec oppida ab hostibus oppugnāta sunt.
3. optimī librī ab hōc poētā scrīptī sunt.
4. mulierēs ā iuvenibus servātae sunt.
5. templum tempestāte dēlētum est.
6. parva puella ā comitibus custōdīta est.
7. ad montem currere coāctus sum.
8. mīlitēs cum hostibus pugnāre iussī sunt.
9. multa oppida ā fortibus incolīs dēfēnsa sunt.
10. cūr hīc ab amīcīs relictī sumus?

Exercise 4.3

Translate into Latin:

1. The food was eaten by our companions.
2. This city has been defended by brave citizens.
3. The boys were immediately called by their teacher.
4. The animal has been wounded by a wicked man.
5. Those soldiers were killed by the enemy.
6. These women have been wounded by arrows.
7. Have you (m. pl.) really been driven to the sea?
8. This book was sought by me in many places.
9. Have not the works of the poet been praised by all?
10. Were you (f. sing.) forced to stay in the ship?

The pluperfect passive

The pluperfect passive is formed from the past participle passive plus the imperfect of sum. Thus amātus eram means literally 'I was in a state of having been loved', which, if you come to think of it, means 'I had been loved'. The participle changes again to the gender, number and case of the noun with which it agrees. Thus:

mulier amāta erat.
The woman had been loved.

puerī amātī erant.
The boys had been loved.

Exercise 4.4

Translate into English:

1. iuvenēs ā parentibus amātī erant.
2. ō ancillae, ā rēgīnā amātae erātis.
3. hoc oppidum ōlim ā iuvenibus aedificātum erat.
4. nōnne ā crūdēlī duce in flūmen contendere coāctī erāmus?
5. longa itinera facere iussus eram.
6. num ā cīvibus cōnspectā erās?
7. multum aurum ab illīs captum erat.
8. malī puerī ā magistrīs pūnītī erant.
9. quid ā vōbīs factum erat?
10. ā duce monitī erāmus.

Exercise 4.5

Translate into Latin:

1. We (f.) had been called by our friends.
2. You (m. pl.) had been punished by the teacher.
3. The horses had been driven into the field.
4. Had you (m. sing.) really been forced by the farmer to flee?
5. Had I not been ordered to overcome many dangers?
6. Had not these cities been defended by old men?
7. The boys and girls had been praised by the teachers.
8. Many things had been taken by the enemy.
9. The horses had been moved into a bigger field.
10. Hadn't you (pl.) been warned?

alius

And now let's turn to something completely new – a very useful word indeed which needs careful handling. It is alius, meaning 'other'. It belongs to the highly double-faced (can one be highly double-faced? I don't see why not) tribe of words in '-us', which go like ūnus = 'one' and sōlus = 'alone, only'. Perhaps it's to its credit that, unlike ūnus and sōlus, which start off so innocently, it puts us on our guard right from the word go with its neuter singular nominative and accusative, aliud. So here it is:

alius, -a, -ud = 'other'			
Singular			
	Masculine	**Feminine**	**Neuter**
Nominative	alius	alia	aliud
Accusative	alium	aliam	aliud
Genitive	alterīus	alterīus	alterīus
Dative	aliī	aliī	aliī
Ablative	aliō	aliā	aliō

Notes:
(i)   Remember is and ille had similar forms in the neuter singular, namely id and illud.
(ii) For its genitive, alius dislikes the form which would come naturally from it on the analogy of ūnīus and sōlīus from ūnus and sōlus. Instead alius begs, borrows or steals (whichever you prefer) alterīus, the genitive singular of alter, which means 'one or the other of two'. The 'i' of alterīus is sometimes short.

In spite of all the trouble it causes, alius is indeed a very useful word, and we shall soon learn some very nice ways in which it is used. Moreover, it does show true penitence in its plural, which is immaculately regular. Here it is:

aliī, -ae, -a = 'other (plural), others'			
Plural			
	Masculine	**Feminine**	**Neuter**
Nominative	aliī	aliae	alia
Accusative	aliōs	aliās	alia
Genitive	aliōrum	aliārum	aliōrum
Dative	aliīs	aliīs	aliīs
Ablative	aliīs	aliīs	aliīs

Note:
In the singular, alius can often be translated as 'another'.

Exercise 4.6

Translate into English:

1. hōs librōs omnēs lēgī; nōnne aliōs habētis?
2. in nostrō oppidō aliud templum nōn est.
3. crās aliī puerī et aliae puellae hīc aderunt.
4. herī cum aliīs comitibus ad mare festīnāvimus.
5. aliōrum mīlitum gladiī in agrō sunt.
6. aliārum puellārum rēs hīc nōn sunt.
7. hanc pecūniam aliī fēminae dā.
8. nōn hīs servīs dominus dōnum dedit, sed aliīs.
9. illa mulier rēgīna est alterīus īnsulae.
10. alia oppida peiōra sunt nostrō.

Exercise 4.7

Translate into Latin:

1. Did you really believe the other messenger?
2. I made a difficult journey with another companion.
3. The boys have eaten this food; have you (pl.) any[1] other food?
4. These horses are bad; I want some[2] others.
5. Other teachers will go to that town tomorrow.
6. Will you (pl.) really be led by other leaders?
7. I shall soon see another town.
8. Isn't this young man another woman's son?
9. Do you (sing.) really like the works of other poets?
10. They were being ruled then by another queen.

[1] Ignore 'any'.
[2] Ignore 'some'.

nōlō

Here comes another verb; recently we learnt volō = 'I wish, want'. So now we shall turn to nōlō = 'I do not wish, want'. It can best be understood as being a combination of nōn + volō; this should be easy enough now that we know all about the preposterous volō; but is it? You've guessed. It isn't! Needless to say, nōlō is mixed-up, poor thing. At times it plunges forth on its own; at others it crumbles up into two separate words; and this is how it happens:

Present tense of nōlō, nōlle, nōluī = 'I do not wish, want'

1st person singular	nōlō	I do not wish, want
2nd person singular	nōn vīs	you (sing.) do not wish, want
3rd person singular	nōn vult	he, she, it does not wish, want
1st person plural	nōlumus	we do not wish, want
2nd person plural	nōn vultis	you (pl.) do not wish, want
3rd person plural	nōlunt	they do not wish, want

You see what I mean?

Well, after this, anyway, nōlō is nearly a spent force in the indicative: its future is nōlam, its imperfect is nōlēbam and its perfect is nōluī. Its infinitive is nōlle and its imperfect subjunctive is nōllem.

N.B. nōluī (past) often means 'I refused to'. And nōlēbam is often best translated by 'I was unwilling'.

nōlō has no supine and no passive.

But there is something very special about nōlō, which we learnt in *Latin Prep* Book 2 (p.89). We promised you then that we would learn nōlō in Book 3, and, lo and behold! we are (of course!) keeping our promise.

The very special thing, I need hardly say, is the irregular imperative, nōlī (sing.), nōlīte (pl.), which, followed by an infinitive, means 'do not wish to …', in other words 'don't'. Just to remind you:

> nōlī (nōlīte) clāmāre!
> Do not shout!

nōlī clāmāre!

Exercise 4.8

Write out in full all the tenses of nōlō; and repeat them to yourself day and night, including the present infinitive and the imperfect subjunctive. And when you are pretty sure that you know them all, sing them out yet again.

Exercise 4.9

Translate into English:

1. cum Rōmānīs pugnāre nōlumus.
2. quis mēcum ad mūrōs currere nōlet?
3. cūr nōbīscum rīdēre nōn vīs?
4. hī servī in agrīs labōrāre nōlunt.
5. puerōs et puellās iuvāre nōn vultis.
6. cum illīs mīlitibus īre nōluī.
7. ō incolae, senēs vulnerāre nōlīte!
8. saepe hoc facere nōlēbātis.
9. malum est rēs bonās facere nōlle.
10. cūr puer hōs librōs legere nōn vult?

Exercise 4.10

Translate into Latin:

1. Why don't the women wish to come down from the mountain to the sea?
2. They will not wish to attack the city.
3. Marcus, do not drink much wine!
4. These soldiers do not want to remain in this city.
5. Why do you (sing.) not wish to do that which[1] the teacher orders you to do?
6. He refused to go into the fields with the other citizens.
7. We do not wish to wound the other young men.
8. This little boy does not wish to sing in the temple alone.
9. She was unwilling to make a difficult journey without her friends.
10. Why don't you (pl.) wish to hurry to the river?

[1] For 'that which' say id quod.

And now for the continuation of the story of Jason.

Exercise 4.11

Read the following passage carefully and answer the questions on it:

The story of Jason (2): Pelias sends Jason to fetch the Golden Fleece

1	rogāvit Peliās iuvenem 'quis es?' 'Iāsōn sum,' respondit ille, et ipse Peliam rogāvit: 'et tū, quis es?' respondit Peliās: 'Peliās sum, rēx Iōlcī.' 'nōn es,' dīxit Iāsōn, 'nam Aesōn, pater meus, ā tē
5	inclūsus, rēx esse dēbet.' Peliās magnopere territus dīxit: 'ad Colchidem nāvigā et inde pellem aureī arietis īn silvā Mārtis in rāmīs arboris pendentem cape et eam mihi dā: et ego tibi rēgnum tuum trādam.' tum Argus nāvem
10	Argō Minervae auxiliō aedificābat; ea prīma nāvis longa erat; et inter comitēs ab Iāsone collēctōs, quī Argonautae vocābantur, multī nōtissimī erant. nam Herculēs aderat et Orpheus et Lynceus, quī optimōs oculōs habuit. sīc iter
15	parābātur.

inclūdō, -ere, inclūsī, inclūsum (here) = I imprison
dēbeō, -ēre, dēbuī, dēbitum = I ought
Colchis, -idis, f. = Colchis (see below)
inde = thence, from there
pellis, -is, f. = fleece
aureus, -a, -um = golden
ariēs, -etis, m. = ram
silva, -ae, f. = forest
Mārs, Mārtis, m. = Mars (see below)
rāmus, -ī, m. = bough, branch
arbor, -oris, f. = tree
pendeō, -ēre, pependī, (no supine) = I hang (intrans.)
rēgnum, -ī, n. = kingdom
Argō, Argūs, f. = Argo (see below)
Minerva, -ae, f. = Minerva, goddess of wisdom (see below)
oculus, -ī, m. = eye

Notes:

(i) We met Hercules, the greatest of the Greek heroes, more than once in *Latin Prep* Book 1 and Orpheus the singer of songs in *Latin Prep* Book 2. Lynceus is famous for his wonderful eyesight, and Argus is famous as the builder of the Argo.

(ii) Argō is another Greek feminine noun in 'ō' (accusative Argō, genitive Argūs); compare Tȳrō the mother of Aesōn in Chapter 3.

(iii) Colchis, -idis, f. is a region east of the Black Sea.

(iv) The famous name Argonauts (Argonautae, -ārum, m. pl.) means 'the crew (nautae) of the Argo'.

(v) Mars is the god of war.

(vi) Minerva is the goddess of wisdom, the arts, the sciences and much else.

1. Answer the following questions:

    (a) nōn es (lines 3-4); to what words of Pelias do these two words apply?
    (b) In lines 4-5, what had Pelias done to Aeson, Jason's father?
    (c) In lines 5-6, how did Pelias react to this speech of Jason's?
    (d) In lines 8-9, what did Pelias promise to give Jason in return for the Golden Fleece?
    (e) In lines 9-10, did Argus build the ship alone? Explain your answer.
    (f) In lines 11-12, what had Jason done meanwhile?
    (g) In line 12, why were Jason's companions called Argonautae?
    (h) In lines 12-14, were his crew just a lot of ordinary men? Explain your answer.
    (i) In line 14, why was Lynceus particularly useful?

2. Translate the passage adventurously.

3. Answer the following questions:

    (a) In line 2, if, instead of '(he) replied', we had wanted to say '(he) will reply', to what would we have had to change respondit?
    (b) 'Peliās sum, rēx Iōlcī.' (line 3); how does the word rēx relate to the word Peliās? Mention and translate any other examples of this feature in the passage.
    (c) In line 5, what part of inclūdō is inclūsus? Mention and translate any other examples of this part in the passage.
    (d) In line 7, what is the case of rāmīs? Why is this case used here?
    (e) In line 8, what part of its verb is pendentem? Translate it.
    (f) In line 8, to what does eam refer?
    (g) In line 8, what part of which verb is dā? Mention and translate any other examples of this part in the passage.
    (h) In line 10, what is the case here of auxiliō? And how would you translate it?
    (i) In line 12, put vocābantur into the perfect passive tense.
    (j) nōtissimī (line 13); what part of nōtus is this? Mention and translate any other example of this part in the passage.

A further use of ipse

We have learnt sē, which is a reflexive pronoun for the third person singular or plural and is used in all genders and all cases, except the nominative and vocative. Thus:

hic mīles sē amat.
This soldier loves himself.

me ipsum amō

illa mulier sibi dōnum dedit.
That woman gave a present to herself.

By adding the appropriate gender, number and case of ipse to the first person or second person pronouns, we can make them reflexive also. Thus:

(ego) mē ipsum laudābam.
I (m.) used to praise myself.

(tū) tē ipsam laudās.
You (f.) are praising yourself.

(nōs) nōbīs ipsīs cibum parābimus.
We shall prepare food for ourselves.

(vōs) ā vōbīs ipsīs vulnerātae estis.
You (f.) have been wounded by yourselves.

I have put the nominative ego, tū, nōs and vōs in brackets, because the persons are revealed anyway by the person of the main verb: thus, laudābam, by itself, means 'I used to praise'.

Exercise 4.12

Translate into English:

1. ō amīcī, in templō nōs ipsōs custōdiēmus.
2. Mārce, tū ā tē ipsō servātus es.
3. ō mīlitēs, cūr vōs ipsōs laudātis?
4. mē ipsam hostibus nōn trādam.
5. mihi ipsī dōnum pulchrum dedī.
6. num ā vōbīs ipsīs vulnerābiminī?
7. nōnne nōbīs ipsīs fidem habēmus?
8. mē ipsum labōrāre coēgī.
9. nōs ipsōs līberāvimus.
10. vōs ipsōs clāmantēs audīte!

Exercise 4.13

Translate into Latin:

1. Girls, you saw yourselves in the water of the river.
2. Sulpicia, you were saved by yourself.
3. We said many words to ourselves.
4. Young men, why are you always praising yourselves?
5. I (f.) often hear myself singing.
6. We (m.) defended ourselves with swords and spears.
7. You (sing.) gave yourself a beautiful present.
8. We (f.) will defend ourselves with spears.
9. I (m.) never praise myself.
10. 'Give yourselves swords!' said the general.

A little piece on locus

The word locus, -ī, m. (= place) has a regular plural locī, but it also has a neuter plural form loca.

(i) The plural form locī regularly refers to individual places; it also refers to places or passages in a book.
(ii) The form loca generally refers to places combined together to form a region or neighbourhood.

īdem, eadem, idem

And here is something more difficult: it is īdem meaning 'the same'. And this is how it goes:

īdem, eadem, idem = 'the same'

Singular

	Masculine	**Feminine**	**Neuter**
Nominative	īdem	eadem	idem
Accusative	eundem	eandem	idem
Genitive	eiusdem	eiusdem	eiusdem
Dative	eīdem	eīdem	eīdem
Ablative	eōdem	eādem	eōdem

Notes:

(i) īdem, eadem, idem is closely based on our old friend is, ea, id (see *Latin Prep* 2, Chapter 6, page 64) strengthened by the termination '-dem'. Note that the 'ī' in the nominative masculine singular is long, whereas in the neuter it is short.

(ii) In the accusative singular the 'm' of eum and eam regularly changes to 'n' before the 'd' that follows it.

(iii) For the genitive eiusdem see the note on cuius (Chapter 1, page 5).

Exercise 4.14

Translate into English:

1. puellae saepe ab eōdem magistrō laudantur.
2. idem oppidum iterum ab hostibus oppugnātum est.
3. hōc annō senex eīdem iuvenī praemium dedit.
4. omnēs illī hominēs cīvēs sunt eiusdem oppidī.
5. cīvis ille eandem urbem habitat quam[1] ego.
6. Mārcus et Aulus, ut eundem sapientem[2] convenīrent, in urbem festīnāvērunt.
7. eiusdem poētae opera amāmus et ego et tū.
8. hic mīles in eōdem proeliō pugnāvit quō[3] ille.
9. hī iuvenēs eandem mulierem amant.
10. nōs omnēs eundem magistrum habēmus.

[1] Translate quam (here) by 'as' (lit. 'which').

[2] sapiēns, -entis (= 'wise') is very frequently used to mean 'a wise man', 'a sage', 'a philosopher'.

[3] Translate quō by 'as' (lit. '(in) which').

Exercise 4.15

Translate into Latin:

1. We heard the same boy in the temple singing.
2. My friend and I made a long journey in order to see the same city again.
3. Are they really the sons of the same mother?
4. I have always believed the same leader.
5. You (pl.) were seeking the same gold as[1] your friends.
6. This old man was wounded by the same sword as[2] that one.
7. We citizens are all ruled by the same queen.
8. We all wish to read the same book.
9. All these books belong to[3] the same teacher.
10. Give all those gifts to the same woman.

[1] For 'as' (here) say 'which'.
[2] For 'as' (here) say 'by which'.
[3] For 'belong to' (here) say 'are of'.

Numbers: 30-100 and 1000

It's far too long since we exhibited our mathematical genius. So let's go racing on, now. We ended last time on a mere twenty. Well certainly we can do better than that.

Numbers: 30-100 and 1000

30	XXX	trīgintā	70	LXX	septuāgintā
40	XL	quadrāgintā	80	LXXX	octōgintā
50	L	quīnquāgintā	90	XC	nōnāgintā
60	LX	sexāgintā	100	C	centum
			1000	M	mīlle

All these words are safely indeclinable.

Exercise 4.16

Translate into English:

1. trīgintā annōs per terrās et maria errābat.
2. mīlle hominēs in hōc oppidō habitant.
3. cum septuāgintā comitibus iter fēcī.
4. quadrāgintā equī in eōdem agrō stant.

5. hīc quīnquāgintā puerī librōs legent.
6. illa urbs ā centum iuvenibus servāta est.
7. hās octōgintā puellās omnēs magistrī laudāvērunt.
8. hīs centum mīlitibus centum gladiōs dā.
9. dux noster dominus est nōnāgintā servōrum.
10. centum puerī ā cīvibus audītī sunt cantantēs.

Exercise 4.17

Translate the following sums into Latin words, using et for '+' and sunt for '=':

1. XL + L = XC
2. XXX + LXX = C
3. LX + X = LXX

4. LXXX + XX = C
5. XXX + XX = L
6. L + L = C

Exercise 4.18

Translate into Latin, using words for the numbers, not symbols:

1. In this land there are forty towns.
2. We remained in the city for seventy days.
3. I hurried through the fields with a hundred companions.
4. We gave books to sixty boys.
5. A thousand soldiers attacked this city.
6. These men are the guards of eighty women.
7. Fifty old men were fighting in that battle.
8. Did thirty horses really run down from the mountain?
9. Ninety young men are present in this field, working.
10. I saw a hundred citizens in the town.

Compound numerals

Compound numerals are formed as follows: either the larger number is followed by the smaller, or the smaller comes first followed by et and the larger. Thus:

sexāgintā septem

and

septem et sexāgintā

are both right for 67. Compare English 'sixty seven' or 'seven and sixty'.

dum

And now for something entirely different – a new construction; we haven't had one for ages. This one is all about dum, which means a number of things, but we are only interested in its meaning 'while'.

1. If we wish to say 'while something was happening, something else was happening throughout the same period of time', there is no problem. Thus:

puerī, dum agricolae in agrīs labōrābant, in templō cantābant.

While (i.e. 'during the whole time in which') the farmers were working in the fields, the boys were singing in the temple.

The imperfect tense is used both in the main clause and in the dum clause. I'm sure, though, that you didn't think we were going to get off so lightly. Here it comes:

2. If we wish to say 'while something was happening, some new thing happened' –
out of the blue, as it were – then the verb in the dum clause is in the present
tense, even though the whole thing happened in the past. Thus:

dum per agrōs ambulō, clāmōrem magnum audīvī.

While I was walking through the fields, I heard a great shout.

If the main verb is in the present tense, there is no problem; dum would be
followed by the present tense, whatever the meaning.

Exercise 4.19

Translate into English:

1. cīvēs, dum hostēs in urbe manēbant, magnopere timēbant.
2. Sulpicia, dum Mārcus cum Aulō pugnat, subitō: 'nōlīte pugnāre!' clāmāvit.
3. dum in oppidum festīnō, senem vīdī vulnerātum.
4. vōs omnēs, dum urbs oppugnābātur, fortissimī erātis.
5. nautae, dum vīnum petunt, aquam subitō invēnērunt.
6. dum montēs spectō, subitō equum vīdī.
7. poēta, dum scrībit, cantat.
8. dum nox est, tempestāte territī sumus.
9. dum dormit mīles, laetissimī sumus.
10. dum librum legimus, magister subitō discessit.

Exercise 4.20

Translate into Latin:

1. While I was drinking in the city, I suddenly heard Marcus' voice.
2. While the girls were singing in the temple, the boys were playing in the fields.
3. While she was reading a book, the master arrived.
4. While his mother was preparing food, Marcus suddenly laughed.
5. While the enemy were attacking the city, Quintus was writing his book.
6. The slaves are working while they are listening to their master.
7. While we were watching the road, Aulus crossed it.
8. While the soldiers were defending the city, the citizens were safe.
9. While the boys were holding swords, Titus was wounded.
10. While the old men are walking, the young men are running.

And now let's return to the Argonauts.

Exercise 4.21

Read the following passage carefully, and answer the questions on it:

The story of Jason (3): Jason gets hold of the fleece

1   tandem nāvigāvērunt Argonautae et post multa
perīcula ad Colchidem advēnērunt; ibi rēx
Aeētēs dīxit Iāsonī: 'duo <u>taurōs</u> <u>ignem</u> <u>spīrantēs</u>
<u>iunge</u> et <u>arā</u> agrum <u>Mārtis</u> et <u>sere</u> ibi <u>dentēs</u>
5   <u>serpentis</u>; et <u>pellem</u> tibi trādam.' fīlia rēgis
Mēdēa, quod Iāsonem <u>adamāverat</u>, <u>artibus</u>
<u>magicīs</u> iūvit eum; illīus auxiliō <u>taurōs</u> <u>iūnxit</u>,
agrum <u>arāvit</u>, <u>dentēs</u> <u>sēvit</u>; hī, mīlitēs <u>factī</u>, <u>alius</u>
<u>alium</u>, aut interfēcērunt aut vulnerāvērunt. sed
10   Aeētēs <u>pellem</u> trādere nōluit. ea <u>pellis</u> ā <u>dracōne</u>
custōdiēbātur ingentissimō, quī numquam
dormīvit; eum Mēdēa <u>sōpīvit</u> et Argonautae
<u>pellem</u> cēpērunt; et cum Mēdēā in nāve
effūgērunt.

taurus, -ī, m. = bull
ignis, -is, m. = fire
spīrō, -āre, -āvī, -ātum = I breathe
iungō, -ere, iūnxī, iūnctum =
     I join, (here) = I yoke
arō, -āre, -āvī, -ātum = I plough
Mārs, Mārtis, m. = Mars, the god
     of war
serō, -ere, sēvī, satum = I sow
dēns, dentis, m. = tooth
serpēns, -entis, c. = serpent
pellis, -is, f. = fleece
adamō, -āre, -āvī, -ātum (here) =
     I fall in love with (+ acc.)
ars, artis, f. = art
magicus, -a, -um = magic
factī (here) = having been turned
     into (lit. having been made)
alius alium = one another
dracō, -ōnis, m. = dragon
sōpiō, -īre, -īvī, -ītum = I send to
     sleep

1. Answer the following questions:

    (a) In lines 1-2, did the Argonauts have an easy journey to Colchis? Give a
        reason for your answer.
    (b) In lines 3-5, why do you think Aeetes gave these instructions to Jason?
    (c) et...trādam (line 5); what did Aeetes promise?
    (d) In line 6, why did Medea help Jason?
    (e) In lines 6-7, how particularly was Medea's help so effective?
    (f) In line 8, what did the serpent's teeth become?
    (g) In line 10, what is the best translation for nōluit here?
    (h) In lines 11-12, what made this dragon a particularly awkward customer?
    (i) In line 12, how did Medea cope with the dragon?

2. Translate the passage magically (or otherwise!)

3. Answer the following questions:

    (a) In lines 1-2, what is the case of multa perīcula, and why are these two words
        in that case?
    (b) rēx Aeētēs (lines 2-3); how does the word Aeētēs relate to rēx?
    (c) In line 3, what part of its verb is spīrantēs? Translate it.
    (d) In line 4, what part of its verb is iunge? Translate it and any other such parts
        in the passage.
    (e) In line 5, what tense is trādam and of what verb?
    (f) In line 6, what tense is adamāverat?
    (g) In line 7, if, instead of '(she) helped', we had wished to say '(she) will help',
        to what would we have had to change iūvit?
    (h) In line 8, what part of faciō is factī?
    (i) ea pellis (line 10); put this into the dative singular.
    (j) ingentissimō (line 11); how does this word relate to ingēns?

Exercise 4.22

Translate into Latin:

1. The good boy was singing in the big temple.
2. The strong citizens are building a wall with the help of the brave soldiers.
3. The happy young men were defending the wretched old men.
4. The noble king heard the famous poet.
5. We were moving all the shields.
6. We hurried into the city to save the citizens.
7. Has that city really been destroyed by the enemy?
8. While we were reading our books, a soldier was killed.
9. Why do the teachers not wish to praise the boys?
10. Tomorrow we shall make the same journey.

Vocabulary 4

Vocabulary 4

trīgintā = thirty
quadrāgintā = forty
quīnquāgintā = fifty
sexāgintā = sixty
centum = a hundred

celer,[1] celeris, celere = swift, quick
rēs, reī, f. = thing, matter, affair
spēs[2], speī, f. = hope
īdem, eadem, idem = the same
alius, alia, aliud = other

[1] celer is a 3rd declension adjective in -er. Note that it has different nominative and vocative forms for the three different genders
[2] Note that spēs does not have a genitive, dative or ablative plural

So, here we are once again, becoming ever more learned with every chapter!

Chapter 5

eīdem, eaedem, eadem

Let's start straight off with the plural of īdem:

eīdem, eaedem, eadem = 'the same'			
Plural			
	Masculine	**Feminine**	**Neuter**
Nominative	eīdem	eaedem	eadem
Accusative	eōsdem	eāsdem	eadem
Genitive	eōrundem	eārundem	eōrundem
Dative	eīsdem	eīsdem	eīsdem
Ablative	eīsdem	eīsdem	eīsdem

Notes:

(i)   This seemingly innocent lay-out is not really quite as innocent as it looks, since eīdem and eīsdem are usually contracted to īdem and īsdem. However, we shall stick to the longer, regular forms.

(ii) The 'm' of eōrum and eārum becomes 'n' in front of the 'd'.

Exercise 5.1

Translate into English:

1. semper per eāsdem viās currit.
2. haec mulier eundem cibum eīsdem puerīs parābat.
3. crās ego cum eīsdem comitibus iter faciam.
4. hī gladiī eōrundem mīlitum sunt.
5. eadem verba dīcēbāmus quae vōs.
6. magistrī eadem dōna eīsdem puellīs dabant.
7. semper eōsdem librōs legitis.
8. omnēs eīsdem mūris dēfendimur.
9. eīdem puerī eadem faciunt.
10. omnēs puerī et puellae in eīsdem agrīs lūdunt.

Exercise 5.2

Translate into Latin:

1. We always see the same horses standing in the same fields.
2. Many women departed from the same cities.
3. All these books belong to[1] the same girls.
4. Those teachers punished the same boys.
5. We were giving the same shields to the soldiers.
6. We shall make the same journeys as[2] you.
7. These sailors always sail in the same ships.
8. Give (pl.) the same things to these citizens.
9. The same old men were wounded by the same soldiers.
10. They all praise the same leaders.

[1] For 'belong to' say 'are of'.
[2] For 'as' say 'which'.

ferō

And here comes the most outrageously irregular verb in the Latin language. It is ferō = 'I carry, bear, bring'. Let us deal first with its active forms. Not only are its present tense, its imperative, its present infinitive and therefore its imperfect subjunctive round the bend, but its principal parts too are uniquely weird. Let's start with its present tense active.

Present tense active of ferō, ferre, tulī, lātum = 'I carry, bear, bring'

1st person singular	ferō	I carry, bear, bring
2nd person singular	fers	you (sing.) carry, bear, bring
3rd person singular	fert	he, she, it carries, bears, brings
1st person plural	ferimus	we carry, bear, bring
2nd person plural	fertis	you (pl.) carry, bear, bring
3rd person plural	ferunt	they carry, bear, bring

The principal parts of ferō are beyond belief. They are ferō, ferre, tulī, lātum. Yes, it's true. I'm not pulling your leg, I'm not making it up. It's true! For some reason, ferō looks to a different stem altogether to form its perfect and to yet another different stem to form its supine. At least, even Latin can't get more irregular than that.

The perfect itself, tulī, while odd to look at, has perfectly regular endings (tulī, tulistī, tulit etc.)

I need hardly say that ferō is much commoner than portō. In fact it is one of the commonest words in Latin.

Notes:
(i)   The imperative of ferō is fer in the singular; the plural is ferte.
(ii)   The present infinitive is ferre.
(iii) The imperfect subjunctive is ferrem.
(iv)   The future is regular (double bluff!) feram, ferēs etc, which shows that if it has a
       conjugation at all, it is 3rd. The imperfect is ferēbam.

In the second book of Virgil's *Aeneid*, Laocoon, the wise Trojan prophet, tries to
persuade his fellow Trojans not to take the wooden horse into Troy. He utters words
which have become famous:

>   timeō Danaōs et dōna ferentēs.
>   I fear the Danai (= Greeks) even when they bear (lit. 'bearing') gifts.

I couldn't resist bringing in this present participle of ferō here.

Exercise 5.3

Set out the present tense active of ferō, as it is set out above, and then say it to
yourself (yes, you've guessed it!) day and night and (guessed again!) night and day.
Then write out the future, imperfect and perfect tenses, to prove that you know them.

Exercise 5.4

Translate into English:

1.   quid fertis, mīlitēs? gladiōs ferimus et hastās.
2.   cūr multōs librōs fers? eōs legere volō.
3.   ō Mārce, fer mihi[1] auxilium.
4.   Aenēās patrem ex urbe ferēbat.
5.   dominus servōs, ut aurum in templum ferrent, collēgit.
6.   senex hic miserrimus multa mala[2] fert.
7.   cūr ego semper īram rēgis ferō?
8.   ventī mox in oppidum nostrum tempestātem ferent.
9.   hās omnēs rēs ferre nōlō.
10.   cūr illī haec scūta ferunt? quod vōs ea nōn fertis.

[1] ferō (+ acc.) is regularly followed by the dative, when you are bringing help to
   someone.
[2] mala (here) = 'woes' (lit. bad things).

Exercise 5.5

Translate into Latin; for 'carry' 'bring' or 'bear' use ferō.

1.   The slaves were not able to bear the anger of their master.
2.   The old men were carrying water to the city.
3.   Sulpicia, aren't you carrying food and wine?
4.   That soldier is carrying a sword and a shield.

5. The wicked sailors were going through the city carrying spears.
6. I am bringing gold from the river and from the mountains.
7. The women are bringing help to the wounded citizens.
8. Will this horse really carry you to Rome?
9. Why are you happy? Because we are bringing gold into our city.
10. You (pl.) are bearing great dangers bravely.

Compounds of faciō

Remember, compounds of faciō, such as interficiō, unlike faciō itself, have a full house of passive forms. For example, interficitur = 'he is being killed', interficiēbantur = 'they were being killed' and so on.

tōtus, tōta, tōtum

Here's a very useful new word, namely tōtus. It is one of the insidious gang, declining like ūnus and sōlus, and it means 'whole'.

tōtus, tōta, tōtum = 'whole, whole of'			
Singular			
	Masculine	**Feminine**	**Neuter**
Nominative	tōtus	tōta	tōtum
Accusative	tōtum	tōtam	tōtum
Genitive	tōtīus	tōtīus	tōtīus
Dative	tōtī	tōtī	tōtī
Ablative	tōtō	tōtā	tōtō

Note:
The 'i' of the genitive tōtīus is sometimes short. tōtus is very common in the singular and less so in the plural, which is completely straightforward, as follows:

tōtī, tōtae, tōta = 'whole, whole of'			
Plural			
	Masculine	**Feminine**	**Neuter**
Nominative	tōtī	tōtae	tōta
Accusative	tōtōs	tōtās	tōta
Genitive	tōtōrum	tōtārum	tōtōrum
Dative	tōtīs	tōtīs	tōtīs
Ablative	tōtīs	tōtīs	tōtīs

This is how tōtus is used:

> oppidum tōtum oppugnātur.
> The whole (of the) city is being attacked.

> hunc librum tōtum laudō.
> I praise the whole of this book.

There is a specially nice use of tōtus, namely:

> tōtus in amōre est. (amor, -ōris, m. = love)
> He is, every bit of him, in love.

One might translate this last use of tōtus into English by the adverb 'totally'.

Exercise 5.6

Translate into English:

1. tōtum oppidum sagittīs oppugnābant.
2. cum hostibus in tōtō proeliō pugnābam.
3. ut sapiēns esset, hōs tōtōs librōs lēgit.
4. dum in templō cantābant, per tōtum agrum ambulābāmus.
5. per tōtam viam lūdunt puerī?
6. ō servī, dominus tōtus in īrā est!
7. nōlī partem mūrī aedificāre, sed tōtum mūrum aedificā!
8. huic tōtī locō[1] septem partes sunt.
9. saevī ventī tōta flūmina movent.
10. illa urbs pars maxima est tōtīus nostrae patriae.

[1] Remember the dative of the possessor (see *Latin Prep* Book 1, p.47)?

Exercise 5.7

Translate into Latin:

1. Whole cities were destroyed by winds.
2. The whole of the enemy's forces were conquered by our soldiers.
3. We have read the whole of the book which the teacher gave us.
4. The good young men built the whole of this wall.
5. That boy does not hear the teacher, because he is totally asleep.
6. The whole island has[1] nine parts.
7. The whole of this journey is very difficult.
8. In the whole war there was not a worse battle.
9. These words are a part of a whole work written by a poet.
10. Did you (pl.) really sail along the whole of the river?

[1] Use the dative of the possessor.

It's now time to return to Aeneas, whom we left long ago just after his escape from Troy.

Exercise 5.8

Read the following passage carefully, and answer the questions on it:

The story of Aeneas (4): Aeneas at last reaches Italy

1   <u>Aenēān</u> cum patre et fīliō et comitibus in montibus relīquimus; hī omnēs, ut novam patriam invenīrent, <u>classem</u> nāvium multārum aedificābant. et tandem nāvigāvērunt; sed dea

5   Iūnō, quae Troiānōs nōn amāvit, Aeolum, ventōrum deum, <u>classem</u> eōrum ventīs dēlēre iussit; Neptūnus tamen eōs <u>dēsistere</u> coēgit. tum <u>classis</u>, paene dēlēta, ad terram vēnit in quā Dīdō rēgīna ex suā patriā cum comitibus <u>expulsa</u>

10   novam urbem <u>Carthāginem</u> aedificābat; huius auxiliō Aenēās <u>classem</u> <u>refēcit</u>; et diū <u>Carthāgine</u> manēbat; nam Dīdō, ubi <u>ruīnam</u> Troiae ab eō nārrātam audīvit, eum <u>adamāvit</u>; sed Mercurius, ā Iove missus, eum discēdere iussit. tandem

15   Ītaliam advēnit. ibi urbem <u>condidit</u>, nōmine <u>Lāvīnium</u>; posteā Ascanius fīlius eius <u>Albam Longam</u> <u>condidit</u>; et <u>posterī</u> Aenēae, Rōmulus et Remus, <u>condidērunt</u> Rōmam.

Aenēān is the Greek accusative of Aenēās, commonly used by Latin authors

classis, classis, f. = fleet

dēsistō, -ere, dēstitī, dēstitum = I stop (intrans.), cease

expellō, -ere, expulī, expulsum = I drive away

Carthāgō, Carthāginis, f. = Carthage

reficiō, reficere, refēcī, refectum = I repair

ruīna, -ae, f. = downfall, fall

adamō, -āre, -āvī, -ātum (+ acc.) (here) = I fall in love with

Alba Longa, -ae, f. = Alba Longa

condō, -ere, condidī, conditum = I found, establish

Lāvīnium, -iī, n. = Lavinium

posterī, -ōrum, m. pl. = descendants

Notes:
(i) For Troiānōs (line 5) and Troiae (line 12) see p.1 on cuius.
(ii) Dīdō (line 8) is yet another Greek feminine name ending in '-ō'.
(iii) Iūnō (Juno, line 5), the equivalent of the Greek Hera, the wife of Jupiter, was one of the most powerful of the deities. Iūnō is a Latin name; the genitive is Iūnōnis.
(iv) Aeolus (line 5) was the god of the winds.
(v) Neptūnus (line 7), god of the sea, was a very mighty god indeed. His Greek name was Poseidon.
(vi) Mercurius (line 13), known to the Greeks as Hermes, was, among other things, the messenger of the gods.
(vii) After Aeneas' desertion of Dido, Rome and Carthage ultimately became bitter enemies. Aeneas was regarded as the fore-father of Romulus and Remus, the founders of Rome. Rome was founded in 753 BC.

1. Answer the following questions:
   (a) In lines 1-2, where was Aeneas when we last mentioned him?
   (b) In lines 3-4, what was he doing there with all his companions?
   (c) In lines 2-3, why were they doing this?
   (d) In lines 5-7, how did Juno plan to destroy the Trojan fleet?
   (e) In line 7, how was her plan foiled?
   (f) In lines 8-9, why was Dido in the land to which Aeneas came with his damaged fleet?
   (g) In line 10, what was she doing in that land?
   (h) In lines 12-13, what caused Dido to fall in love with Aeneas?
   (i) In line 14, why was Mercury's order so effective?
   (j) In lines 15-18, was Aeneas famous for founding Rome? Answer in full.

2. Translate the passage fore-fatherishly (I hope you like this word).

3. Answer the following questions:
   (a) comitibus (line 1); what case is this word here, and what is its nominative singular?
   (b) relīquimus (line 2); what tense is this and of what verb? Translate it.
   (c) invenīrent (line 3); what is the mood of this verb? Why is it in this mood?
   (d) In lines 4-5, how does Iūnō relate to dea in this sentence? Mention and translate any other examples of this feature.
   (e) In line 7, if, instead of '(she) ordered', we had wished to say '(she) will order', to what would we have had to change iussit?
   (f) dēlēta (line 8); what part of what verb is this? Mention and translate any other examples of this part.
   (g) huius auxiliō (lines 10-11); what case is auxiliō? Translate these two words.
   (h) In lines 12-13, discuss the position of the clause ubi...audīvit? in the sentence.
   (i) In line 15, put advēnit into the imperfect subjunctive.
   (j) In line 16, what part of speech is posteā? (See *Latin Prep* 2, p.57)

Indirect command

And now – we've been saving this one up – we've got a really magnificent new construction. It is called an indirect command, and it works as follows.

A direct command is an 'imperative'. For example,

> hōs librōs portā!
> Carry these books!

The command becomes indirect if, instead of using an imperative, we say 'I ask you to carry these books'. The regular way of translating 'to carry' into Latin is not to use the infinitive, as we do in English, but to use our old friend ut plus the subjunctive. And don't forget the sequence of tenses. In other words, in the sentence, 'I asked him to carry those books', 'to carry' would be ut + the imperfect subjunctive. Thus:

> I asked him to carry those books.
> eum ut illōs librōs portāret rogāvī.

A quick word before you expostulate (I hope you like this word also) – I agree, by the way – that 'ask' is hardly a word of command. To be quite honest, this construction applies to any sentence in which the subject of the main verb is trying to get someone else to do something.

And do I hear another expostulation? I think I do. After all we've been following iubeō, which means 'I order', with an infinitive happily for ages. What about that? I can only hang my head at this and confess very feebly that iubeō is an exception. And so is cōgō, before you come at me again. However, we can, nay must, use rogō and moneō with our new construction, and here are two splendid other verbs which we can add to them:

imperō, -āre, -āvī, -ātum (+ dat.) = I order, command
persuādeō, -ēre, persuāsī, persuāsum (+ dat.) = I persuade

(imperō is much stronger than iubeō.)

Note that both these new verbs are followed by the dative.

So here are a few examples of this construction:

parentēs nostrī nōs ut bene labōrārēmus monēbant.
Our parents used to advise us to work well.

magister puerōs ut librōs portārent rogāvit.
The teacher asked the boys to carry the books.

rēgīna mulieribus ut in templō cantārent persuāsit.
The queen persuaded the women to sing in the temple.

dux mīlitibus ut fortiter pugnārent imperāvit.
The leader commanded the soldiers to fight bravely.

The negative of ut is nē. Thus:

nē iterum clāmārēs tē monuī.
I warned you not to shout again.

Exercise 5.9

Translate into English:

1. magister puerōs ut librum legerent monuit.
2. nautās ut discēderent rogāvimus.
3. dominī servōs nē male labōrārent monuerant.
4. saepe rēgem incolae ut senibus auxilium daret rogābant.
5. hostēs nōs ut in urbe manērēmus monuērunt.
6. agricola puerōs nē in agrō lūderent rogābat.
7. cūr vōs ut ad flūmen currerētis monēbant?
8. num tē ut multum vīnum biberēs rogāverant?

Exercise 5.10

Translate into Latin:

1. I advised the boys to play in the fields.
2. We asked the soldier not to wound the old man.
3. The leader warned us to stay in the city.
4. Did they ask you (sing.) to read those books?
5. I warned you (pl.) not to stand in the road.
6. I asked them to depart.
7. They advised us to watch the sea.
8. He asked us not to shout near the temple.

Exercise 5.11

Translate into English:

1. dux mīlitibus ut in hostēs ruerent imperāvit.
2. puerīs ut sē bene gererent persuāsimus.
3. rēgīna ancillīs ut cibum parārent imperāverat.
4. puellīs nē in viā lūderent persuāsī.
5. magistrī nōbīs nē clāmārēmus saepe imperābant.
6. agricolae incolīs ut mūrum aedificārent persuāsērunt.
7. illīs malīs iuvenibus nē equōs vulnerārent imperāvī.
8. cīvibus ut urbem dēfenderent persuāsī.

Exercise 5.12

Translate into Latin, always using ut/nē (+ the subjunctive):

1. Our mother persuaded us to read many good books.
2. The king ordered the inhabitants to build ten walls.
3. Who persuaded you (pl.) to depart from the city?
4. Had not the leader commanded the young men to work in the fields?
5. We persuaded the enemy not to attack our city.
6. Who commanded our forces to depart from the island?
7. Did I not order you (pl.) not to do that[1] again?
8. Had the old men really persuaded the young men to save the captured citizens?

[1] For 'that' use the neuter of ille.

The passive of ferō

And now we come to the passive of ferō.

The imperfect and future passive are regular, producing: ferēbar and ferar, which go like regēbar and regar. The present passive, however is not so obliging. This is how it goes:

Present tense passive of ferō:
feror = 'I am being carried, borne, brought'

1st person singular	feror	I am being carried, borne, brought
2nd person singular	ferris	you (sing.) are being carried, borne, brought
3rd person singular	fertur	he, she, it is being carried, borne, brought
1st person plural	ferimur	we are being carried, borne, brought
2nd person plural	feriminī	you (pl.) are being carried, borne, brought
3rd person plural	feruntur	they are being carried, borne, brought

The 2nd person singular is the strangest part here; the third person singular remains irregular but less oddly so, whereas the plural performs a double bluff and is oh! so innocently regular: indeed butter wouldn't melt in its mouth.

N.B. fertur often means 'it is said'; feror often means 'I rush'.

The perfect passive is lātus sum.

Exercise 5.13

Write out the present passive of ferō as it is written above, and repeat it to yourself in Latin – day and night, I need hardly say, not to mention night and day.

Exercise 5.14

Translate into English:

1. quid ad mē fertur?
2. nāvibus per mare ferimur.
3. magnīs undīs ad terram feruntur.
4. cūr ā puerīs ferris?
5. in proelium feror.
6. num īn flūmen feriminī?
7. equus vulnerātus ad agricolam fertur.
8. hastae ā iuvenibus ad mīlitēs feruntur.

Exercise 5.15

Translate into Latin, using ferō:

1.   Food is being brought to me.
2.   The old men are being carried by the young men.
3.   We are being carried to the river.
4.   What is being brought to the leader?
5.   Why are you (sing.) being carried by the citizens?
6.   Are you (pl.) being brought to the island by these ships?
7.   I am being carried to the temple.
8.   The women are being carried to the city.

Idioms

Now for some nice idioms involving some of the words which we have recently learnt:

(i) aliī...aliī

aliī...aliī means 'some...others'. For example:

> aliī urbem dēlēbant, aliī dēfendēbant.
> Some were destroying the city, others were defending it.

alius can be in an oblique (i.e. one other than the nominative or vocative) case. Thus:

> aliī aliōs laudant.
> Some praise some men and others praise others.

(ii) is quī and eī quī

is quī means 'one who…', 'a man who…', 'he who…'
eī quī means 'they who…', 'men who…', 'those who…'

Thus:

> is quī celeriter currit = a swift runner
> eī quī animālia amant = animal lovers

is might well be in an oblique case. Thus:

> eōs, quī bene cantant, amāmus.
> We love good singers.

The neuter singular (id quod = 'that which') also occurs very often.

(iii) īdem

And now for something about īdem.

> Titus parvus est, īdem validissimus.
> Titus is small, yet (that same Titus) is very strong.

Here īdem has introduced a new idea which contains an unexpected contrast to the previous one. A good English translation here would be 'Though Titus is small, he is very strong'.

Two more nice little things and we are done.

(iv) multus

When multus is followed by an adjective and a noun, it is regularly joined to the adjective by et (remember?). Thus:

> Many beautiful cities
> multae et pulchrae urbēs

But when the adjective is used as a noun, the word et is omitted. Thus:

> Multī bonī
> Many good (men)

(v) And, finally, the present infinitive

The present infinitive can often be translated as an abstract noun. Thus:

> labōrāre est ōrāre
> To work is to pray (i.e. work is prayer)

> dulce est vincere (dulcis, -e = sweet)
> It is sweet to conquer (i.e. victory is sweet)

A note on using vocabularies and dictionaries

Take a word such as 'concerning'. You cannot find it in your English-Latin vocabulary. Do not lose heart, but think of a synonym of 'concerning'. Ah! yes, here it is – 'about'. Look up 'about' and there it is – dē. Again, you have to translate 'we hastened'. Alas! It is not in the vocabulary. But what about 'hurry'? We don't even need to look up this old friend, and the answer is festīnāvimus. I hope you will find this useful – and good for your English too.

And so, we come at last to our next story.

Exercise 5.16

Read the following passage carefully, and answer the questions on it:

Horatius holds the bridge

1 Lars Porsenna, rēx Clūsiī, urbis Etruscae, bellum cum Rōmānīs gerēbat. Rōma mūrīs et flūmine Tiberī dēfēnsa est, sed pōns fuit ligneus nōmine Sublicius trāns quem flūmen trānsīre facile erat.

5 Etruscī ad pontem ruēbant, et Rōmānī territī fugiēbant, sed vir ūnus, Horātius Cocles nōmine, eōs, nē hostēs flūmen transīre possent, pontem dēlēre iussit; intereā ipse in parte pontis ulteriōre plūrimīs mīlitibus Etruscīs prīmō sōlus, deinde

10 cum duōbus comitibus Sp. Lartiō et T. Herminiō resistēbat; hōs tamen Horātius, ubi pōns iam paene dēlētus est, trāns eum quam celerrimē currere iussit, sed ipse mānsit hostēs dērīdēns et sē scūtō dēfendēns. tandem cecidit pōns, et

15 Horātius patrem Tiberim ut sibi auxilium ferret ōrāvit et īn flūmen dēsiluit et, quamquam multīs vulneribus vulnerātus est, tūtus ad rīpam Rōmānam adnāvit.

Clūsium, -iī, n. = Clusium, a city in Etruria
Etruscus, -a, -um = Etruscan
Tiberis, -is, m. = the river Tiber (see below)
pōns, pontis, m. = bridge
ligneus, -a, -um = wooden
ulterior, -ōris = further
prīmō = at first
resistō, -ere, restitī (+ dat.) = I resist
dērīdeō, -ēre, dērīsī, dērīsum = I laugh at, mock
cadō, -ere, cecidī, cāsum = I fall
ōrō, -āre, -āvī, -ātum = I pray, beg
dēsiliō, -īre, desiluī, dēsultum = I jump down
rīpa, -ae, f. = bank, shore
adnō, -āre, -āvī, -ātum = I swim to

Notes:

(i)   The story of Horatius (6th Century BC) is told by the great Roman historian Titus Līvius (59 BC–17 AD), whom we call Livy, in Book 2 of his work entitled 'ab urbe conditā', 'From the Foundation of the City' (lit. 'from the city having been founded').

(ii)   The river Tiber is Tiberis, -is, m. and its accusative is regularly Tiberim. Its ablative singular is Tiberī.

(iii)   The Etruscans were a great and important people in Italy, with whom Rome was frequently in conflict.

1.   Answer the following questions:

(a) In line 1, who was Lars Porsenna?

(b) In lines 3-4, was there any weak point in Rome's defences? Explain your answer.

(c) In line 5, why were the Romans terrified?

(d) In lines 7-8, why did Horatius tell the Romans to destroy the bridge?

(e) In line 8, where was Horatius while the Romans were destroying the bridge?

(f) In lines 9-11, was he alone all the time?

(g) In lines 15-16, to whom did he turn when the bridge collapsed?

(h) In lines 15-16, what did he ask for?

(i) In lines 17-18, did he receive this? Explain your answer.

(j) quamquam...adnāvit (lines 16-18); what makes this feat all the more remarkable?

2.   Translate the passage pontifically.

3. Answer the following questions:

(a) In line 1, how does rēx relate to Lars Porsenna? Mention and translate any other examples of this feature in the passage.

(b) In line 3, what tense is dēfēnsa est?

(c) In line 4, what part of what verb is trānsīre? Mention and translate any other such parts in the passage.

(d) In line 4, what is the gender of facile?

(e) ne...possent (line 7); what kind of clause is this?

(f) sōlus (line 9); write the genitive and dative singular of this word.

(g) quam celerrimē (line 12); what part of speech is celerrimē? (see *Latin Prep 2*, p.88)

(h) In lines 13-14, what part of their verbs are dērīdēns and dēfendēns?

(i) ut...ferret (line 15); what construction is this?

(j) In line 18, if, instead of 'he swam to', we wanted to say 'he had swum to', to what would we have to change adnāvit?

nō

A little story about nō.

Believe it or not, adnō is a compound of nō, nāre, nāvī, nātum = 'I swim'.

A very long time ago a grandfather asked his little grandson whether he could swim. 'No' answered the boy, whereupon the grandfather, delighted at this affirmative answer in Latin, presented his grandson with five shillings.

Exercise 5.17

Match up the Latin words 1 – 7 with the English ones a – g. Explain the connexion between them:

	Latin		English
1.	volō	a.	millennium
2.	tōtus	b.	deride
3.	somnus	c.	imperious
4.	paene	d.	voluntary
5.	mīlle	e.	peninsula[1]
6.	imperō	f.	insomnia
7.	rīdeō	g.	total

[1] '-ae' in a Latin word often becomes 'e' in English.

Exercise 5.18

Translate into Latin:

1. The little boys praised the brave young men.
2. The cruel soldier killed the wretched old man with a sword.
3. The happy citizens were hearing beautiful words.
4. The enemy attacked our city with many arrows.
5. You (sing.) have read all my books.
6. We hastened into the city in order to defend it.
7. Did you (pl.) really warn the soldiers not to cross the river?
8. He walked through the fields laughing.
9. Forced to work, we were unhappy.
10. Though the task is difficult, we shall do it well.

Vocabulary 5

Vocabulary 5

septuāgintā = seventy
octōgintā = eighty
nōnāgintā = ninety
mīlle = a thousand

ferō, ferre, tulī, lātum = I carry, bear, bring
imperō, -āre, -āvī, -ātum (+ dat.) = I order, command
interficiō, -ere, interfēcī, interfectum = I kill
lentē = slowly
persuādeō, -ēre, persuāsī, persuāsum (+ dat.)
    = I persuade

And now for a glorious chapter of lovely stories!

Chapter 6

Exercise 6.1

Read the following passage (do not write a translation) and answer the questions below in English. Complete sentences are not required.

Homer's Iliad (The Wrath of Achilles): Achilles and Agamemnon quarrel

1 Graecī puellam ex oppidō <u>Chrȳsā</u> captam
Agamemnonī dederant; pater illīus, <u>sacerdōs</u>
Apollinis, ad Graecōs, ut fīliam <u>redimeret</u>,
plūrima et pulcherrima dōna tulit; sed,

5 quamquam mīlitēs <u>sacerdōtī</u> <u>favēbant</u>,
Agamemnōn eī <u>maledīxit</u> et ut discēderet
imperāvit. ille Apollinem ut sibi auxilium ferret
<u>ōrāvit</u>; et Apollō plūrimōs Graecōs <u>morbō</u>
interficiēbat. tandem <u>vātem</u> Calchantem rogāvit

10 Achillēs: 'cūr nōs pūnit Apollō?' respondit
Calchās perterritus: 'quod Agamemnōn fīliam
patrī <u>reddere</u> nōluit'. Agamemnōn īrātissimus
erat, sed Achillēs <u>vātem</u> dēfendit. tum
Agamemnōn et Achillēs <u>inter sē</u> <u>altercātī sunt</u>; et

15 tandem huīc ille dīxit: 'ego <u>sacerdōtī</u> fīliam eius
<u>reddam</u>, sed puellam tuam <u>Brīsēida</u> <u>prō eā</u>
capiam.' tum dīxit Achillēs: '<u>nōn iam</u> in proelium
inībō,' et cum Patroclō, amīcō suō, discessit; et
<u>Brīsēida</u> cēpit Agamemnōn.

Chrȳsa, -ae, f. = Chryse (a town near Troy)
sacerdōs, -ōtis, c. = priest/priestess
redimō, -ere, redēmī, redēmptum (here) = I ransom
faveō, -ēre, fāvī, fautum (+ dat.) = I favour, support
maledīcō, -ere, maledīxī, maledictum (+ dat.) = I abuse, curse (lit. 'speak badly')
ōrō, -āre, -āvī, -ātum = I beg, pray
morbus, -ī, m. = disease
vātēs, -is, c. = prophet, poet
reddō, -ere, reddidī, redditum = I give back
inter sē (here) = with each other
altercor, -ārī, -ātus sum = I quarrel
Brīsēida is the Greek accusative of Brīsēis, -idis, f.
prō eā (here) = instead of her, in her place
nōn iam = no longer

(a) In lines 2-3, who was the girl's father?
(b) In line 3, why did the girl's father come to the Greeks?
(c) In line 4, what did he bring with him?
(d) In line 5, what did the Greek army feel about him?
(e) In lines 6-7, did Agamemnon feel the same?
(f) In lines 7-8, what did the father do?
(g) In line 10, what did Achilles ask the prophet?
(h) In lines 12-13, why was Agamemnon īrātissimus?
(i) In lines 16-17, what threat did Agamemnon deliver to Achilles?
(j) In lines 17-18, what threat did Achilles deliver in return?

Exercise 6.2

Translate the following passage into good English:

Achilles refuses to fight

1 Achillēs mātrem suam <u>Thetin</u>, quae dea erat, ut
sibi auxilium ferret <u>ōrāvit</u>; et illa <u>Iovem</u> ut Troiānīs
<u>favēret</u> <u>ōrāvit</u>; et dum Achillēs pugnāre nōlēbat,
Hector, dux Troiānōrum, <u>nātū maximus</u> fīliōrum
5 Priamī rēgis, omnēs Graecōs superābat.
Agamemnōn magnopere <u>perturbābātur</u> et
tandem trēs ducēs, Phoenīcem, Aiācem, Ulixem,
ut Achillem in proelium <u>revocārent</u>, ad <u>māgālia</u>
<u>Myrmidonum</u> mīsit. Phoenīx, quī senex erat,
10 Achillem <u>ā puerō</u> <u>ēducāverat</u> et ab eō maximē
amābātur; Aiāx post Achillem optimus erat
<u>hērōum</u> Graecōrum; Ulixēs <u>callidissimus</u> erat et
<u>vaferrimus</u>. hī Achillī persuādēre ut in proelium
redīret <u>temptāvērunt</u>: dōna plūrima et
15 pulcherrima <u>prōmīserat</u> Agamemnōn; <u>reddere</u>
cōnstituerat <u>Brīsēida</u>. sed quamquam Graecī ā
Troiānīs et ab Hectore <u>praecipuē</u> superābantur,
quamquam in maximō perīculō erant,
quamquam Achillem maximē <u>dēsīderābant</u>,
20 Achillēs in proelium nōn rediit.

Thetin is the Greek accusative of
 Thetis
ōrō, -āre, -āvī, -ātum (here) = I beg
Iuppiter, Iovis, m. = Jupiter
faveō, -ēre, fāvī, fautum (+ dat.) =
 I favour, support
nātū maximus = oldest
perturbō, -āre, -āvī, -ātum = I upset
revocō, -āre, -āvī, -ātum = I call back
māgālia, -ium, n. pl. = huts
Myrmidonēs, -um, m. pl. =
 Myrmidons (a people of Thessaly
 ruled over by Achilles)
ā puerō = from his boyhood
ēducō, -āre, -āvī, -ātum = I educate
hērōs, hērōis, m. = hero
callidus, -a, -um = clever
vafer, vafra, vafrum = cunning
temptō, -āre, -āvī, -ātum = I try
prōmittō, -ere, prōmīsī, prōmissum
 = I promise
reddō, -ere, reddidī, redditum =
 I give back
Brīsēida is the Greek accusative of
 Brīsēis
praecipuē = chiefly, especially
dēsīderō, -āre, -āvī, -ātum = I long
 for, miss

Exercise 6.3

Study the following passage and answer the questions below in good English.
Complete sentences are not required.

At last Achilles returns to the battle

1   Patroclus, dum Graecī superantur, ut arma sibi
        optima et validissima <u>commodāret</u> Achillem
        <u>ōrābat</u>; Achillēs, quod eum magnopere amāvit,
        sua arma eī <u>commodāvit</u>; et Patroclus in
5   proelium iit; ibi cum Hectore pugnāvit et ab eō
        occīsus est; et Hector arma Achillis, in quibus
        scūtum erat <u>magnificum</u>, <u>abstulit</u>. Achillēs, ubi
        mortem Patroclī <u>cognōvit</u>, maximē <u>doluit</u> et
        tandem in proelium rediit; sed <u>anteā</u> mātrem
10   <u>Thetin</u> ut nova sibi arma ā deō <u>Volcānō</u>
        <u>impetrāret</u> <u>ōrāvit</u>; et arma, in quibus scūtum erat
        <u>magnificentissimum</u>, fēcit <u>Volcānus</u>; eīs <u>armātus</u>
        Achillēs cum Hectore pugnāvit; et eum interfēcit
        et corpus eius circum mūrōs Troiae <u>trāxit</u>.
15   Priamus senex, pater Hectoris, ā dīs dēfēnsus,
        ad <u>māgālia</u> Graecōrum iit et Achillem ut sibi fīliī
        corpus <u>redderet</u> <u>ōrāvit</u>; Achillēs, patris suī
        <u>memor</u>, corpus Hectoris patrī <u>reddidit</u>; et Troiānī
        Hectorem <u>sepelīre</u> parābant.

commodō, -āre, -āvī, -ātum = I lend
ōrō, -āre, -āvī, -ātum (here) = I beg
magnificus, -a, -um = magnificent
auferō, auferre, abstulī, ablātum =
  I carry off
cognōscō, -ere, cognōvī, cognitum
  = I get to know about, learn of (+
  acc.)
doleō, -ēre, doluī, dolitum = I grieve
anteā = beforehand
Thetin is the Greek accusative of
  Thetis
Volcānus, -ī, m. = Vulcan, the god of
  fire, son of Jupiter and his wife
  Juno
impetrō, -āre, -āvī, -ātum = I obtain
  something by asking for it
magnificentissimus; superlative of
  magnificus, -a, -um = magnificent
armō, -āre, -āvī, -ātum = I arm
  (trans.)
trahō, -ere, trāxī, tractum = I drag
māgālia, -ium, n. pl. = hut
reddō, -ere, reddidī, redditum =
  I give back
memor, -oris (irreg.) = mindful (of)
sepeliō, -īre, -īvī, sepultum = I bury

(a) optima (line 2); of which adjective is optimus the superlative?
(b) In line 2, why is commodāret in the subjunctive?
(c) in proelium (lines 4-5); what is the case of proelium? Why is it in this case?
(d) doluit (line 8); if, instead of 'he grieved', we had wished to say 'they grieved', to what would we have had to change doluit?
(e) In line 9, what part of which verb is rediit?
(f) In line 10, how does Volcānō relate to deō?
(g) In line 14, what case of which noun is corpus?
(h) Mention and translate all the prepositions in this passage together with the nouns or pronouns which they govern.
(i) dēfēnsus (line 15); what part of which verb is this?
(j) In line 17, put patris into the genitive plural.

Exercise 6.4

Using the vocabulary given below, translate into Latin:

(i) The cruel enemy were attacking the big city with arrows.

cruel = crūdēlis, -e   enemy = hostēs, -ium, c. pl.
I attack = oppugnō, -āre, -āvī, -ātum   big = magnus, -a, -um
city = urbs, -is, f.   arrow = sagitta, -ae, f.

(ii) The brave soldier defended the frightened old man with a sword.

brave = fortis, -e   soldier = mīles, -itis, c.
defend = dēfendō, -ere, dēfendī, dēfēnsum   frightened = perterritus, -a, -um
old man = senex, senis, m.   sword = gladius, -iī, m.

Exercise 6.5

Read the following passage (do not write a translation) and answer the questions below in English. Complete sentences are not required.

Nero becomes Emperor: things go well

1 post Claudium fuit Nerō: dē eō, ubi <u>nātus est</u>,
   pater eius, 'nēmō' dīxit 'ex mē et Agrippīnā
   <u>nātus esse</u> potest quī nōn <u>dētestābilis</u> erit.'
   Agrippīna māter fuit Nerōnis. is, sub Caligulā
5 <u>avunculō</u> suō, <u>paedagōgōs</u> habuit duo,
   <u>saltātōrem</u> et <u>tōnsōrem</u>; ā Claudiō, quī
   Agrippīnam <u>dūxerat</u>, quamquam fīlium suum ille
   habuit Britannicum, <u>adoptātus</u> est; et
   <u>paedagōgum</u> habuit Senecam. ubi Claudius
10 <u>mortuus est</u>, <u>septimō decimō</u> annō suō, prīnceps
   factus est. mātrem suam maximē laudāvit; prīmō
   diē <u>imperiī</u> suī <u>excubitōribus</u> <u>signum</u> dedit
   'optima māter'. sed illa, ubi ab eō nōn <u>satis</u>
   <u>potestātis</u> accēpit, Britannicō <u>fāvit</u>; hunc,
15 quattuordecim <u>annōs nātum</u>, Nerō <u>venēnō</u>, <u>ut</u>
   dīcēbant hominēs, interfēcit. <u>plērumque</u> tamen
   sē <u>benignē</u> gerēbat et omnibus <u>placēre</u>
   <u>temptābat</u>; ubi <u>dē suppliciō</u> <u>subscrībere</u> <u>dēbuit</u>,
   'volō' dīxit 'scrībere nōn posse.' per quīnque
20 annōs paene omnia Senecae, quī rēs omnēs
   mōre maiōrum gerēbat, trādidit; ipse <u>sibi</u>
   <u>indulgēbat</u>; et hī annī fēlīcissimī vocātī sunt.

nātus, -a, -um sum = I was born
dētestābilis, -e = hateful
avunculus, -ī, m. = uncle (maternal)
paedagōgus, -ī, m. = tutor
saltātor, -ōris, m. = dancer
tōnsor, -ōris, m. = barber
dūcō, -ere, dūxī, ductum (here) =
   I marry (of men)
adoptō, -āre, -āvī, -ātum = I adopt
mortuus est = (he) died
septimus decimus = seventeenth
imperium, -iī, n. = rule, power
excubitor, -ōris, m. = sentryman
signum, -ī, n. = sign; (here) =
   password
satis (+ gen.) = enough (of)
potestās, -ātis, f. = power
faveō, -ēre, fāvī, fautum (+ dat.) =
   I favour, support
x annōs nātus = x years old
venēnum, -ī, n. = poison
ut (+ indicative) = as
plērumque = on the whole
benignus, -a, -um = kind
placeō, -ēre, -uī, -itum (+ dat.) =
   I please
temptō, -āre, -āvī, -ātum = I try
dē suppliciō subscrībō (here) = I
   sign a death sentence
dēbeō, -ēre, -uī, -itum = I must, have
   to
sibi indulgēbat (here) = (he) enjoyed
   himself

Notes:

(i) Seneca (line 9) (c.5 BC – 65 AD) is one of the most famous Roman authors; he wrote many philosophical works and letters which have survived.

(ii) mōre maiōrum (line 21) means 'in the way of our ancestors'; (see *Latin Prep 2*, p.82).

(a) In lines 1-3, what do we learn about Nero's father (who, incidentally, died when Nero was three years old)?

(b) In lines 5-6, does it sound as if Caligula took Nero seriously? Explain your answer.

(c) In lines 6-8, is it strange that Claudius adopted Nero? Explain your answer.

(d) In line 10, do you think Nero was old enough to be Emperor?

(e) In lines 11-13, what do we learn about Nero's feelings for his mother? Answer in full.

(f) In lines 13-14, why was she dissatisfied with Nero?

(g) In lines 13-14, what did she do about this?

(h) In lines 14-16, how is Nero said to have solved this problem?

(i) In lines 18-19, what did Nero feel about having to sign a death-sentence?

(j) In lines 19-21, did Nero have much to do with the administration of the Empire during these five years? Answer in full.

Exercise 6.6

Translate the following passage into good English:

Things go less well with Nero

1   māter Nerōnis, Agrippīna, contrā fīlium <u>cōnsilia</u>
     inībat; hic eam <u>magis</u> <u>magis</u>que timēbat:
     tandem eam necāre cōnstituit; mīlitī quī eam
     interficiēbat, '<u>ventrem</u> <u>ferī</u>' dīxit; post <u>necem</u>
5   mātris nōn, <u>ut</u> timēbat, ab hominibus <u>culpābātur</u>,
     sed, quod illa <u>invidiōsissima</u> erat, maximē
     laudābātur. uxōrem suam Octāviam, fēminam
     <u>innocentem</u>, quam <u>sextō decimō</u> annō <u>dūxit</u>,
     quod eam nōn amābat, <u>repudiāvit</u>; haec tandem
10   occīsa est. Octāviae <u>dissimillimam</u> Poppaeam,
	cōnsilium, -iī, n. (here) = plan, plot
	magis = more
	venter, ventris, m. (here) = womb
	feriō, -īre, (no perfect or supine) =
	   I strike
	nex, necis, f. = murder
	ut (+ indic.) = as
	culpō, -āre, -āvī, -ātum = I blame
	invidiōsus, -a, -um = hated
	innocēns, -entis = innocent
	sextus decimus = sixteenth
	dūcō, -ere, dūxī, ductum (here) =
	   I marry (of a man)
	repudiō, -āre, -āvī, -ātum = I divorce
	dissimillimus, -a, -um (+ gen. or dat.)
	   = most unlike

quam <u>ūnicē</u> amāvit, <u>dūxit</u>; sed ōlim, ubi <u>domum</u>
<u>sērō</u> rediit, ab eā <u>reprehēnsus</u>, īrātus eam <u>calce</u>
<u>percussit</u>; et <u>mortua est</u>. Nerō <u>artēs</u> Graecōrum
maximē amābat; <u>senātōribus</u> ut eī quoque illās
15   amārent persuādēre volēbat; fēminās et virōs
<u>gravissimōs</u> <u>saltāre</u> et <u>partēs agere</u> coēgit; ipse
<u>carmina</u> scrībēbat et aliīs ut scrīberent persuāsit;
ipse īn <u>scaenā</u> cantābat. etiam multōs occīdit, ā
multīs pecūniam cēpit, sē <u>turpissimē</u> gerēbat. et
20   tum urbs Rōma ingentī <u>incendiō</u> <u>vastāta</u> est.

ūnicē = outstandingly
domum = home
sērō = late
reprehendō, -ere, reprehendī,
   reprehēnsum = I reproach
calce percussit = he kicked
   (percutiō, -ere, percussī,
   percussum = I strike; calx, calcis,
   f. = heel)
mortua est = she died
ars, artis, f. = art
senātor, -ōris, m. = senator
gravis, -e (here) = dignified
saltō, -āre, -āvī, -ātum = I dance
partēs agō, agere, ēgī, āctum = I act
   (in a play)
carmen, -inis, n. = song, poem
scaena, -ae, f. = stage
turpis, -e = disgraceful
incendium, -iī, n. = a fire
vastō, -āre, -āvī, -ātum = I lay waste

Exercise 6.7

Study the following passage and answer the questions below in good English. Complete sentences are not required.

Nero comes to a bad end

1	incendium maximum magnam partem Rōmae
	dēlēvit. cīvēs, quamquam Nerō eīs omne genus
	auxiliī dedit, quod magnificam sibi domum
	auream, ubi parva domicilia fuerant, aedificāvit,
5	eum maximē ōderant. 'Nerō' dīcēbant, 'dē
	industriā, ut urbem pulcherrimam faceret,
	incendiō eam dēlēvit.' sīc quoque dīcēbant: 'Nerō
	dum flammās spectābat, eās, quod tam pulchrae
	erant, laudābat et dē eīs carmen ā sē dē Troiae
10	ruīnā scrīptum cantābat.' Chrīstiānōs incēnsiōnis
	arguit, et eōs crūdēlissimē pūnīvit. tum coniūrātī
	Nerōnem interficere et Pīsōnem, hominem nōn
	multō meliōrem, prīncipem facere temptāvērunt;
	sed prōditī sunt et ipsī interfectī; deinde Nerō in
15	Graeciam discessit et ibi in multīs urbibus cantāvit
	et ab omnibus praemia accēpit; et tōtam
	prōvinciam Graeciam ā Rōmānīs līberāvit. ubi
	Rōmam rediit, ducēs mīlitum sēditiōnēs fēcērunt;
	ā senātōribus hostis iūdicātus 'quālis artifex
20	pereō' dīxit et, mortem timēns saevissimam, sē
	ipse famulī auxiliō aegrē occīdit.

incendium, -iī, n. = a fire
genus, -eris, n. = sort, kind
magnificus, -a, -um = magnificent
domus, f. (irregular) = house
aureus, -a, -um = golden
domicilium, -iī, n. = dwelling
ōderant = hated (see below)
dē industriā = on purpose
flamma, -ae, f. = flame
tam = so
carmen, -inis, n. = song, poem
ruīna, -ae, f. = (the) fall
Chrīstiānus, -ī, m. = a Christian
incēnsiō, -ōnis, f. = arson
arguō, -ere, arguī, argūtum = I accuse
coniūrātus, -ī, m. = conspirator
temptō, -āre, -āvī, -ātum = I try
prōdō, -ere, prōdidī, prōditum = I betray
Graecia, -ae, f. = Greece
praemium, -iī, n. (here) = prize
prōvincia, -ae, f. = a (Roman) province
sēditiō, -ōnis, f. = mutiny
senātor, -ōris, m. = senator
iūdicō, -āre, -āvī, -ātum = I judge, (here) = I proclaim
quālis artifex = what an artist
famulus, -ī, m. = servant
aegrē = with difficulty

Notes:

(i)   ōdī (line 5) = I hate: it is perfect in form but present in meaning; thus ōderam is pluperfect in form and perfect/past in meaning.

(ii)   multō (line 13); 'much' followed by a comparative becomes multō in Latin, the ablative case meaning 'by much'.

(a) In line 1, what is the case of maximum?
(b) In line 2, give the case and gender of omne.
(c) maximē (line 5); what part of speech is this word?
(d) faceret (line 6); what part of which verb is this? Explain its use here.
(e) In line 7, if, instead of 'they used to say', we wanted to say 'they said', to what would we have to change dīcēbant?
(f) In line 8, put spectābat into the subjunctive.
(g) In line 12, how does hominem relate to Pīsōnem?
(h) In line 18, why is there no preposition before Rōmam?
(i) ā senātōribus (line 19); this means 'by the senators'. Why is ā necessary here?
(j) In line 20, what part of timeō is timēns? Translate it.

Exercise 6.8

Using the vocabulary given below, translate into Latin:

(i) The brave citizens sought great rewards.

brave = fortis, -e	citizen = cīvis, cīvis, c.
I seek = petō, -ere, petīvī, petītum	great = magnus, -a, -um
reward = praemium, -iī, n.	

(ii) The happy young men were reading good messages.

happy = laetus, -a, -um	young man = iuvenis, iuvenis, m.
I read = legō, -ere, lēgī, lēctum	good = bonus, -a, -um
message = nūntius, -iī, m.	

Exercise 6.9

Study the following passage (do not write a translation) and answer the questions below in English. Complete sentences are not required.

The birth and upbringing of Perseus

1   Acrisius, rēx <u>Argōrum</u>, fīliōs nōn habuit, sed fīliam habuit ūnam, <u>Danaēn</u>: rogāvit igitur <u>ōrāculum</u>: 'fīliumne habēre poterō?' respondit <u>sacerdōs</u>: 'fīlium habēre nōn poteris; et <u>nepōs</u>
5   tuus tē interficiet.' Acrisius, ubi hoc audīvit, fīliam in <u>carcere</u> <u>inclūsit</u>, cuius <u>iānuae</u> <u>aēneae</u> erant; ibi ā saevīs <u>canibus</u> custōdiēbātur. sed Iuppiter, quī eam amāvit, in <u>imbrem</u> <u>aureum</u> <u>conversus</u>, ad <u>Danaēn</u> <u>pervēnit</u>; et <u>genuit</u> illa
10   <u>Persea</u>; hoc ubi <u>cognōvit</u> Acrisius, maximē īrātus est; et <u>Danaēn</u> cum fīliō in <u>arcā</u> <u>ligneā</u> <u>inclūsit</u>; et <u>arcam</u> in mare iēcit; ea īnsulae appropinquāvit <u>Serīphō</u>; et ibi ā <u>piscātōre</u> <u>rēte</u> capta est; is, ubi <u>arcam</u> <u>aperuit</u>, mātrem et fīlium <u>adhūc</u> vīvōs
15   invēnit; eōs ad frātrem suum, <u>Polydectam</u>, rēgem īnsulae, <u>contulit</u>; et is <u>Persea</u> <u>apud</u> sē <u>ēducāvit</u>.

Argī, -ōrum, m. pl. = Argos (see below)
Danaēn is the Greek accusative of Danaē
ōrāculum, -ī, n. = oracle
sacerdōs, -ōtis, c. (here) = priestess
nepōs, nepōtis, m. = grandson
carcer, carceris, m. = prison
inclūdō, -ere, inclūsī, inclūsum = I shut in
iānua, -ae, f. = door
aēneus, -a, -um = made of bronze
canis, canis, c. = dog, bitch
imber, imbris, m. = shower
aureus, -a, -um = made of gold
convertō, -ere, convertī, conversum = I turn into (trans.)
perveniō, -īre, pervēnī, perventum (+ ad + acc.) = I reach
gignō, -ere, genuī, genitum = I bear (a child)
Persea is the Greek accusative of Perseus
cognōscō, -ere, cognōvī, cognitum = I discover, learn
arca, -ae, f. = a chest
ligneus, -a, -um = made of wood
Serīphus, -ī, f. = Seriphus
piscātor, -ōris, m. = fisherman
rēte, -is, n. = net (abl. sing. rēte)
aperiō, -īre, aperuī, apertum = I open
adhūc = still
Polydectes, -ae, m. = Polydectes
cōnferō, cōnferre, contulī, collātum (here) = I take
apud (+ acc.) = at the house of
ēducō, -āre, -āvī, -ātum = I bring up

Notes:

(i)   Argos (line 1) is a very old city in the N.E. of the Peloponnese.

(ii) Note that the 'aē' of Danaēn (line 2) and the first 'aē' of aēneae (line 6) are not diphthongs but two individual vowels: thus Da-na-ēn has three syllables, and a-ē-ne-ae has four. See *Latin Prep* 1, p.6.

(iii) Seriphus (line 13) is a small island in the Aegean sea (the sea between Greece and Asia Minor).

(a)   In lines 1-2, how many children did Acrisius have?
(b)   In lines 4-5, how would you describe the priestess' response?
(c)   In lines 5-6, what did it make Acrisius do?
(d)   In line 8, why was Jupiter interested in Danae's fate?
(e)   In lines 8-9, how did he manage to reach her?
(f)   In lines 10-11, why was Acrisius so angry when he heard that Danae had given birth to a son? (See lines 4-5)
(g)   In lines 11-12, what did he do about this?
(h)   ea (line 12); to what does this word refer?
(i)   In lines 13-15, what did the fisherman find in his catch?
(j)   In lines 15-16, what did he do with his find?

Exercise 6.10

Translate the following passage into good English:

Perseus promises Polydectes the Gorgon Medusa's head

1   Perseus, ubi iuvenis fuit, mātrem suam contrā
Polydectam, quī eam <u>dūcere</u> volēbat, dēfendit;
sed ubi ille Hippodamīam <u>dūcere</u> velle vidēbātur,
Perseus eī laetissimus dīxit: 'dōnum tibi <u>spōnsāle</u>
5   dabō, <u>caput</u> Gorgonis Medūsae.' Polydectēs
quoque, quod Perseus opus difficillimum
<u>suscēperat</u>, laetissimus erat. Medūsa <u>serpentēs</u>
<u>prō</u> <u>capillīs</u>, <u>dentēs</u> ingentissimōs, <u>linguam</u>
<u>prōminentem</u> habuit; eī quī <u>caput</u> eius vīdērunt,
10   in <u>lapidēs</u> <u>conversī</u> sunt. Minerva igitur iuvenī
scūtum dedit quod omnia <u>repercutiēbat</u>.
Mercurius eī <u>falcem</u> dedit <u>adamantinam</u> quae
<u>caput</u> <u>abscīdere</u> potuit. etiam <u>crepidās</u> <u>ālātās</u>,
<u>pēram</u> maximam, <u>galeam</u> quae eōs ā quibus
15   gerēbātur <u>invīsōs</u> faciēbat habēre <u>dēbuit</u>; hās
omnēs rēs custōdiēbant Nymphae Stygiae:
locum in quō eae habitābant Graeae <u>sciēbant</u>
sōlae; hae trēs sorōrēs erant, quae ūnum sōlum
<u>oculum</u> habēbant et ūnum <u>dentem</u>.

dūcō, -ere, dūxī, ductum (here) =
   I marry (of a man)
spōnsālis, -e = for a betrothal
caput, capitis, n. = head
suscipiō, -ere, suscēpī, susceptum
   = I undertake
serpēns, -entis c.= snake
prō (here) = instead of
capillus, -ī, m. = hair
dēns, dentis, m. = tooth
lingua, -ae, f. = tongue
prōmineō, -ēre, -uī, no supine = I jut
   out, protrude
lapis, -idis, m. = a stone
convertō, -ere, convertī, conversum
   = I turn (trans.) into
repercutiō, -ere, repercussī,
   repercussum = I reflect
falx, falcis, f. = scythe, sickle
adamantinus, -a, -um = adamantine,
   i.e. very tough
abscīdō, -ere, -īdī, -īsum = I cut off
crepida, -ae, f. = sandal
ālātus, -a, -um = winged
pēra, -ae, f. = a bag
galea, -ae, f. = helmet
invīsus, −a, -um (here) = invisible
dēbeō, -ēre, -uī, -itum = I must, have
   to
sciō, -īre, -īvī, -ītum = I know
oculus, -ī, m. = eye

Notes:

(i)   The Gorgons (line 5) were three sisters of whom Medusa was by far the most
famous and most terrible. They were daughters of Phorcys, a sea-god.

(ii)   The Nymphae Stygiae (line 16) were nymphs of the Underworld. The adjective
Stygius, -a, -um comes from Styx, Stygis, f. = one of the rivers of the
Underworld. On earth, Nymphs were natural spirits, generally benevolent to
men.

(iii) The Graeae (line 17) were also three sisters; they were sisters of the Gorgons and
were grey-haired from birth.

Exercise 6.11

Study the following passage and answer the questions below in good English.
Complete sentences are not required.

Perseus cuts off the Gorgon's head, rescues Andromeda and returns home

1   Perseus <u>oculum</u> Graeārum cēpit et eās locum
    dīcere in quō Stygiae Nymphae habitābant
    coēgit; ab hīs omnēs rēs quās habēre voluit
    accēpit. tum <u>caput</u> Medūsae dum dormit
5   <u>abscīsum</u> in <u>pērā</u> posuit; <u>crepidārum</u> <u>ālātārum</u>
    auxiliō sorōrēs eius effūgit; et, dum <u>volat</u>,
    pulcherrimam mulierem in <u>catēnis</u> <u>vīnctam</u>
    cōnspexit; eam <u>mōnstrum</u> <u>marīnum</u>
    crūdēlissimum cōnsūmere volēbat; sed Perseus
10   <u>mōnstrī</u> <u>caput</u> <u>abscīdit</u> et sēcum mulierem
    Andromedam ferēbat. omnibus quī <u>obstābant</u>
    <u>caput</u> ostendit Medūsae; et illī in <u>lapidēs</u>
    <u>conversī sunt</u>. tandem Serīphum vēnit. ibi
    Polydectēs Hippodamīam nōn <u>dūxerat</u> et
15   <u>Danaēn</u> sibi <u>nūbere</u> cōgēbat; sed eī et omnibus
    quī eī auxilium dabant Perseus <u>caput</u> Medūsae
    ostendit. deinde Andromedam <u>dūxit</u> et <u>Argōs</u>
    nāvigāvit et ibi Acrisium, <u>avum</u> suum, <u>discō</u>
    <u>fortuītō</u> interfēcit; nam hoc fuit quod ōlim
20   <u>praedictum erat</u>. <u>postrēmō</u> Perseus rēx fuit in
    <u>Argolide</u>.

oculus, -ī, m. = eye
caput, capitis, n. = head
abscīdō, -ere, abscīdī, abscīsum = I
   cut off
pēra, -ae, f. = bag
crepida, -ae, f. = sandal
ālātus, -a, -um = winged
volō, -āre, -āvī, -ātum = I fly
catēna, -ae, f. = chain
vinciō, -īre, vīnxī, vīnctum = I bind
mōnstrum, -ī, n. = monster
marīnus, -a, -um = of the sea
obstō, -āre, obstitī, obstitum (+ dat.)
   = I obstruct, get in the way of
lapis, lapidis, m. = stone
convertō, -ere, convertī, conversum
   = I turn (trans.)
dūcō, -ere, dūxī, ductum (here) =
   I marry (of man)
Danaēn is the Greek accusative of
   Danaē
nūbō, -ere, nūpsī, nūptum (+ dat.) =
   I marry (of woman)
Argī, -ōrum, m. pl. = Argos (see
   below)
avus, -ī, m. = grandfather
discus, -ī, m. = discus, quoit
fortuītō (here) = accidentally
praedīcō, -ere, praedīxī, praedictum
   = I predict
postrēmō = finally
Argolis, Argolidis, f. = the Argolid
   (see below)

Notes:

(i) pōnō (line 5) is regularly followed by in (+ abl.)

(ii) Argos, Tiryns and Mycenae were very famous ancient cities in the Argolid (line 21), a large region in the North-East of the Peloponnese.

(a) In line 3, what part of what verb is voluit? What is its meaning and what is its infinitive?

(b) In line 5, what tense is posuit and from what verb does it come?
(c) In line 6, what is the case here of auxiliō? What does it mean here?
(d) Mention any superlatives in this passage and translate them.
(e) dum volat (line 6); translate these words.
(f) In line 10, translate sēcum.
(g) In line 13, Serīphum vēnit means 'he came to Seriphus'. What does the Latin tell us about this island?
(h) In line 14, if, instead of '(he) had not married', we wanted to say '(he) was not marrying', to what would we change nōn dūxerat?
(i) In line 18, how does avum relate to Acrisium?
(j) In line 20, what are the tense and voice of praedictum erat?

Exercise 6.12

Using the vocabulary given below, translate into Latin:

(i) All the masters punished the sad slaves with savage wounds.

all = omnis, -e master = dominus, -ī, m.
I punish = pūniō, -īre, īvī, ītum sad = trīstis, -e
slave = servus, -ī, m. savage = saevus, -a, -um
wound = vulnus, vulneris, n.

(ii) Tired girls love easy journeys.

tired = fessus, -a, -um girl = puella, -ae, f.
I love = amō, -āre, -āvī, -ātum easy = facilis, -e
journey = iter, itineris, n.

Crossword 1

Across

1. They persuade (10)
9. Go out! (5)
10. 9 (2)
11. Queen of Carthage (4)
12. We know – well, not quite (5)
14. You will rush (6)
15. With a kiss (5)
18. Let it be (3)
19. Him (beheaded) (2)
20. (O) bottom-most (man) (3)
22. Stand! (3)
24. Thus (3)
26. Mistress (backwards) (3)
28. To my most loving son (abbrev.) (2)
29. (With) his own (woman) (3)
31. (With) a wife (5)
33. Courage (6)
35. Halls (5)
36. My (men) (acc.) (4)
38. He's going (2)
39. 100 East winds (1, 4)
40. Those leisurely (women) (acc.) (3, 7)

Down

1. With feet (7)
2. Go out! (3)
3. You laugh (5)
4. I stand (3)
5. Hooray (backwards) (2)
6. You will say (5)
7. You go out (6)
8. Your (man) (4)
12. I nearly am (2)
13. I shall be sent (6)
14. A very, very special city (4)
16. He lost (6)
17. I went (2)
21. A master (4)
23. By weary (men) (1, 6)
25. You're running (6)
27. Out of (2)
30. By Titus (1, 4)
32. O! god (1, 4)
33. (With) a prophet (4)
34. (Backwards) Ow! (2)
36. (With) my (man) (3)
37. Pray! (3)
39. 101 (2)

The following words will help you:

āmittō, -ere, āmīsī, āmissum = I lose
ātrium, -iī, n. = hall
au = an exclamation of pain
bāsium, -iī, n. = a kiss
erus, -ī, m. = master
era, -ae, f. = mistress
eu = an exclamation of approval
Eurus, -ī, m. = East wind
fīliō amantissimō = to my most loving son
īmus, -a, -um = bottom-most
ōrō, -āre, -āvī, -ātum = I pray, beg
ōtiōsus, -a, -um = leisurely
pēs, pedis, m. = foot
sciō, -īre, -īvī, -ītum = I know
sit = let it be (3rd person sing., pres. subj. of sum)
vātes, vātis, c. (here) = priest, prophet

Vocabulary 6

Vocabulary 6
animal, animālis, n. = animal
gēns, gentis, f. = race, family, clan, nation
tōtus, -a, -um (goes like ūnus) = whole
nec, neque = nor, neither, and…not
volō, velle, voluī (irreg.) = I want, wish
nōlō, nōlle, nōluī (irreg.) = I do not want, wish
custōs, custōdis, c. = guard
opus, operis, n. = work, task
somnus, -ī, m. = sleep
dum = while

Having got this far, I'm sure I can't prevent you from leaping into the next four chapters, which are very special indeed.

Chapter 7

We now move on to even more advanced things, suitable for you budding scholars. Let's start with something fairly mild and keep our fistful of fireworks to be unleashed as we go along.

The perfect infinitive active

Well, so far we've met the present infinitives over and over again in every principal part we have learnt. Now we can reveal the fact that there is also a perfect (or past) infinitive. The present infinitive was formed by removing the final 'ō' from the first person of the present tense and adding '-āre', '-ēre', '-ere' or '-īre', according to the conjugation to which the verb belonged. To form the perfect infinitives active, we must take the first person singular of the perfect indicative tense and add '-sse' to it. Thus, the perfect infinitive active of amō is amāvisse and it means 'to have loved'; similarly monuisse means 'to have warned, advised', rēxisse means 'to have ruled', audīvisse means 'to have heard', and cēpisse means 'to have taken'. It's all rather insultingly easy!

Exercise 7.1

Give the perfect infinitives of the following:

1. superō
2. līberō
3. dēleō
4. habeō
5. videō

6. dēfendō
7. ruō
8. cōnsūmō
9. veniō
10. pūniō

Exercise 7.2

Give the Latin for:

1. To have said
2. To have praised
3. To have done
4. To have come
5. To have helped

6. To have drunk
7. To have replied
8. To have slept
9. To have caught sight of
10. To have feared

Perfect infinitives: irregular verbs

Even sum, possum, ferō and volō have the spirit knocked right out of them and are all submissively regular:

sum	produces	fuisse
possum	produces	potuisse
ferō	produces	tulisse
volō	produces	voluisse
nōlō	produces	nōluisse

However, eō generally produces īsse; and its compounds follow suit (e.g. redīsse, adīsse etc.)

gradus – the 4th declension

Now for some more nouns.

I'm sure you have wondered why we went straight from the 3rd to the 5th declension. Admittedly the Romans were not very wonderful at mathematics, but they weren't quite as bad as that! No. There is indeed a 4th declension, but we have not had it yet because it is very muddling. To begin with it ends in '-us' and, at first sight, looks like an innocent 2nd declension noun. But it is not. Instead, it goes like this:

gradus, gradūs, m. = 'step'

	Singular	Plural
Nominative	gradus	gradūs
Vocative	gradus	gradūs
Accusative	gradum	gradūs
Genitive	gradūs	graduum
Dative	graduī	gradibus
Ablative	gradū	gradibus

The form gradubus is also found for the dative and ablative plural, but we shall stick to gradibus.

Note that in this declension quantities are supremely important: the genitive singular is gradūs and the nominative, vocative and accusative plural are gradūs. This certainly does not make the 4th declension easy!

Here are three useful 4th declension nouns:

portus, portūs, m. = harbour, port
exercitus, exercitūs, m. = army
manus, manūs, f. = hand

Nearly all 4th declension nouns are masculine, but note that manus is feminine.

Exercise 7.3

Set out exercitus, portus and manus in full, as gradus has been set out above.

Exercise 7.4

Translate into English:

1.   tandem, dux cum exercitū in urbem advēnit.
2.   rēx exercituī ut cum hostibus fortiter pugnāret imperāvit.
3.   nōs omnēs tūtī in portum nāvigāvimus.
4.   in portibus multae nāvēs sunt et nautae multī.
5.   serve, quid in manū fers? num aurum est?
6.   illa puella pulcherrimās manūs habet.
7.   duo exercitūs hanc urbem, ut malōs cīvēs pūnīrent, oppugnābant.
8.   in ūnō oppidō turba erat exercituum.

Exercise 7.5

Translate into Latin:

1.   Many ships had been left in the small harbour.
2.   We ordered the soldiers to carry swords in[1] (their) hands.
3.   In order to see the ships sailing into the harbour, we remained there.
4.   In this army the soldiers are very bad.
5.   Many ships sail from many places into those harbours.
6.   While he was fighting with this young man, he was watching his[2] hands.
7.   The king ordered the commander to give gold to the army.
8.   The soldiers of these armies are very brave.

[1] Omit 'in'.
[2] Note how ambiguous 'his' is in English. Give two Latin versions of 'his' here, making clear what each version means.

The present infinitive passive

Back to verbs!

Here is yet another part for us to learn, namely the **present infinitive passive**.

We have known for a long time how to use the present infinitive meaning 'to love', 'to advise', 'to hear' and so on. Now we shall be able to use the present infinitive passive meaning 'to be loved', 'to be advised', 'to be heard' and so on.

In the first, second and fourth conjugations, the present infinitive passive is formed very easily. We take the present infinitive active, e.g. amāre, remove the final 'e' and replace it with a long 'ī'. Thus:

> from amāre, hey presto, we get amārī = 'to be loved'
> from monēre we get monērī = 'to be advised, to be warned'
> from audīre we get audīrī = 'to be heard'

Needless to say, it is the 3rd conjugation which lets the side down with a bang. It must go a step further than the other three, cutting out the whole of the present infinitive ending and replacing it with a long 'ī'. Thus:

> regere becomes regī[1] = 'to be ruled'

The mixed conjugation does the same as the 3rd. Thus:

> capere becomes capī = 'to be taken'

[1] Note the difference between regī = 'to be ruled' and rēgī = 'to or for a king'. Conversely, note dūcī = 'to be led' and ducī = 'to/for a leader'. Oh! the joy of quantities.

N.B. The present infinitive passive of ferō is ferrī.

Solemn note

There is **no** present infinitive passive of faciō. But its compounds, such as interficiō, have a regular present infinitive passive.

Exercise 7.6

Give and translate the present infinitive passive of the following (note the deliberate 'trick' question):

1. videō
2. cōnsūmō
3. vulnerō
4. pūniō
5. interficiō
6. faciō
7. cōnspiciō
8. custōdiō
9. gerō
10. laudō

Exercise 7.7

Read the following passage carefully, and answer the questions on it:

dē nūtrīcibus – On nurses

1 et Graecī et Rōmānī parentēs <u>līberōs</u> suōs
   <u>nūtrīcibus</u>, ut eōs <u>cūrārent</u>, trādēbant; <u>nūtrīcēs</u>
   illae saepe puerōs eōs et puellās <u>magis</u> quam
   parentēs eōrum amābant. īn <u>fābulā</u> Hippolytō,
5 quam scrīpsit Eurīpidēs, Phaedra, ubi <u>prīvignum</u>
   suum Hippolytum <u>adamāvit</u>, <u>pudōre</u> et <u>miseriā</u>
   maximē <u>affecta est</u>; <u>dolōrem</u> eius <u>nūtrīx</u> <u>lēnīre</u>
   <u>temptāvit</u>. In <u>Homērī</u> <u>Odyssēā</u>, ubi tandem post
   vīgintī annōs <u>domum</u> <u>suam</u> Ulixēs <u>mendīcī</u>
10 <u>speciē</u> rediit, statim Euryclēa <u>nūtrīx</u> <u>pedem</u> eius
   <u>lavāns</u> <u>cicātrīcem</u> ōlim ab <u>aprō</u> <u>īnflīctum</u> <u>agnōvit</u>
   et 'Ulixēs es!' clāmāvit. Nerōnis <u>reliquiās</u> Eclogē
   et Alexandra <u>nūtrīcēs</u> eius et Actē, quam
   amāverat, in <u>monumentō</u> gentis Domitiae
15 <u>condidērunt</u>. Domitiānī, quī <u>senātuī</u> <u>odiōsissimus</u>
   erat prīncipum, <u>cadāver</u> Phyllis <u>nūtrīx</u> īn
   <u>suburbānō</u> suō <u>fūnerāvit</u> et <u>reliquiās</u> eius in
   templum gentis Flāviae <u>clam</u> <u>intulit</u>.

nūtrīx, nūtrīcis, f. = nurse
līberī, -ōrum, m. pl. = children (see below)
cūrō, -āre, -āvī, -ātum = I look after, I take
   care of
magis (adverb) = more
fābula, -ae, f. (here) = a play
prīvignus, -ī, m. = step-son
adamō, -āre, -āvī, -ātum (here) = I fall in
   love with (+ acc.)
pudor, pudōris, m. = shame
miseria, -ae, f. = wretchedness
afficiō, -ere, affēcī, affectum = I affect
dolor, dolōris, m. = grief
lēniō, -īre, lēnīvī, lēnītum = I soften,
   assuage
temptō, -āre, -āvī, -ātum = I try
Homērus, -ī, m. = Homer (see below iii)
Odyssēa, -ae, f. = the Odyssey (see
   below iii)
domum suam = to his home
mendīcus, -ī, m. = beggar
speciēs, speciēī, f. = appearance; see
   note (iv) below
pēs, pedis, m. = foot
lavō, -āre, lāvī, lautum, lavātum or lōtum
   = I wash
cicātrīx, cicātrīcis, f. = scar
aper, aprī, m. = boar
īnflīgō, -ere, īnflīxī, īnflīctum = I inflict
   (+ acc. and dat.)
agnōscō, -ere, agnōvī, agnitum =
   I recognise
reliquiae, -ārum, f. pl. = remains
monumentum, -ī, n. = monument
condō, -ere, condidī, conditum (here) =
   I lay to rest
senātus, senātūs, m. = the Senate
odiōsus, -a, -um = hateful
cadāver, cadāveris, n. = corpse
suburbānum, -ī, n. = a home in the
   suburbs
fūnerō, -āre, -āvī, -ātum = I conduct the
   funeral of
reliquiae, -ārum, f. pl. = remains
clam = secretly
īnferō, īnferre, intulī, illātum = I bring in

The pieces about Nero and Domitian are derived from Suetonius, whom we have already met.

Notes:

(i)   līberī (line 1) always means 'children of somebody'. You cannot see the little līberōs playing in the garden, but you can see e.g. līberōs Claudiī = 'the children of Claudius'. 'Children' in general, are puerī (unless they are specifically girls, in which case they would be puellae).

(ii)   Euripides (line 5) was the youngest of the three great Athenian tragedians. He lived from 485? to 406? BC. The *Hippolytus* tells the story of Phaedra's ill-fated love of her stepson, which results in both their deaths.

(iii)   The hero of Homer's *Odyssey* (line 8) is Odysseus in Greek. In Latin he became Ulixēs. We call him Ulysses.

(iv)   The phrase here (lines 9-10) means 'in the appearance of (i.e. 'disguised as') a beggar'.

(v)   reliquiae (lines 12 and 17) refers especially to the ashes of the dead person preserved after cremation.

(vi)   Nero belonged to the gēns Domitia (line 14).

(vii)   The Emperor Domitian (Domitiānus, -ī, m.) (line 15) belonged to the gēns Flavia.

(viii) Eclogē (line 12) and Actē (line 13) are Greek names.

1.   Answer the following questions:
        (a) In lines 1-2, why did Greek and Roman parents hand over their children to nurses?
        (b) In lines 2-4, what was frequently the result of this practice?
        (c) In lines 5-7, why was Phaedra so miserable?
        (d) In lines 7-8, what did her nurse try to do?
        (e) In lines 10-11, what was Euryclea doing when she noticed Ulysses' scar?
        (f) In line 11, how had Ulysses received this scar?
        (g) Why do you think Euryclea was so familiar with this scar?
        (h) In lines 15-16, what do you think the Senate felt when Domitian was murdered?
        (i) In line 18, why do you think Phyllis acted clam?
        (j) In line 18, to what gēns did Domitian's father belong?

2.   Translate the passage nursefully (I think I've made up this word).

3.   Answer the following questions:
        (a) In line 2, what are the tense and mood of cūrārent?
        (b) In line 6, what is the case of miseriā, and how do we know it?

(c) In line 9, what is the case of vīgintī? And how do you explain this?

(d) In line 10, how does the word nūtrīx here relate to the word Euryclēa?

(e) In line 11, what part of lavō is lavāns? Translate it.

(f) In line 11, why do we have ab in front of aprō?

(g) senātuī (line 15); what is the case and number of this word? To what declension does it belong? And what would its genitive singular be?

(h) odiōsissimus (line 15); how does this word relate to odiōsus? And what would the Latin for 'more hateful' be?

(i) In line 16, what is the case of cadāver?

(j) In line 18, if, instead of '(she) brought into' we had wanted to say (i) 'to bring into', or (ii) 'to have brought into', what ought we to have written?

The perfect infinitive passive

We've been dealing recently with various infinitives; so here's another: the perfect infinitive passive, i.e. 'to have been loved'. This is formed by taking the past participle passive and adding esse (= 'to be'). Thus:

The perfect infinitive passive of amō is amātus, -a, -um esse = 'to have been loved'.

The perfect infinitive passive of moneō is monitus, -a, -um esse = 'to have been warned, to have been advised'.

The perfect infinitive passive of regō is rēctus, -a, -um esse = 'to have been ruled'.

The perfect infinitive passive of audiō, is audītus, -a, -um esse = 'to have been heard'.

The perfect infinitive passive of capiō is captus, -a, -um esse = 'to have been taken.

N.B. Since there is a perfect participle passive of faciō (i.e. factus, -a, -um), there is also a perfect infinitive passive, factus, -a, -um esse = 'to have been done, to have been made'.

Since the perfect participle passive is an adjectival form, it can be in a different case (especially the accusative), gender and number. We shall be handling this infinitive extensively very soon indeed; so let's practise its formation.

Exercise 7.8

Give the perfect infinitive passive, complete with translation, as above, of the following:

1.   laudō
2.   dēleō
3.   dūcō
4.   moveō
5.   pōnō

6.   custōdiō
7.   cōnspiciō
8.   mittō
9.   terreō
10. inveniō

Indirect statement

And now we come to something supremely important, which lies at the very heart of the Latin language: indirect statement.

When dealing with a *direct* statement, we are dealing with the actual words spoken by someone, placed between inverted commas. Thus:

He says, 'Caesar is approaching.'

An *indirect* statement occurs when the words spoken are not put between inverted commas, but are preceded by the word 'that'. Thus:

He says that Caesar is approaching.

In Latin, indirect statements are **not** introduced by a word meaning 'that'.

How, then, are they expressed? They are expressed by a wonderful, magical construction called the Accusative and Infinitive.

Indirect statement introduced by a primary tense

So let's see this construction at work, first when introduced by the present tense:

He says that Caesar is approaching.

becomes

He says Caesar to be approaching.
Caesarem (acc.) appropinquāre
(infin.) dīcit.

Caesarem appropinquāre dīcit

or   He says that Caesar's forces fight well.
      Caesaris cōpiās bene pugnāre dīcit.

Just look at these, say them to yourself at all hours and then repeat them!

The Accusative and Infinitive construction is used not only after verbs of 'speaking' but also after verbs that convey information by means other than speech, such as 'writing'; it is also used after verbs of 'perceiving' and 'thinking'. The following verbs that we have already learnt could introduce an indirect statement:

crēdō	dīcō
nūntiō	respondeō
clāmō	audiō
inveniō	scrībō
nārrō	legō

Exercise 7.9

Translate into English:

1. rēgīna ancillās suās cantāre dīcit.
2. dux mīlitēs male pugnāre nūntiat.
3. hic iuvenis hostēs appropinquāre legit.
4. nōnne magister puerōs bene labōrāre crēdit?
5. pecūniam meam omnem abesse inveniō.
6. parvās puellās dormīre respondēmus.
7. dominī servōs lentē currere clāmant.
8. rēgem ex urbe discēdere vōbīs nārrō.
9. mātrem suam iam advenīre audiunt.
10. līberōs tuōs ad flūmen ambulāre scrībis.

Exercise 7.10

Translate into Latin:

1. I say that the enemy are fleeing.
2. The citizens reply that the farmers are working in the fields.
3. We discover that the women are departing.
4. This boy is shouting that the soldiers are coming.
5. She writes to me that her sons run quickly.
6. He reads that the enemy are returning.
7. They believe that the old men always remain in the city.
8. He announces that our forces are hurrying into battle.
9. We hear that the boys are walking into the temple.
10. Who tells us that horses sing?

So far, so good.

But what happens when the indirect statement itself is not in the present tense? How do we translate it into Latin?

For example:

He says that Caesar approached, has approached, had approached, was approaching, has been approaching, or had been approaching.

How do we cope with this? It's easy. There is no imperfect or pluperfect infinitive in Latin; all the above meanings can thus only be expressed by the perfect/past infinitive. So all of the above are translated by:

> Caesarem appropinquāvisse (what a splendid word!) dīcit.

Exercise 7.11

Translate into English:

1. mātrem meam advēnisse dīcit.
2. puerī mīlitēs nostrōs vīcisse clāmant.
3. puellam per agrōs errāvisse audiō.
4. quis cōpiās nostrās fūgisse crēdit?
5. senēsne in urbem festīnāvisse respondēs?
6. magistrī puerōs male labōrāvisse inveniunt.
7. hostēs tum urbī appropinquāvisse legō.
8. mīlitī puerōs et puellās in viā lūsisse nārrat.
9. fēminās omnēs in oppidō mānsisse scrībit.
10. dux hostēs subitō discessisse nūntiat.

Exercise 7.12

Translate into Latin:

1. He says that the enemy fled quickly.
2. I believe that the leader has returned.
3. They reply that the teacher departed at the fourth hour.
4. He tells me that the girls sang.
5. The king announces that our soldiers have conquered.
6. We hear that the teacher has arrived.
7. She reads that animals wandered through the streets.
8. They discover that the slaves have hurried to the mountains.
9. Do you (sing.) write that the citizens remained in the city?
10. The farmers shout that the sailors have sailed to the island.

Once again, so far, so good. Do I detect a slight *soupçon* (French!) of smugness creeping in?

I hope not; surely you must have known deep down that sooner or later there would be trouble looming and here it is. It occurs when an indirect statement is introduced by a historic tense (see page 23).

Indirect statement introduced by a historic tense

How do we put 'He said that Caesar was approaching' into Latin?

We must immediately work out what the speaker's actual spoken words were.

They were, 'Caesar is approaching' (present tense). Therefore we use the present infinitive. Thus:

>   Caesarem appropinquāre dīxit. = He said that Caesar was approaching.

Again, in, 'He said that Caesar had approached',

the speaker's words were, 'Caesar approached/has approached', so we use the perfect/past infinitive:

>   Caesarem appropinquāvisse dīxit.

The same principle applies whatever verb introduces the indirect statement. Thus, 'He believed that Caesar was approaching', would be: Caesarem approprinquare crēdidit.

In all the following sentences I am treating the perfect/past form introducing an indirect statement as a simple past tense (i.e. dīxī = I said) and I suggest translating the perfect/past infinitive as e.g. 'had approached'.

This is a good place to remind you that there are plenty of infinitives in Latin; there is a present infinitive active and passive and a perfect/past infinitive active and passive; there is also a future infinitive active, but alas, it does not come into our syllabus.

Exercise 7.13

Translate into English:

1. illōs omnēs redīre dīxit.
2. nōnne iuvenēs adesse nūntiāvistī?
3. dominī servōs suōs festīnāvisse respondērunt.
4. clāmāvit dux hostēs appropinquāre.
5. tē in urbe esse audīvī.
6. scrīpsit mihi exercitum suum fortiter pugnāvisse.
7. illōs hominēs vulnerārī crēdidimus.
8. mīlitēs in viā stetisse invēnit.
9. nārrāvērunt nōbīs urbem oppugnārī.
10. ducem ab hostibus vulnerārī lēgī.

Exercise 7.14

Translate into Latin:

1. They said that the sailors were in the island.
2. He announced that our armies were fighting well.
3. I heard that the leader was standing near the temple.
4. He wrote to the king that the citizens had escaped.
5. The inhabitants shouted that the enemy were near the town.
6. We told you (pl.) that the old men were sleeping.
7. I believed that much food was being eaten.
8. He replied that war was being prepared.
9. Did you read that the farmers had departed into the fields?
10. He discovered that the boys were in the street.

Indirect statement: agreement

(i) When we are handling a perfect infinitive passive, we must make sure that the participle involved is in the accusative and is of the right gender and number. Thus:

He said that the girls had been praised.
puellās laudātās esse dīxit.

He said that the soldier had been wounded.
mīlitem vulnerātum esse dīxit.

(ii) If you are using the verb 'to be', remember that an adjective describing the noun in the accusative must agree with the noun in case, gender and number. Thus:

He says that the women are beautiful.
mulierēs pulchrās esse dīcit.

He said that the old man was alive.
senem vīvum esse dīxit.

Exercise 7.15

Translate into English:

1. nāvem dēlētam esse audīmus.
2. dux hostēs victōs esse nūntiāvit.
3. ancillās ā rēgīnā vocātās esse dīcō.
4. senēs miserōs esse respondimus.
5. illās puellās pulcherrimās esse invēnērunt.
6. num crēdidistī tuam urbem magnam esse?

7. illōs equōs validōs esse lēgī.
8. mīlitēs arma collēcta esse clāmant.
9. nārrāvī cīvibus mūrōs dēfēnsōs esse.
10. scrīpsit mihi praemia ā mīlitibus petīta esse.

Exercise 7.16

Translate into Latin:

1. Did you say that the women had been saved?
2. Did you read that new walls had been built.
3. They replied that the slaves had been set free.
4. I discovered that the swords had been moved.
5. Did you (sing.) tell us that the girls had been very good?
6. I believed that all the weapons had been handed over.
7. They wrote that the old men were tired.
8. The teacher announced that the bad boys had been punished.
9. The sailors shouted that the farmers had been overcome.
10. Did you (sing.) really hear that our forces had been captured?

Negative indirect statements

Finally (almost...), here is a solemn rule about dīcō:

In translating 'He said that Caesar had not come', you never use dīcō followed by nōn, but instead you must use negō, -āre, -āvī, -ātum = 'I say that...not'. Thus:

'He said that Caesar had not come.'

would be:

Caesarem vēnisse negāvit.

We're not quite through even yet, for there is still something in this construction that frequently and shamelessly raises its ugly head. And that is ambiguity. For example:

> Caesarem Gallōs vīcisse dīxit.

could mean

> 'He said that Caesar had conquered the Gauls.'

or

> 'He said that the Gauls had conquered Caesar.'

What do we do about this one? Wait for it. Yes, you've got it. It all depends on our old friend, who hasn't appeared for quite a long time, namely the context, i.e. common sense. We really can't have Gauls having conquered Caesar, so it must be the other way round! Or must it?

Exercise 7.17

Translate into English:

1. nostrōs mīlitēs victōs esse negābō.
2. urbem dēfēnsam esse negāvērunt.
3. ducem fortem esse negō.
4. urbem nostram ille pulcherrimam esse negat.
5. magistrōs puerōs pūnīvisse negō.
6. crūdēlēs mīlitēs fessōs senēs vulnerāvisse crēdō.
7. agricolās in agrīs esse negāvī.
8. iuvenēs mulierēs dēfendere nūntiāvimus.
9. malōs hominēs equōs vulnerāre invēnī.
10. parentēs cum līberīs in urbe relictōs esse negāmus.

Exercise 7.18

Translate into Latin:

1. He said that the enemy were not brave.
2. He said that the walls had not been built.
3. The old men said that the young man was not in the temple.
4. We believed that the young men were defending the women.
5. I said that the parents had not punished their children.
6. Do you (sing.) really believe that the master has set free his slaves?
7. She said that the enemy were not able to conquer the Romans.
8. They said that the city had not been taken.
9. Did you really believe that the boys had overcome the young men?
10. The leader told the citizens that the poet was wise.

Exercise 7.19

In the following exercise you are asked to turn a direct statement into an indirect statement introduced by dīxit. For example:

>   Caesar ā Brūtō necātus est.

would become

>   Caesarem ā Brūtō necātum esse dīxit.

and

>   exercitus flūmen trānsit.

would become

>   exercitum flūmen trānsīre dīxit.

1. hostēs a proeliō fugiunt.
2. puerī ā magistrīs laudantur.
3. multī cīvēs ā mīlitibus occīsī sunt.
4. omnēs fēminae ex urbe discessērunt.
5. puellae librum lēgērunt.
6. pulchrae mulierēs in oppidō habitant.
7. bonī agricolae in agrīs labōrant.
8. fortēs nautae circum īnsulam nāvigāvērunt.
9. bonī puerī ā parentibus amantur.
10. parva puella in urbe relicta est.

Oratio Obliqua

An indirect statement, together with all its subordinate clauses, is traditionally known as 'Oratio Obliqua'. I can't resist bringing in this splendid name here. In the good old days, 'Oratio Obliqua' was used instead of the much feebler 'Indirect Statement' (ōrātiō, -ōnis, f. = 'speech, statement'; oblīquus, -a, -um (here) = 'indirect'). I shall henceforth use this expression (a) because I like it and (b) to avoid the horrible potential for muddle caused by 'direct statement', 'in direct statement', 'indirect statement' and 'in indirect statement'. The opposite of 'Oratio Obliqua' is 'Oratio Recta' (rēctus, -a, -um (here) = 'direct').

In Orato Obliqua, the verbs in the subordinate clauses must be in the subjunctive.

Note that I have not marked the quantities on the expressions 'Oratio Obliqua' and 'Oratio Recta'. This is because I regard them as being part of the English language, and they should be prounced as such.

Indirect statement is often referred to as indirect speech.

Personal pronouns in 'Oratio Obliqua'

As we learnt long ago, the personal pronoun as a subject is generally concealed in the verb. Thus advēnī = 'I arrived'. The pronoun ego is not written, being tucked away in the ending '-ī'.

Hence, if we put advēnī into Oratio Obliqua it becomes dīcit mē advēnisse. = 'He says that I have arrived.' The ego tucked away in advēnī has been put into the accusative – mē.

Similarly advēnistī would become tē advēnisse; and the same applies to nōs and vōs. Thus:

> bonae estis = you (f. pl.) are good

would become:

> vōs bonās esse dīcit. = 'He says that you (f. pl.) are good.'

Remember always that these pronouns can be any gender.

The pronouns can be strengthened by the accusative of ipse, which we met in Chapter 4, always in the right gender and number. Thus:

> mē ipsum advēnisse dīcō. = 'I say that I myself have arrived.'

> nōs ipsās bonās esse dīcunt. = 'They say that we (fem.) ourselves are good.'

In this construction, sē is particularly common. (Have you noticed how often people talk about themselves?) Thus:

> 'advēnī,' dīxit. = 'I have arrived,' he said.

would become

> sē advēnisse dīxit. = 'He said that he (himself) had arrived.'

To strengthen sē we can again use ipsum etc. (remembering that sē can mean 'himself, herself, itself' or 'themselves').

However, if the 'he' with the infinitive is someone other than the 'he' of the main verb we should use 'eum' Thus:

> ʹadvēnīt,ʹ dīxit. = 'He has arrived,' he said (i.e. someone other than himself
> has arrived).

would become

> eum advēnisse dīxit. = 'He said that he (someone else) had arrived.'

Again, we can use any gender or number of eum, and whatever form we choose can be strengthened by the right gender and number of ipsum.

Exercise 7.20

Translate into English:

1. quis tē mūrum aedificāvisse nūntiāvit?
2. senēs nōbīs sē rēs magnās fēcisse respondērunt.
3. num sē victōs esse nārrant?
4. eum necārī clāmāvērunt.
5. nūntius mihi vōs servātās esse lēgit.
6. nōs ipsōs omnēs superāvisse crēdimus.
7. id ipsum factum esse invēnit.
8. num nōs superārī audīs?
9. cūr tē ipsum sapientissimum esse dīcis?
10. sē in portū manēre scrīpsērunt.

Exercise 7.21

Translate into Latin:

1. I said that I myself was a good soldier.
2. The leader told me that he had fought for a long time.
3. You (pl.) announced that you were very good citizens.
4. They shouted that you (pl.) were fighting bravely.
5. Surely they heard that the enemy were defeated by you (pl.)?
6. We replied that they had fled swiftly.
7. She believed that she herself was both beautiful and wise.
8. They wrote that they themselves were sailing out of the harbour.
9. I discovered that he was a very bold young man.
10. He read that he (someone else) had done good things.

Exercise 7.22

Translate into Latin:

1. I told the king that you (sing.) had arrived.
2. The farmer is shouting that a wind is destroying the walls.
3. He replied to me that he had read the books himself.
4. She read that she herself was wise.
5. The master believed that the slaves were working well.
6. The leader announced to the citizens that the enemy had been defeated.
7. I wrote to the lucky young men that the journey was easy.
8. He replied to the teacher that the girl had been found.
9. The king wrote that all the leaders were very brave.
10. The happy old man heard that we were approaching.

Exercise 7.23

Of what English words do the following Latin ones remind you?

1. manus
2. portus
3. gradus
4. domus (see Vocabulary 7, below)
5. negō
6. ōrātiō

Exercise 7.24

Translate into Latin (some gentle revision):

1. The new town was being attacked by the cruel enemy.
2. All the girls were reading their books in the city.
3. The good farmers were working in these fields.
4. The tired teachers are hearing the good words of the boys and girls.
5. The brave young men were walking across the road.
6. The bad soldiers were being punished by the leader.
7. The girls played with the boys in the field.
8. All the animals have departed from high mountains.
9. The savage sailors have drunk all the water and eaten all the food.
10. The happy old man is writing wise words to the young man.

Exercise 7.25

Read the following passage carefully and answer the questions on it:

dē <u>rīsū</u> – About laughter

1   in <u>Īliade</u> <u>Homērī</u>, postquam <u>inter sē</u> Iuppiter et
     Iūnō <u>dissēnsērunt</u>, Volcānus, fīlius eōrum, <u>pācem</u>
     inter eōs fēcit et omnibus dīs <u>nectar</u>, deōrum
     vīnum, <u>effūdit</u>; tum dī, ubi eum per <u>sēdēs</u> suās
5   vīdērunt <u>discurrentem</u>, <u>rīsūs</u> <u>ēdidērunt</u>
     <u>inextinguibilēs</u>. iterum in <u>Īliade</u>, ubi Hector, dux
     Troiānōrum, ā pugnā ad uxōrem fīliumque
     <u>īnfantem</u> rediit et hunc manibus <u>tollere</u> volēbat,
     <u>īnfāns</u> <u>galeam</u> <u>cristātam</u> timēns <u>flēvit</u> et īn <u>sinū</u>
10   sē <u>nūtrīcis</u> <u>abdidit</u>; tum rīsērunt pater et māter,
     galeamque Hector <u>humī</u> posuit et fīlium <u>fōvit</u>.
     Caligulam iam <u>lēgimus</u> <u>cēnantem</u> <u>rīsū</u> <u>abstinēre</u>
     nōn potuisse; nam <u>meminerat</u> sē servīs ut
     <u>convīvās</u> occīderent imperāre posse. dum
15   Claudius opus suum plūrimīs legit, <u>subsellia</u>
     multa <u>obēsitāte</u> <u>audītōris</u> <u>dētracta sunt</u>; Claudius
     hoc <u>accidisse</u> iterum <u>atque</u> iterum <u>meminerat</u> et
     <u>rīsū</u> superātus <u>aegrē</u> opus suum <u>perlēgit</u>.

rīsus, rīsūs, m = a laugh, laughter
Īlias, Īliadis, f. = the Iliad
Homērus, -ī, m. = Homer
inter sē (here) = with each other
dissentiō, -īre, dissēnsī, dissēnsum
   (here) = I quarrel
pāx, pācis, f. = peace
nectar, nectaris, n. = nectar
effundō, -ere, effūdī, effūsum = I pour
   out
sēdēs, -is, f. (here) = house, abode
discurrō, -ere, discurrī, discursum
   (here) = I bustle about
ēdō, -ere, ēdidī, ēditum = I give forth
inextinguibilis, -e (here) =
   unquenchable
īnfāns, īnfantis, c. = baby
tollō, -ere, sustulī, sublātum (here) =
   I lift up
galea, -ae, f. = helmet
cristātus, -a, -um = crested
fleō, -ēre, flēvī, flētum = I weep, I cry
sinus, sinūs, m. (here) = bosom
nūtrīx, nūtrīcis, f. = nurse
abdō, -ere, abdidī, abditum = I hide
   (trans.)
humī (here) = on the ground
foveō, -ēre, fōvī, fōtum = I caress
cēnō, -āre, -āvī, -ātum = I dine
abstineō, -ēre, abstinuī, abstentum =
   I abstain
meminī (see below) = I remember
convīva, -ae, c. = guest
subsellium, -iī, n. = bench
obēsitās, obēsitātis, f. = fatness
audītor, audītōris, m. = member of an
   audience
dētrahō, -ere, dētrāxī, dētractum
   (here) = I knock over
accidō, -ere, accidī, no supine =
   I happen
atque (see below) = and
aegrē = with difficulty
perlegō, -ere, perlēgī, perlēctum =
   I read to the end

Notes:

(i)   rīsus is a typical 4th declension verbal noun (formed from the supine of rīdeō).

(ii)   Homer's Iliad (line 1) is all about a great crisis which occurred when the Greeks were besieging Troy, in order to win back Helen, wife of Menelaus, whom Paris, son of Priam, King of Troy, had stolen. The crisis was caused by a quarrel between Achilles, the greatest fighter among the Greeks, and Agamemnon, the great king, as you read in Chapter 6. (Īlium, -iī, n. = Troy).

(iii)   Vulcan (line 2) was the god of fire.

(iv)   memini (line 13) has no present tense; thus, memini = 'I remember'. Its pluperfect acts as its past; thus, memineram = 'I remembered'. A similar verb is ōdī, which means 'I hate'. 'I hated' would be ōderam. Verbs of this type are called defective verbs.

(v)   imperāre (line 14); though this is the present infinitive, the sequence of tense in the whole sentence is taken from the main verb which introduces the Oratio Obliqua, namely meminerat, and is therefore historic; hence the imperfect subjunctive occīderent.

(vi)   atque (line 17) is yet another word for 'and'. So is ac, which is not used before a vowel. Don't mix up ac = 'and' with at, another word for 'but'.

1.   Answer the following questions:
        (a) In lines 3-4, how did Vulcan make things more cheerful for the gods?
        (b) In lines 4-6, what particularly caused the gods to laugh?
        (c) In lines 6-7, what was Hector's role during the siege of Troy?
        (d) In line 8, what did Hector want to do with his son?
        (e) In lines 9-10, how did the child react to his father's approach? Answer in full.
        (f) In line 10, how did both parents react to their son's reaction?
        (g) In line 11, why was the baby no longer afraid of his father?
        (h) In lines 13-14, what did Caligula remember, which made him laugh so much?
        (i) In lines 15-16, why were many benches knocked over?
        (j) In lines 16-18, why did Claudius hardly manage to deliver his lecture to the end?

2.   Translate the passage uncontrollably.

3. Answer the following questions:
    (a) dīs (line 3); what case and number of what word is this? What is its vocative singular?
    (b) In line 5, from what part of discurrō does discurrentem come?
    (c) In line 5, what part of rīsus is rīsūs here?
    (d) In line 8, if instead of saying, 'he returned', we had wanted to say, 'he will return', to what would we have had to change rediit?
    (e) Mention and translate any examples of apposition in the passage.
    (f) sinū (line 9); what would the dative singular of this word be?
    (g) In line 15, what is the case and number of opus here? Give its genitive singular and meaning.
    (h) legit (line 15); why is this verb in the present tense here, although the whole story is about the past?
    (i) How do we know that legit line 15 is the present tense and not the past?
    (j) In line 17, what part of accidō is accidisse and why is this part used here? Answer in full.

Vocabulary 7

Vocabulary 7
exercitus, -ūs, m. = army
portus, -ūs, m. = harbour
manus, -ūs, f. = hand
domus, -ūs, f. (irregular) = house, home

We shall deal with domus (poor thing!) anon. (I hope you know what this means.)

In spite of manus and domus, nearly all 4th declension nouns are masculine.

Believe it or not, we've still got some goodies left for you; indeed the next two chapters promise to be very exciting.

Chapter 8

This chapter starts with something that can only be described as crazy. Trust the Romans to have thought it up!

We've learnt all about the active and the passive voices, with their different endings and meanings. I have heard, I must admit, of a very primitive language which did not find it necessary to distinguish between actives and passives, so that if some beating went on it made no difference at all who did the beating and who was beaten. I must confess that I find this hard to believe. Yet, here, in this overwhelmingly advanced language, we suddenly come across the following frequent feature:

Deponent verbs

A deponent verb is a verb which is passive in form but active in meaning. In other words, nearly all its parts have every appearance of being passive and yet they are active. Nor is there any way of recognising that a verb is deponent other than knowing! So let us immediately learn some of these monstrosities. Let us start with hortor (1st conjugation):

Present tense of hortor, hortārī, hortātus sum = 'I encourage, urge'

1st person singular	hortor	I encourage, urge
2nd person singular	hortāris	you (sing.) encourage, urge
3rd person singular	hortātur	he, she, it encourages, urges
1st person plural	hortāmur	we encourage, urge
2nd person plural	hortāminī	you (pl.) encourage, urge
3rd person plural	hortantur	they encourage, urge

Its principal parts consist of the 1st person singular, present tense; the present infinitive; and the 1st person singular, perfect tense. The future tense is hortābor; the imperfect tense is hortābar.

Note: Deponent verbs cannot have a passive, i.e. you cannot say, 'I am encouraged' or, 'you were encouraged' etc. using hortor.

Another deponent verb is cōnor (1st conjugation) = 'I try' (intransitive); this forms its parts in exactly the same way as hortor. Let us play about a bit with these two verbs.

Exercise 8.1

Translate into English:

1. dux mīlitēs ut oppidum fortiter oppugnārent hortābātur.
2. mātrēs fīliās ut bene sē gererent hortātae sunt.
3. magister puerōs dum currunt hortātur.
4. hoc opus facere cōnābor.
5. nōnne illud flūmen trānsīre cōnābiminī?
6. sē in agrō frūstrā labōrāre cōnātam esse dīxit.
7. īdem magister equōs, puerōs, puellās, nautās eīsdem verbīs semper hortābitur.
8. illās mulierēs ut in templō bene cantārent hortātus sum.
9. ō iuvenēs, num senēs dēfendere cōnātī estis?
10. nōnne eōs, quī bene scrībere cōnantur, semper hortāris?

Exercise 8.2

Translate into Latin:

1. I wish to encourage all these farmers.
2. We were urging the citizens to defend the city bravely.
3. They had tried to do all things well.
4. We are trying to sail round the island.
5. Did you (sing.) really encourage the boys to make that difficult journey?
6. I encouraged my friend not to go to Rome.
7. We shall all try to write a book about these things.
8. We are trying in vain to encourage the frightened women.
9. The father encouraged his son to cross the road here.
10. Although the leader urged the citizens to flee, they remained in the town and tried to fight.

We'll soon be bringing in some more deponent verbs for your pleasure. For the moment, however, let's turn to something else.

The pluperfect subjunctive active: amāvissem

This magnificent sounding tense and mood is really quite a softie. In other words it is extremely easy to form and is remarkably regular. I'm sure you remember that the imperfect subjunctive active was formed by adding the relevant endings to the present infinitive; i.e. the imperfect subjunctive of amō is amāre + '-m', '-s', '-t' etc. We do exactly the same sort of thing to produce the pluperfect subjunctive. In other words, we take the perfect infinitive active and again add the endings '-m', '-s', '-t' etc. Thus, the pluperfect subjunctive active is amāvissem, and it goes as follows:

The pluperfect subjunctive active of amō

1st person singular	amāvissem
2nd person singular	amāvissēs
3rd person singular	amāvisset
1st person plural	amāvissēmus
2nd person plural	amāvissētis
3rd person plural	amāvissent

Exercise 8.3

Write out in full as amāvissem is written out above the pluperfect subjunctive active of:

1. moneō
2. regō
3. audiō
4. līberō
5. bibō

6. pūniō
7. faciō
8. appropinquō
9. videō
10. veniō

You may wonder why I seem to be making an extra-special fuss about the pluperfect subjunctive. It isn't just that I like the sound of it, though I do. It is also because the Romans also seem to have liked the sound of it, especially in one particular construction. So let us, mysteriously for the moment, turn to, of all things!, the little word cum.

cum, the conjunction

We heard long ago of cum (+ the abl.) meaning 'with'. Well, cum is not content to be a preposition, although these words, as you will remember, have a fine time governing poor old nouns. No: cum has to be a conjunction, too, introducing a subordinate (there's the attraction, no doubt) clause. Yes, cum is a bossy little word, throwing its weight about all over the place. For the moment, however, we shall confine ourselves, with much blowing of trumpets, to this enormously frequent and totally illogical cum with the pluperfect subjunctive.

When all the shouting has died down, cum followed by the pluperfect subjunctive means nothing more than 'when', when 'when' (I hope you like these three 'when's) means 'after'. I have never discovered why the subjunctive is used here. Could it really be because the Romans liked the solid, authoritative sound of it? There seems to be no obvious reason for it. It certainly has a very special glamour. From now on, let's tend to use cum instead of ubi when 'when' means 'after'; thus we can feel that we are true masters of one of the favourite bits of Latin parlance (a glossy word for 'speech', coming from the French '*parler*').

> Caesar, cum in castra vēnisset, mīlitēs laudāvit.
> When Caesar had come into the camp, he praised the soldiers.
> or
> After having come into the camp, Caesar praised the soldiers.

Exercise 8.4

Translate into English:

1. senēs, cum hostēs cōnspexissent, fūgērunt.
2. magister, cum puerōs audīvisset, omnēs laudāvit.
3. iuvenēs, cum vīnum bibissent, dormīvērunt.
4. dux mīlitēs, cum perīculum effūgissent, pūnīvit.
5. cum verba nūntiī audīvissem, maximē timuī.
6. cum librum illum lēgisset, alium legere voluit.
7. cum iter illud fēcissēmus, maximē fessī fuimus.
8. cum urbem bene dēfendissētis, ab omnibus laudātī estis.
9. cūr, cum tandem advēnissem, mē nōn salūtāvistis?
10. cum quam celerrimē per agrōs cucurrissem, in templum intrāvī.

Exercise 8.5

Translate into Latin:

1. The parents were happy when they had heard their sons' voices.
2. The old men were frightened when they had seen the enemy.
3. Everyone praised this master when he had freed the good slave.
4. When they had bravely defended the city, the young men were praised by all.
5. After having given rewards to the best boys, the teacher encouraged them to play.
6. When they had taken everything out of the city, there was nothing left.
7. When the women had prepared the food, the men ate it.
8. When the old men had warned the citizens about the danger, the young men laughed.
9. When the leaders had led the boys back into the city, all the parents were happy.
10. After having carried[1] the weapons into the town, he departed as quickly as possible.

[1] Use ferō.

And now for a new story.

Exercise 8.6

Read the following passage carefully, and answer the questions on it:

dē duōbus somniīs: **About two dreams**

1   dē somniō Aenēae in quō Hector eum nē Troiam
      dēfenderet et ut dīs Troiānīs novam urbem
      conderet hortātus est, nūper lēgimus; hoc
      somnium vērāx erat. in Īliade Homērī, Thetis,
5   māter Achillis fortissimī Graecōrum, cum
      Agamemnōn, rēx, Achillem temere offendisset,
      Iovem, rēgem deōrum ut Troiānōs iuvāret et ut
      Graecōs laederet ōrāvit; nam Achillēs īrātissimus
      ā proeliō discesserat. Iuppiter igitur ad
10   Agamemnonem somnium mīsit perniciōsum, cui
      hoc dīxit: 'ī, ō somnium perniciōsum, ī et haec
      verba Agamemnonī dīc: "hodiē tū urbem Troiam
      capiēs; nam nōn iam dī deaeque inter sē
      dissentiunt; surge, igitur, Graecōs tuōs armā, et
15   hostēs tuōs superābis; nam sīc Iuppiter
      cōnstituit."' iit somnium et sīc Agamemnonem
      hortātus est. 'dormīre nōlī!' dīxit et verba Iovis
      addidit. surrēxit Agamemnōn laetissimus, et, cum
      ducēs omnēs convocāvisset, dē somniō eīs
20   nārrāvit; somnium tamen fallācissimum erat; et
      Agamemnōn, cum sē imprūdentissimē gessisset,
      nōn sōlum Troiānōs nōn superāvit, sed etiam ipse
      maximō perīculō paene superātus est.

duōbus is the ablative masculine and
  neuter of duo
somnium, -iī, n. = dream
condō, -ere, condidī, conditum =
  I found, I establish
nūper = recently
vērāx, vērācis = truthful
Īlias, -adis, f. = The Iliad (Homer's
  epic poem)
temere = rashly
offendo, -ere, offendī, offēnsum
  (here) = I offend
laedō, -ere, laesī, laesum = I hurt,
  I harm
ōrō, -āre, -āvī, -ātum (here) = I beg
perniciōsus, -a, -um = destructive
nōn iam = no longer
inter sē = with each other
dissentiō, -īre, dissēnsī, dissēnsum =
  I disagree
surgō, -ere, surrēxī, surrēctum =
  I arise
armō, -āre, -āvī, -ātum = I arm (trans.)
addō, -ere, addidī, additum = I add
convocō, -āre, -āvī, -ātum = I call
  together
fallāx, fallācis = deceitful
imprūdēns, imprūdentis = unwise

1.   Answer the following questions:
    (a) In lines 1-3, what did Hector urge Aeneas to do in the dream?
    (b) In lines 4-6, why did Thetis intervene?
    (c) In lines 7-8, why did Thetis beg Jupiter to harm the Greeks?
    (d) hodiē...capiēs (lines 12-13): was this true?
    (e) In lines 13-14, what reason was Agamemnon to be given to encourage him
        to believe that he would capture Troy?
    (f) In line 17, what did the dream tell Agamemnon not to do?

(g) In line 18, why was Agamemnon laetissimus?

(h) What was the essential difference between the two dreams?

(i) What do we learn about Agamemnon from this passage?

(j) In line 22, what did he fail to achieve?

2. Translate the passage veraciously.

3. Answer the following questions:

(a) In line 2, if, instead of just 'for the gods', we had wished to say 'for the gods and for the goddesses', how would we write 'and for the goddesses'?

(b) In lines 4-5, how does the word māter relate to the word Thetis? Mention and translate any other examples of this feature in the passage.

(c) In line 10, give the principal parts and meaning of the verb from which mīsit comes.

(d) In line 11, what is the case of perniciōsum? What would it be if it were accusative singular neuter?

(e) dīc (line 12); comment on this word.

(f) armā (line 14); what part of which word is this?

(g) dormīre nōlī! (line 17); what would this become if addressed to more than one person?

(h) In line 19, if we had wanted to put ducēs into the genitive plural, what should we have written?

(i) In line 20, comment on anything special about the use of the word tamen. Is there any other word in the passage about which you could make the same comment?

(j) In line 21, if, instead of the pluperfect subjunctive gessisset, we had wished to write the imperfect subjunctive of this verb, what should we have written?

Here are some more deponent verbs:

loquor, loquī, locūtus sum = I speak
sequor, sequī, secūtus sum = I follow
proficīscor, proficīscī, profectus sum = I set out (on a journey)

These are all 3rd conjugation.

Exercise 8.7

Translate into English:

1. cum magistrō dē praemiīs, quae puerīs puellīsque dare cōnstituerāmus, locūtus sum.
2. nōnne iuvenēs ad montēs sequēbāminī?
3. cum omnia parāvissēmus, ex urbe quam celerrimē profectī sumus.
4. dē multīs rēbus dux loquētur.
5. celeria animālia sequī difficillimum est.
6. iam herī senēs ex urbe profectī erant.
7. mulierēs omnēs bene cantāre cōnātae sunt.
8. cūr puerōs ut viam trānsīrent hortābāminī?

Exercise 8.8

Translate into Latin:

1. When we had done everything, we urged everyone not to fear.
2. Though we tried to speak with the old men, they were unable to reply to us.
3. The women were in the fields because they had followed the old men out of the town.
4. Who will set out with me to the very beautiful land?
5. It is easier to follow than to lead.
6. When we had already returned, you (pl.) were setting out.
7. She said that she had not followed the boys out of the temple.
8. The masters replied that they had spoken with the children and were speaking with the slaves.

Deponent verbs: the present participle

The present participle of deponent verbs was just too much for the Romans! They were certainly up against it here, since there is no present participle passive in Latin. It simply doesn't exist. So what could they do? Well, very simply, they forgot for the moment all this business about 'passive in form but active in meaning' and treated these verbs as if they were just ordinary verbs. Thus, the present participle of hortor is formed from an imaginary 'hortō' and, being first conjugation, is hortāns, hortantis; the present participle of loquor, third conjugation, is loquēns, loquentis, and so on.

Exercise 8.9

Translate into English:

1. cīvēs ducem multa loquentem audiēbant.
2. mīlitēsne ad proelium proficīscentēs vīdistī?
3. dā puerō auxilium opus suum facere cōnantī.
4. vōcem magistrī puerōs hortantis audīvimus.
5. clāmōrēs audīvī iuvenum nōs sequentium.
6. agricolae cum nautīs pugnābant equōs terrēre cōnantibus.
7. parvās puellās bene cantāre cōnantēs laudāvimus.
8. puerī ā magistrīs pūnītī sunt multa loquentibus.
9. turbam senum ex urbe proficīscentium cōnspexī.
10. ducem vīdī mīlitēs exercitum hostium sequentēs hortantem.

Note: Latin present participles are often best translated into English by a clause. Thus, puerōs cantantēs audiō could be rendered 'I am listening to the boys as they sing' or 'I am listening to the boys who are singing'.

puerōs cantantēs audīre nōn vult

Exercise 8.10

Translate into Latin, using a present participle in each sentence:

1.   He listened to the messengers as they spoke.
2.   This is the work of a boy who tries to do everything well.
3.   We gave food to the girls who were following us.
4.   Those are the arms of the soldiers who are setting out.
5.   He stood in the same place, encouraging the boys and girls.
6.   The master praised the slaves as they tried to work well.
7.   The young men setting out from the city were very happy.
8.   We gave beautiful presents to the wives who were following their husbands.
9.   Where are the books of the boys and girls who are speaking about our fatherland?
10.   We all praised the leader as he spoke in the middle of the city.

Note: Although we are using present participles here, to practise, they are not very frequent in the nominative case.

Deponent verbs: the past participle

This is something really exciting. I'm sure you remember the dear old past participle passive, the very backbone of the Latin language. But there's no past participle active in Latin. So you can't say 'having eaten a meal, he walked in the field'. But I'm sure you can see what's coming. Yes! What a wonderful thing! With a deponent verb, the past participle, looking passive of course, is active in meaning. Thus we can say 'having urged' (hortātus), 'having set out' (profectus) and really go to town with a meaning which cannot be achieved with an ordinary verb. So let's bask in this sudden freedom.

Exercise 8.11

Translate into English:

1.   crās ex urbe profectī iter ad montēs faciēmus.
2.   magister puerōs ut quam celerrimē currerent hortātus, librum legēbat.
3.   hostēs ad mare secūtī pugnāre coēgērunt.
4.   hostēs, oppidum frūstrā occupāre cōnātī, discessērunt et fessī et īrātī.
5.   virtūs mīlitum iam profectōrum maxima est.
6.   nūntiī, cum cīvibus locūtī, discessērunt.
7.   malōs hominēs ad montēs secūtī, aurum invēnimus.

8.   hās rēs iuvenibus profectīs nōn dedimus.
9.   omnēs magistrum puerōs et puellās bene hortātum laudābant.
10.   quid senī dīxistī perīculum effugere cōnātō?

Exercise 8.12

Translate into Latin, using a past participle in every sentence:

1.   Who will announce these things to Caesar, who has set out from the city?
2.   These books belong to[1] the boys who have spoken about the battles.
3.   Having encouraged the girl to sing, the teacher was happy.
4.   The leader praised the soldiers who had followed the army of the enemy.
5.   I gave the best prize to the woman who had tried to save her husband.
6.   Having set out from the island, I wished to return.
7.   Do not praise the young men who have not tried to do their work.
8.   These wise men, having spoken much about many things, did nothing.
9.   Having followed the farmers into the field, the soldiers found many horses there.
10.   The young men urged the old men to be brave, and fled.

[1] For 'belong to' say 'are of'.

Two nice little idioms for purpose clauses

Now for two little things that you really ought to know about purpose clauses:

1.   In translating a sentence such as 'He sent soldiers to save the citizens', instead of saying:

      mīlitēs mīsit ut cīvēs servārent

it is better to say

      mīlitēs mīsit quī cīvēs servārent
      (lit. he sent soldiers who should save the citizens)

2.   If there is a comparative in the purpose clause, we must introduce this clause by quō rather than ut.

      e.g. copiīs suīs, quō melius pugnārent, optima arma dedit.
      He gave his forces excellent weapons in order that they might fight better.

I thought you would like these.

Exercise 8.13

Translate into English:

1. exercitūs mīsimus quī hostēs vincerent.
2. per agrōs, quō celerius ad urbem advenīrent, currēbant.
3. mē haec omnia loquentem multī malī terrēre cōnābantur.
4. dominus saevum servum mīserat quī aliōs pūnīret.
5. cūr nōs domum euntēs sequiminī?
6. multae et pulchrae mulierēs aderant.
7. hostēs mūrōs quō facilius in urbem intrārent dēlēverant.
8. puellās in templum mīsimus quae ibi cantārent.
9. hodiē profectī ad montēs iuvenēs rediērunt
10. cīvēs, quō melius proelium vidērent, prope mūrum steterant.

Exercise 8.14

Translate into Latin:

1. The good boys have been praised by the happy teacher.
2. The cruel master was punishing the sad slaves.
3. We were eating much food.
4. The little girls were running through the big field.
5. The proud sailors have sailed through many seas in big ships.
6. You (pl.) came down from the mountain to defend the town better.
7. After the long night, we sent citizens into the city to prepare weapons.
8. The queen sent maid-servants to find food.
9. The leaders sent soldiers to overcome the enemy.
10. The tired old men were walking on the high walls to watch the battle more easily.

Exercise 8.15

Read the following passage carefully, and answer the questions on it:

dē somnō: About sleep

1	Graecī somnum <u>dulcem</u> esse dīcēbant; Rōmānī eum dōnum esse dīcēbant deōrum; nam ad hominēs <u>quiētem</u> fert; sed negat Homērus fīlium <u>Ulixis</u> dē patre <u>perturbātum</u> dormīre
5	posse. Mēdēa propter perīcula quibus <u>Iāsōn</u>, quem amāvit, <u>circumdatus</u> est, <u>commōta</u> dormīre nōn poterat. et Dīdō, dum <u>ubīque</u> regēbat somnus, dormīre nōn poterat; nam Aenēās, quem amāvit, ā Mercuriō ut ad Ītaliam
10	nāvigāret monitus, discēdere cōnstituerat. circum manūs Claudiī dormientis antequam prīnceps factus est, <u>soccī</u> pōnēbantur; et ille statim <u>experrēctus</u> <u>faciem</u> hīs <u>cōnfricābat</u>; et rīdēbant omnēs. In Graeciā Vespasiānus, dum
15	Nerō cantat, <u>obdormīvit</u>; īrātissimus Nerō eum ad Iūdaeam mīsit; nam ibi bellum gerēbātur saevissimum; et posteā, cum Nerō et trēs aliī prīncipēs perīssent, Vespasiānus ā <u>legiōnibus</u> quārum dux erat prīnceps factus, per decem
20	annōs rem pūblicam bene et <u>sapienter</u> <u>gubernāvit</u>.

dulcis, -e = sweet
quiēs, quiētis, f. = quietness, rest
Ulixes, -is, m. = Ulysses
perturbō, -āre, -āvī, -ātum = I disturb, upset
Iāsōn, Iāsonis, m. = Jason
circumdō, -are, circumdedī, circumdatum = I surround
commoveō, -ēre, commōvī, commōtum = I move deeply
ubīque = everywhere
soccus, -ī, m. (here) = slipper
expergīscor, -ī, experrēctus sum = I wake up (intrans.)
faciēs, faciēī, f. (here) = face
cōnfricō, -āre, -āvī, -ātum = I rub vigorously
obdormiō, -īre, obdormīvī, obdormītum = I fall asleep
legiō, legiōnis, f. = a legion
sapienter = wisely
gubernō, -āre, -āvī, -ātum = I govern

1. Answer the following questions:

   (a) In lines 2-3, why did the Romans say that sleep was the gift of the gods?
   (b) In lines 3-5, why was Ulysses' son unable to sleep?
   (c) In line 6 and line 9, what same reason did Medea and Dido have in common for being so deeply upset?
   (d) In lines 9-10, why had Aeneas decided to depart?
   (e) In line 14, why did everyone laugh?
   (f) In lines 14-15, why was Nero so angry?
   (g) In lines 15-16, how did Nero punish Vespasian?
   (h) In lines 18-19, how did Vespasian become Emperor?
   (i) Read from line 17 to the end. What do you think Nero would have thought about the way in which things turned out for Vespasian?
   (j) In lines 20-21, what sort of an emperor was Vespasian?

2. Translate the passage sleepily (but not too sleepily).

3. Answer the following questions:

> (a) In line 3, what part of what verb is fert? Give its principal parts and meaning.
> (b) filium (line 4); what is the vocative singular of this noun?
> (c) In line 6, what part of commoveō is commōta?
> (d) In line 7, if, instead of saying 'he was not able', we had wanted to say 'he will not be able', to what would we have had to change poterat?
> (e) dum (lines 7-8 and lines 14-15); explain the different usages of dum in these lines.
> (f) In line 10, what is the tense of cōnstituerat? Put it into the subjunctive.
> (g) In line 11, what could the case of manūs be? What case is it here?
> (h) antequam (line 11); discuss the way in which this word is regularly used. (See *Latin Prep* 2, p.51)
> (i) In line 17, put saevissimum into the comparative.
> (j) In line 18, what part of which verb* is perīssent. Why is this part used here?

*The correct term for giving the precise grammatical details of a word or words is 'parsing'. For example we could have said, parse perīssent.

Vocabulary 8

> **Vocabulary 8**
> cōnor, -ārī, -ātus sum = I try
> hortor, -ārī, -ātus sum = I encourage, urge
> loquor, loquī, locūtus sum = I speak
> proficīscor, proficīscī, profectus sum = I set out (on a journey)
> sequor, sequī, secūtus sum = I follow

And now at last we are embarking upon the chapter of chapters, containing a fantastic feature which will put everything else into the shade. It really will; so here goes.

Chapter 9

domus

Let's start this chapter with a uniquely mixed-up noun. It is domus, which we first met in Chapter 7, and it can't make up its mind whether to be 2nd or 4th declension. Anyway, here it is:

domus, -ūs, f. = 'a house, home'

	Singular	**Plural**
Nominative	domus	domūs
Vocative	domus	domūs
Accusative	domum	domōs (or domūs)
Genitive	domūs	domuum (or domōrum)
Dative	domuī	domibus
Ablative	domō	domibus

There are some variations on this theme but we have only mentioned those that are common, and in this volume we shall stick to the first form given.

Notes:
Parts of domus are used without prepositions as follows:

(i)   domum = 'home' in the sense of 'to home'. For example:

domum rediī.
I returned home.

You can also say

domum meam rediī.
I returned to my home.

and

domum Caesaris iī
I went to Caesar's home.

(ii) domī is an old locative form, giving 'place where' (locus, -ī, m. = 'place'; remember?). Thus: domī = 'at home'.

domī meae
at/in my home

domī Caesaris
at/in Caesar's home

(iii) domō = 'from home'

Exercise 9.1

Translate into English:

1. domus illīus cīvis pulcherrima est.
2. domūs illōrum cīvium pulcherrimae sunt.
3. cuius est domus haec?
4. mox tuae domuī appropinquābō.
5. ō optima domus, quis in tē habitat?
6. puerī parva animālia in illīs domibus esse dīxērunt.
7. dux senibus ut ab illīs domibus exīrent et in hās domōs intrārent imperāvit.
8. fīlius meus, cum domum amīcī vīdisset, eam adiit.
9. hic vir, quamquam clārissimus est, suam domum nōn habet.
10. num in hōc oppidō domus est nostrā domō melior?

Exercise 9.2

Translate into Latin:

1. The leader's house is very high.
2. Those houses belong to[1] those old men.
3. Can you (sing.) see the houses of the well-known citizens?
4. This house is the best of all the houses.
5. He said that the boys were not in those houses.
6. Who built the house in which you (pl.) live?
7. Nothing was left in that house.
8. The king ordered the soldiers to destroy the leaders' houses.
9. Who is the master of this huge house?
10. Who is approaching our house?

[1] Say 'are of'.

And here are some exercises on domum, domī and domō:

Exercise 9.3

Translate into English:

1. cum haec verba audīvissent, domum Caesaris fūgērunt.
2. illa mulier fessa dē monte domum rediit.
3. fuitne pater tuus domī herī?
4. sē domī suae manēre velle dīxit.
5. servī omnēs domō discessērunt.
6. quod malī iuvenēs in viīs lūdunt, domum quam celerrimē eō.
7. hominem vīdī domum mātris meae euntem.
8. mē domī amīcī pete.

Exercise 9.4

Translate into Latin:

1. I am at home today, and I shall remain at home tomorrow.
2. He wishes[1] to return to his own house.
3. They were running home in order to escape from the storm.
4. Having set out from home, we hurried to the river.
5. I saw our master going home.
6. Do not (pl.) shout in my mother's home!
7. The slaves have departed to the fields from home.
8. My friend had gone suddenly to the home of his brother.

[1] Use volō.

Revision of participles

We are about to learn a fascinating new construction which relies heavily on participles in all their glory. So before we do this, this is a good time to review our participles.

Latin is very low in participles; it only has three:

(a) The perfect (past) participle **passive**:

amātus, -a, -um = 'having been loved'

(b) The present participle **active**:

amāns, amantis = 'loving'

(c)   The future participle **active**:

amātūrus, -a, -um = 'being about to love'

This last will not feature in this book; but we thought you ought to know about it.

To this we might wish to add, and you will see why in due course, a fourth:

(d)   The past participle deponent:

locūtus = 'having spoken'

This is not anything new, but it is worth while remembering that deponent verbs, being passive in form and active in meaning, are the only verbs that can have a past participle with an active meaning. Store this one up; it will be useful later.

The ablative absolute

So now on to the ablative absolute, which consists of a noun in the ablative and a participle agreeing with it. It tells us with the utmost neatness about something which has happened, is happening or will happen, and is sometimes said to be used to 'set the scene'. It really is the most Latin of all constructions.

Consider the following examples:

hostibus victīs, Caesar Rōmam rediit.
(With) the enemy having been defeated, Caesar returned to Rome.

hostibus and victīs are in the ablative agreeing with each other, and the two words together tell us of something that had happened before Caesar returned to Rome. We might translate it, 'After the enemy had been defeated, Caesar returned to Rome.'

Again:

Nerōne cantante, Vespasiānus obdormīvit.
(With) Nero singing, Vespasian fell asleep.

Nerōne and cantante are in the ablative agreeing with each other, and the two words together tell us of something that was happening at the time that Vespasian fell asleep. We might translate it, 'While Nero was singing, Vespasian fell asleep.'

Note:
Although present participles decline like ingēns, when the participle is part of an ablative absolute, the ablative always ends in '-e' (instead of '-ī'). Hence cantante above.

We shall say some more things about the ablative absolute presently, but let us first practise this regular use of it.

Exercise 9.5

Translate into English:

1. puerī, cibō parātō, domum rediērunt.
2. magistrī, cantantibus puellīs, laetī erant.
3. iuvenēs, appropinquante magistrō, fūgērunt.
4. librīs domī relictīs, ad agrōs ambulāvimus.
5. num, hostibus oppidum oppugnantibus, dormīre potuistis?
6. senēs, altō murō circum urbem aedificātō, sē tūtōs esse crēdēbant.
7. cīvēs, mīlitibus vīnum bibentibus, domī manēbant.
8. urbe hostium captā, Rōmānī sē bene gerēbant.
9. equō vulnerātō, agricolae īrātissimī erant.
10. nāve dēlētā, nautae miserrimī erant.

Exercise 9.6

Translate into Latin, using an ablative absolute in every sentence:

1. While the teacher was laughing, the boys were not happy.
2. The old men having been well defended, the king said that the young men had been very brave.
3. The girls having been praised, the boys said that they also had done well.
4. As the day approached, all the inhabitants kept seeing[1] brighter light.
5. Great walls having been built, the city was very safe.
6. Many weapons having been given to the leader, the citizens cried out that they wished to fight.
7. While the soldiers were fighting, you (pl.) made a difficult journey.
8. The guard having been killed, no one was guarding the road.
9. While this boy was receiving beautiful gifts, that boy received nothing.
10. Many arrows having been shot[2], they believed that the enemy had been overcome.

[1] For 'kept seeing', use the imperfect tense.
[2] For 'shot' say 'thrown'.

More deponent verbs

Here are five more deponent verbs:

> patior, patī, passus sum = I suffer, I allow
> ēgredior, ēgredī, ēgressus sum = I go out / come out
> ingredior, ingredī, ingressus sum = I go into / come into, enter, enter upon
> prōgredior, prōgredī, prōgressus sum = I advance
> morior, morī, mortuus sum = I die

These all belong to the mixed conjugation. We have already met mortuus = 'having died', used as an adjective, 'dead'.

Exercise 9.7

Translate into English:

1. urbem īngressī per viās ambulābant.
2. Aenēās in bellīs multa passus est.
3. hostēs trāns montēs lentē prōgrediēbantur.
4. in hōc itinere multī morientur.
5. quis hōs hominēs in urbem ingredī patiētur?
6. herī septem et vīgintī mīlitēs mortuī sunt.
7. cūr nēminem ex templō ēgredī patiminī?
8. celeriter prōgressī ad flūmen advēnimus.

Exercise 9.8

Translate into Latin:

1. Tomorrow, I shall enter upon a difficult journey.
2. Having suffered great dangers, Aeneas with his gods and comrades entered Italy.
3. When we had caught sight of the enemy, we came out of the city as quickly as possible.
4. Having been freed by the citizens, the sailors advanced to the harbour.
5. Many soldiers who are fighting now, will die tomorrow.
6. I shall not allow you to be cruel in my home.
7. They all suffered many things in order to do these things.
8. Will you (pl.) really allow your friends to die?

It's time now for a new story.

Exercise 9.9

Read the following passage carefully, and answer the questions on it:

dē iuvene et <u>fūre</u>: About a young man and a thief

1   mātrem meam hanc mihi <u>fābellam</u> nārrāvisse
    <u>meminī</u>. ōlim iuvenis domum ad parentēs in
    equō <u>vehēbatur</u>. iam <u>hiems</u> <u>appetēbat</u> et terra
    <u>nive</u> <u>tēcta est</u>. subitō, <u>humī</u> <u>iacentem</u>, senem
5   paene <u>nūdum</u> cōnspexit <u>aegrum</u>, vulnerātum.
    'iuvā mē!' clāmāvit senex, 'nam <u>pauperrimus</u>
    sum; uxōrem habeō et <u>līberōs</u>, quī mox <u>famē</u> et
    <u>frīgore</u> morientur.' cum iuvenis statim dē equō,
    ut senī auxilum ferret, <u>dēscendisset</u>, ille rīdēns,
10   <u>nōn iam</u> senī <u>similis</u>, gladiō <u>dēstrictō</u>, iuvenī ut
    pecūniam sibi omnem, omne aurum, <u>vestēs</u>
    omnēs daret imperāvit. quō factō, dīxit <u>fūr</u> sē
    iuvenem, nē sē sequī cōnstitueret, vulnerāre
    velle. dīxit iuvenis: 'fac mēcum id quod facere
15   vīs, sed hoc ūnum mihi <u>prōmitte</u>.' 'quid?' 'nōlī tē
    hoc fēcisse <u>glōriārī</u>.' 'cūr nōn?' 'quod omnēs quī
    hoc audient, hominī quī <u>rē vērā</u> pauperrimus
    est, auxilium ferre nōlent; et ille cum uxōre et
    <u>līberīs</u> <u>famē</u> et <u>frīgore</u> moriētur.' hōc ā iuvene
20   dictō, <u>fūr</u> <u>nōn</u> <u>iam</u> rīdēns, omnibus rēbus iuvenī
    <u>redditīs</u>, discessit; nec posteā hominēs <u>dēcēpit</u>
    neque vulnerāvit neque eōrum rēs <u>fūrātus est</u>.

fūr, fūris, m. = thief
fābella, -ae, f. = short story
meminī = I remember (see below)
vehō, -ere, vēxī, vectum = I convey
  (see below)
hiems, hiemis, f. (here) = winter
appetō, -ere, appetīvī, appetītum
  (here) = I approach
nix, nivis, f. = snow
tegō, -ere, tēxī, tēctum = I cover
humī (here) = on the ground
iaceō, -ēre, iacuī, iacitum = I lie (e.g.
  on the ground). Not to be mixed up
  with iaciō.
nūdus, -a, -um = naked
aeger, aegra, aegrum = ill
pauperrimus, -a, -um = very poor
līberī, -ōrum, m. pl. = children, with
  reference to their parents. See p.111
famēs, famis, f. (ablative famē) =
  hunger
frīgus, frīgoris, n. = the cold
dēscendō, -ere, dēscendī, dēscēnsum
  = I descend
nōn iam = no longer
similis, -e = similar (+ gen. or dat.)
dēstringō, -ere, dēstrīnxī, dēstrictum
  = I unsheathe
vestis, vestis, f. = garment
prōmittō, -ere, prōmīsī, prōmissum =
  I promise
glōrior, -ārī, -ātus sum = I boast
rē vērā (also written as one word,
  rēvērā) = truly, really
reddō, -ere, reddidī, redditum = I give
  back. Not to be mixed up with
  redeō.
dēcipiō, -ere, dēcēpī, dēceptum =
  I deceive
fūror, fūrārī, fūrātus sum = I steal

pecūniam mihi dā!

Notes:

(i)   meminī (line 2) = 'I remember'; it is one of the defective verbs which have no present tense, but whose perfect is used with present meaning.

(ii) vehor (line 3) = 'I am conveyed', hence 'I ride'.

(iii) famē et frīgore (lines 7-8). In Latin one dies '**with** hunger and cold' while in English one dies '**of** something'. Isn't this jolly?

(iv) quō factō (line 12). It is very common in Latin to start a new sentence with a relative, which joins the new sentence to the preceding one. Thus, quō factō literally means 'which (thing) having been done'. In English we don't use the relative in this way: we would say 'this having been done' or 'when this was done'.

1. Answer the following questions:
    (a) In line 2, where was the young man going?
    (b) In lines 3-4, were the weather conditions favourable for travelling?
    (c) In lines 4-5, what did the young man think he saw?
    (d) In lines 7-8, what did this person say about his wife and children?
    (e) In lines 9-10, why was the person laughing?
    (f) In lines 12-14, why did the thief wish to wound the young man?
    (g) In lines 14-15, was the young man worried by this? Explain your answer.
    (h) In lines 15-16, what did the young man want the thief to promise?
    (i) In line 17, what is the point here of rē vērā?
    (j) In lines 19-22, how did the thief respond to the young man's words?

2. Translate the passage virtuously.

3. Answer the following questions:
    (a) In lines 1-2, mention and explain the construction used in the first sentence.
    (b) iuvenis (line 2); what is the genitive plural of this word? Is it regular? Answer in full.
    (c) In line 4, what part of iaceō is iacentem?
    (d) cōnspexit (line 5); give the principal parts and meaning of the verb from which this word comes.
    (e) In line 7, is famē a regular 3rd declension ablative singular?
    (f) In line 8, if, instead of saying 'they will die', we had wished to say 'they have died', to what we would have had to change morientur?
    (g) In lines 9 and 10-12, explain the two constructions introduced by ut.
    (h) dēscendisset (line 9); parse this word, and explain why this form is used here.
    (i) Mention and translate any ablative absolute in this passage.
    (j) Parse and translate fac (line 14) and vīs (line 15).

More on the ablative absolute

And now for a cunning use of the ablative absolute, enabling us to cope with the lack of a past participle active in Latin.

We can't say, 'Having captured the city, Caesar advanced.' But we can say, 'The city having been captured, Caesar advanced.' i.e.:

> Caesar, urbe captā, prōgressus est.

The context makes it clear who captured the city, and we may be allowed to translate this sentence by: 'Having taken the city, Caesar advanced.' Or by: 'After taking the city, Caesar advanced.' Or even by: 'Caesar took the city and advanced.'

Exercise 9.10

Translate into English:

1. dux, hostĭbus victīs, ad castra rediit.
2. fēmina, cibō parātō, puerōs et puellās domum suam venīre iussit.
3. agricolae, magnō mūrō aedificātō, fessī erant.
4. magistrō cōnspectō, puerī sē bene gerēbant.
5. servī, operĭbus suīs celeriter factīs, laudātī sunt.
6. novō librō scrīptō, poēta laetus erat.
7. puellae, longō et difficilī itinere factō, dormīre volēbant.
8. senēs et iuvenēs, oppidō relictō, per agrōs ambulābant.
9. magistrī, malīs puerīs pūnītīs, discessērunt.
10. rēx, urbĭbus suīs per multōs annōs bene rēctīs, tandem mortuus est.

Exercise 9.11

Translate into Latin, using an ablative absolute in every sentence:

1. We read the book and entered upon a new task.
2. After finding the gold, they returned home.
3. They ate the food and slept.
4. After seeking those things in vain, you (pl.) are wretched.
5. Having conquered the Greeks, the Roman general was praised by all.
6. They left the town and wandered through the fields.
7. The leader praised the citizens and departed.
8. Having killed the woman's husband, the wicked man was punished.
9. After praising the singers[1], the teacher remained in the temple.
10. The enemy destroyed the walls and entered the city.

[1] Say 'those who were singing'.

cum + the imperfect subjunctive

We still have quite a bit more to say about the ablative absolute. However, meanwhile, let us return to our friend cum, which we last met governing the pluperfect subjunctive. As a matter of fact cum as a conjunction is more or less insatiable; in other words, it can be followed by every conceivable part of a verb. We shall confine ourselves to one more only of its uses, which is one of the commonest after its use with the pluperfect subjunctive. And that is cum followed by the imperfect subjunctive.

This construction is very common indeed, and it is far from straighforward, since cum can appear here in three different guises; it can mean 'when, while' or 'because, since' or even 'though, although'.

I can already hear you indignantly asking how you are expected to know which is the correct meaning in any given case. And I'm sure the answer won't surprise you. Yes; it depends more than ever, on the context.

Incidentally, I have just discovered that some old grammarians believed that cum was followed by the subjunctive, even when the sense was purely temporal, simply because the Romans liked the subjunctive so much. I find this view very attractive and very probably true, all the more so because it throws logic to the winds.

So let's try cum with the imperfect subjunctive:

(i) cīvēs, cum hostēs urbem oppugnārent, multa mala patiēbantur.
     While the enemy were attacking the city, the citizens were suffering many evils.

In this sentence, cum couldn't possibly mean 'although'. 'While' seems slightly more likely than 'because', but in a short sentence we can only do our best.

(ii) cum hostēs nōs nōn exspectārent, eōs facile superāvimus.
      Since the enemy were not expecting us, we overcame them easily.

In this sentence, 'since' is clearly right.

N.B. facile, the neuter singular of facilis is used as its adverb. Do not be tempted to pronounce that short final 'e' as if it were long.

(iii) cum iter difficillimum esset, omnēs tūtī erāmus.
       Although the journey was very difficult, we were all safe.

Here, 'although' clearly gives the best sense.

Let's see how it works out in the following sentences; if ever you think two interpretations are equally possible, give both.

Exercise 9.12

Translate into English:

1. puerī, cum librōs legerent, nihil dīcēbant.
2. agricolae, cum nautae appropinquārent, sē dēfendere parābant.
3. illud iter, cum difficillimum esse crēderent, ingredī nōlēbant.
4. hic puer, cum minimus esset, cum magnīs iuvenibus fortiter pugnābat.
5. rēgem illum, cum crūdēlissimus esset, nēmō amāvit.
6. cīvēs, cum maxima tempestās domōs dēlēret, in agrōs fugiēbant.
7. puerōs, cum bene in templō cantārent, omnēs laudāvērunt.
8. cum ventī saevissimī essent, multī cīvēs in viīs ambulābant.
9. iuvenēs, cum cibum cōnsūmerent, cantābant.
10. iuvenēs, cum multum vīnum biberent, magnā vōce clāmābant.

Exercise 9.13

Translate into Latin, using cum in every sentence:

1. While the boys were playing in the streets, the girls were reading their books.
2. Since the queen was calling her maid-servants, they were rushing to her.
3. While the enemy were fighting with our soldiers, I remained at home.
4. Because you were all fleeing, no one was defending us.
5. While he was asking us to go out from home, we were speaking with our father.
6. While the Romans were attacking the city, the citizens did not have (any) food.
7. Though the very great army of the enemy was approaching[1], no one fled.
8. Because the master was punishing them, the boys were sad.
9. While they were drinking the wine, the soldiers were laughing.
10. Because they were drinking much wine, the soldiers were shouting.

[1] Use adeō

And now we must return to the ablative absolute, in stern mood this time.

Solemn warning about the ablative absolute

This warning is very important indeed and will, I hope, forestall many a potential howler. So here it is:

> The noun or pronoun in an ablative absolute must be completely independent of the main verb of the sentence, or any other verb for that matter.

This will be understood more clearly from the following examples:

(i)   Having been conquered the army fled.

Here, 'the army' is the subject of the main verb 'fled', and must therefore be in the nominative, giving us:

>   exercitus victus fūgit.

(ii)   The city having been attacked, the enemy captured it.

This would be:

>   hostēs urbem oppugnātam cēpērunt.

'The city', here, is the object of the main verb and so must go into the accusative.

(iii)   While the boy was playing in the street, the teacher did not give him a gift.

>   magister puerō in viā lūdentī dōnum nōn dedit.

Here 'the boy' has to go into the dative after dedit.

It is very easy to be caught out on this one. So remember, only if the noun that you wish to use in the ablative absolute is totally independent, grammatically, of the rest of the sentence can an ablative absolute be used.

Exercise 9.14

Translate into English:

1.   opere factō, puellae domum rediērunt.
2.   Caesar, hostibus victīs, in Galliam prōgressus est.
3.   Caesar hostēs victōs ad flūmen secūtus est.
4.   puerīs pūnītīs, puellae perterritae sunt.
5.   iuvenī nōbīs appropinquantī ut ex oppidō exīret imperāvimus.
6.   appropinquante magistrō, puerī et puellae sē optimē gerēbant.
7.   senex, multō cibō cōnsūmptō, dormīre voluit.
8.   fēminae optimē cantantī multa et pulcherrima dōna dedērunt.
9.   duce locūtō, cīvēs cum hostibus pugnāre parābant.
10.   servī līberātī māter laeta erat.

Exercise 9.15

Translate into Latin, using a participle in every sentence:

1.   The walls having been built, the citizens were safe.
2.   Many houses having been destroyed, we walked into the fields.
3.   Gold having been found in the city, the leaders wanted to have it.
4.   The soldiers having been wounded, the women tried to help them.
5.   The city having been attacked, the old men fled to the mountains.
6.   The girl having been praised, the teachers gave her a reward.
7.   These words having been said, no one will depart from the town.
8.   The storm having been expected, everyone remained at home.
9.   While these boys were working well, their teachers did not punish them.
10.   While the sailors were watching the city, the farmers decided to defend the fields.

Exercise 9.16

Give an English word derived from the following Latin words; and mention the connexion between the meanings of the Latin and English words. Don't forget to look at all the principal parts of the verbs. If you get stuck, try English compounds:

1.   hortor
2.   loquor
3.   morior
4.   patior
5.   progredior
6.   sequor

Using sum (understood)

And here, now, is just a little bit more about the ablative absolute:

Since there is no present participle of sum, it might appear impossible to construct an ablative absolute using the verb 'to be'; but there is good news: we can simply *understand* it.

Thus:

> Caesare duce
> When Caesar was leader (lit. '(with) Caesar (being) leader')

> C. Caesar nātus est…patre suō et C. Fonteiō Capitōne cōnsulibus.
> Gaius Caesar was born…in the consulship of his father and Gaius Fonteius Capito (lit. '(with) his father and Gaius Fonteius Capito (being) consuls').

Marcus Tullius Cicero (106 – 43BC), most famous of the Roman orators, wrote quite a lot of verse also; this is one of his lines:

> ō fortūnātam nātam mē cōnsule Rōmam!
> Oh! lucky Rome (re)born in my consulship! (lit. '(with) me (being) consul', i.e. 'when I was consul')

This is not considered one of Cicero's best efforts with its nasty jingle in the middle and its ablative absolute producing a rather unsubtle lack of modesty!

By the way, Rōmam, here, is an example of the accusative of exclamation.

Cicero was overjoyed with himself for having put down a dangerous conspiracy. It is rather a nice coincidence that in the same year (63 BC), Octavian, who was later the Emperor Augustus, and who brought peace to the Roman world was born.

Exercise 9.17

Translate into English:

1. mē puerō, mīlitēs nostrī omnēs aliōs vincēbant.
2. quis, tē iuvene, optimus erat cīvium?
3. omnēs hominēs, illō rēge, miserī erant.
4. Caesare duce, omnēs superāvimus.
5. ō puerī puellaeque, mē sene, patrēs eritis et mātrēs.
6. vīsne, mē comite, ad flūmen iter facere?
7. Titō magistrō, puerī nihil dīcēbant.
8. tē custōde, iuvenēs effūgērunt.
9. illō prīncipe, omnēs laetī fuimus.
10. quis tē puellā incolās regēbat?

Exercise 9.18

Translate into Latin, using an ablative absolute in every sentence:

1. During that man's reign, nobody was happy.
2. When I was a boy, many men used to sing in the temple.
3. With this man as leader, we shall conquer all our enemies.
4. When you were a young man, I was a boy.
5. While that man was emperor, few Roman armies were defeated.
6. When I was a girl, everyone was happy.
7. When Aulus is the guard, the slaves work well in the fields.
8. During her reign, all the maid-servants were wretched.
9. When you are teacher, the boys and girls read their books.
10. When I am an old man, Rome will be even more famous.

And now for a really beautiful story:

Exercise 9.19

Study the following passage carefully, and answer the questions on it:

dē tertiō amīcō: About a third friend

1   erat ōlim rēx superbissimus, quem omnēs
        <u>ōderant</u>; is <u>adversāriōs</u> crūdēlissimē pūniēbat;
        inter quōs iuvenis erat nōbilis, <u>capitis damnātus</u>:
        is, in <u>carcere</u> <u>vīnctus</u>, <u>dictā</u> diē morī <u>dēbuit</u>. dīxit

ōdī = I hate (see below)
adversārius, -iī, m. = opponent
capitis damnātus = condemned to death
carcer, carceris, m. = prison
vinciō, -īre, vīnxī, vīnctum = I bind
dictus, -a, -um (here) = appointed
dēbeō, -ēre, dēbuī, dēbitum = I must,
    have to

5 eī nūntius patrem eius senem in <u>lectō</u> <u>iacēre</u>
morientem; pater ille in oppidō <u>longinquō</u>
habitābat nec <u>fātum</u> fīliī <u>cognōverat</u>; fīlius rēgem
ut sibi patrem <u>vīsere</u> <u>licēret</u> <u>ōrāvit</u>. respondit ille:
'tē īre patior, sed <u>anteā</u> amīcus tuus in <u>carcere</u>
10 manēre <u>dēbēbit</u>; et is, <u>nisi</u> tū post ūnum
<u>mēnsem</u> dictā diē redībis, interficiētur. statim
iuvenis, amīcō optimō in <u>carcere</u> <u>vīnctō</u>,
discessit; patrem <u>vīsit</u>, mortuum <u>sepelīvit</u>; et
domum quam celerrimē festīnābat. sed
15 tempestāte subito <u>coortā</u>, <u>arboribus</u> <u>ubīque</u>
<u>collāpsīs</u>, equō vulnerātō, flūminibus
<u>redundantibus</u> <u>aeger</u>, <u>vix</u> vīvus sē domum
<u>trahēbat</u>. intereā rēx amīcum <u>cottīdiē</u> <u>vīsēbat</u>; cui
rīdēns dīcēbat 'numquam veniet amīcus tuus;
20 <u>stultus</u> es quī eī crēdidistī.' vēnit dicta diēs; in
locō <u>caudex</u> positus est, <u>caput</u> <u>inclīnāvit</u> amīcus,
<u>astitit</u> <u>carnifex</u>, cīvēs omnēs aderant trīstēs; vēnit
hōra; rēx <u>tantum nōn</u> amīcum <u>dētruncārī</u> iussit;
et subitō vōx virī audīta est '<u>dēsine</u>' clāmantis.
25 'ego adsum; domum vēnī.' et <u>inter sē</u> duo amīcī
<u>complexī</u> sunt. quibus rēx, maximē <u>commōtus</u>,
<u>plaudentibus</u> omnibus, 'accipite mē,' dīxit, '<u>ōrō</u>
vōs, vestrum tertium amīcum.'

lectus, -ī, m. = bed
iaceō, -ēre, iacuī, iacitum = I lie, recline
longinquus, -a, -um = far, distant
fātum, -ī, n. = fate
cognōscō, -ere, cognōvī, cognitum
(+ acc.) = I learn of
vīsō, -ere, vīsī, vīsum = I visit
licet (+ dat.) = it is permitted to
ōrō, -āre, -āvī, -ātum (here) = I beg
anteā = beforehand
nisi = unless
mēnsis, mēnsis, m. = month
sepeliō, -īre, sepelīvī, sepultum = I bury
coorior, coorīrī, coortus sum = I break out
arbor, arboris, f. = tree
ubīque = everywhere
collābor, -ī, collāpsus sum = I collapse
redundō, -āre, -āvī, -ātum = overflow
aeger, aegra, aegrum = ill
vix = scarcely
trahō, -ere, trāxi, tractum = I drag
cottīdiē = every day
stultus, -a, -um = stupid
caudex, -icis, m. = block
caput, capitis, n. = head
inclīnō, -āre, -āvī, -ātum = I bend
astō, -āre, astitī, astitum = I stand near
carnifex, carnificis, m. = executioner
tantum nōn iussit = was on the point of
ordering
dētruncō, -āre, -āvī, -ātum = I behead
dēsinō, -ere, dēsiī, dēsitum = I stop
(intrans.)
inter sē = each other
complector, -ī, complexus sum =
I embrace
commoveō, -ēre, commōvī, commōtum
= I move deeply
plaudō, -ere, plausī, plausum = I clap,
I applaud

ego adsum!

Notes:

(i)   ōderant (line 2). This comes from ōdī, which does not have a present tense, but its perfect/past tense is present in meaning: thus we translate it as 'I hate' and the pluperfect form ōderam is used for its past/perfect.

(ii)   interficiētur (line 11). Remember that compounds of faciō, such as interficiō, have regular passive forms, unlike faciō itself.

1.   Answer the following questions:
     (a) In lines 1-2, give two reasons why everyone hated the king.
     (b) In lines 2-3, why was the noble youth in prison?
     (c) In lines 4-6, what news was brought to the young man?
     (d) In lines 7-8, for what favour did the young man beg the king?
     (e) In lines 9-11, on what condition did the king grant this favour?
     (f) In lines 15-17, mention three events which hindered the young man's return home.
     (g) In lines 18-19, did the king believe that the young man would return home? Give reasons for your answer.
     (h) In line 20, what did the king think of the young man's friend? Answer in full.
     (i) In line 22, which Latin word tells us how the citizens felt about the impending execution? Translate it.
     (j) In line 27, which words tell us what everyone felt about the outcome of this story? Translate them.

2.   Translate the passage nobly.

3.   Answer the following questions:
     (a) crūdēlissimē (line 2); what part of speech is this word?
     (b) diē (line 4); why is this word feminine here?
     (c) patrem...iacēre (line 5); explain the construction used here.
     (d) ut...ōrāvit (line 8); explain this construction.
     (e) redībis (line 11); what tense and person of what verb is this? Give the principal parts and meaning of this word.
     (f) amīcō...vīnctō (line 12); what is the construction here? Give and translate all other examples of this construction in the passage.
     (g) In line 18, if, instead of saying 'he used to visit', we had wished to say 'he will visit', to what would we have had to change vīsēbat?
     (h) In line 21, what is the case of caput here?
     (i) In line 23, what part of dētruncō is dētruncārī? Translate it.
     (j) In line 24, what is the genitive plural of vōx? Is it regular?

I hope you enjoyed this story.

Exercise 9.20

Translate into Latin:

1. The brave soldiers were being praised by the noble leader.
2. The beautiful girls were singing sacred words.
3. The weary old men walked to the high mountains.
4. The frightened messengers threw their weapons into the deep sea.
5. Among the missiles of the enemy are arrows and spears.
6. The strong young men made a difficult journey into the mountains.
7. The big horses are rushing from the field to the river.
8. The angry parents have punished their sad children.
9. The brave leader led the great army into the battle.
10. The wretched women were listening to the shouts of the savage young men.

Vocabulary 9

Vocabulary 9
morior, morī, mortuus sum = I die
patior, patī, passus sum = I suffer, allow
ēgredior, ēgredī, ēgressus sum = I go forth, come forth.
ingredior, ingredī, ingressus sum = I go into, enter
prōgredior, prōgredī, prōgressus sum = I advance
cum (+ imp. subj.) = while, since, although
cum (+ plup. subj.) = when, after

All these verbs belong to the mixed conjugation.

So there we are; it merely remains now to enter for a scholarship at the school of your choice and to await congratulations!

Such, however, is our generosity that we still have some stories for you, not to mention a treat of the first order, to round everything off with.

Chapter 10

Exercise 10.1

Read the following passage (do not write a translation) and answer the questions below in English. Complete sentences are not required.

The Emperor Galba

1   Nerōne mortuō, ūnō annō quattuor prīncipēs
    erant; quōrum prīmus Galba fuit; is, ūnum et
    septuāgintā annōs <u>nātus</u>, <u>vītae</u> <u>pūblicae</u> <u>perītus</u>
    erat, īdem <u>illīberālissimus</u> et <u>sevērissimus</u>; ā
5   multīs, quibus Nerō dōna dederat, maximam
    partem dōnōrum <u>recipere</u> cōnstituit; mīlitibus,
    cum ab eīs prīnceps factus esset, <u>dōnātīvum</u>
    nōn dedit; nam sē mīlitēs legere <u>glōriābātur</u>, nōn
    <u>emere</u>. Pīsōnem, quī paucīs nōtus erat, <u>nē tum</u>
10   <u>quidem</u> <u>dōnātīvō</u> <u>solitō</u> mīlitibus datō, <u>adoptāvit</u>.
    mox Othō, quī <u>adoptiōnem</u> illam ipse
    exspectāverat, ā mīlitibus prīnceps factus est; et
    Galba et Pīsō interfectī sunt et Galbae <u>caput</u>
    <u>amputātum</u> et in hastā <u>suffixum</u> per castra
15   mīlitum portābātur. Galbam, antequam prīnceps
    factus est, multī <u>prīncipātū</u> maximē <u>dignum</u> esse
    crēdiderant; sed, postquam factus est, sē
    <u>errāvisse</u> <u>intellēxērunt</u>. sīc igitur Galba ā Tacitō
    <u>dēscrīptus</u> est:

20   '<u>capāx</u> <u>imperiī</u> <u>nisi</u> <u>imperāsset</u>.'*

* Tacitus, *Histories*, I, 49

nātus, -a, -um = born
   nātus (+ x annōs) = x years old
vīta, -ae, f. = life
pūblicus, -a, -um = public
perītus, -a, -um (+ gen.) = experienced
   in
illīberālis, -e (here) = mean
sevērus, -a, -um = strict
recipiō, -ere, recēpī, receptum = I take
   back
dōnātīvum, -ī, n. = largesse (gift of
   money)
glōrior, -ārī, -ātus sum = I boast
emō, -ere, ēmī, ēmptum = I buy
nē tum quidem = not even then
solitus, -a, -um (here) = customary
adoptō, -āre, -āvī, -ātum = I adopt
adoptiō, -ōnis, f. = adoption
caput, capitis, n. = head
amputō, -āre, -āvī, -ātum = I cut off
suffīgō, -ere, suffīxī, suffīxum = I fix
   on
prīncipātus, -ūs, m. = emperorship
dignus, -a, -um (+ abl.) = worthy of
errō, -āre, -āvī, -ātum (here) = I make a
   mistake
intellegō, -ere, intellēxī, intellēctum =
   I understand
dēscrībō, -ere, dēscrīpsī, dēscrīptum
   = I describe
capāx, capācis (+ gen.) = capable of
imperium, -iī, n. (here) = rule
nisi = if not
imperāsset is short for imperāvisset

capāx imperiī nisi imperāsset

Hence, Tacitus' judgement was that Galba was 'capable of ruling, had he not ruled'!

(a)　In lines 1-2, in what way was the year following Nero's death remarkable?
(b)　In lines 3-4, which words suggest that Galba would be an efficient emperor?
(c)　In line 4, does it sound as if Galba would be popular?
(d)　In lines 5-6, do you think that Galba's behaviour mentioned here was wise?
(e)　In line 9, does Piso seem a good person for Galba to have adopted as his heir?
(f)　In lines 9-10, do you think that the soldiers were thrilled by this adoption? Answer in full.
(g)　In lines 17-18, what was the general opinion about Galba's brief time as emperor?
(h)　In line 20, how would you describe this summing up by Tacitus of Galba's period in power?

Exercise 10.2

Translate the following passage into good English:

Otho

1	Othō, Galbā interfectō, iam prīnceps ā mīlitibus factus, quamquam amīcus fuerat Nerōnis, melius quam exspectātum est sē gerēbat; sed iam, antequam prīnceps factus est, aliī mīlitēs
5	Vitellium prīncipem facere cōnstituerant. Othō <u>litterīs</u> sē, fīliā Vitelliī <u>ductā</u>, <u>prīncipātum</u> cum eō <u>partīrī</u> velle nūntiāvit; sed iam proelium inter Othōnis et Vitelliī <u>fautōrēs</u> initum erat; vīcērunt hī. tum Othō, quod bellum <u>cīvīle</u> maximē <u>ōderat</u>,
10	aliud proelium facere nōluit et <u>mortem sibi</u> <u>cōnscīvit</u>. de hāc rē poēta Mārtiālis <u>epigramma</u> scrīpsit; <u>odiō</u> Othōnis bellī <u>cīvīlis dēscrīptō</u>, hīs verbīs <u>epigramma fīnit</u>:
15	'sit Catŏ, dum <u>vīvit, sānē vel</u> Caesare maior: 　dum moritur, num <u>quid</u> maior Othōne fuit?*

* Martial, *Epigrams*, Book 6, 32, 5-6

litterae, -ārum, f. pl. = a letter
dūcō, -ere, dūxī, ductum (here) = I marry (of a man)
prīncipātus, -ūs, m. = emperorship
partior, partīrī, partītus sum = I share
fautor, fautōris, m. = supporter
cīvīlis, -e = civil
ōdī, ōdisse = I hate (see p.156)
cōnscīscō, -ere, cōnscīvī, cōnscītum (here) = I inflict
mortem sibi cōnscīscere = to commit suicide
epigramma, epigrammatis, n. = epigram (a short, pithy poem); it is a Greek word
odium, -iī, n. = hatred
dēscrībō, -ere, descrīpsī, dēscrīptum = I describe
fīniō, -īre, -īvī, -ītum = I end
sit (here) = let...be (see below)
vīvō, -ere, vīxī, vīctum = I live
sānē (here) = admittedly
vel (here) = even
quid (here) = in any way

Notes:

(i)   C. Valerius Mārtiālis, whom we call Martial, lived from c.40 to c.104 AD. He wrote fourteen books of Epigrams, many of which are brilliant. He came from Spain.

(ii) sit is the present subjunctive of sum. Here it means 'let…be'.

(iii) This Cato fought against Caesar and, being defeated, committed suicide to avoid being forgiven by him.

Exercise 10.3

Study the following passage and answer the questions below in good English. Complete sentences are not required.

Vitellius and Vespasian

1	Vitellius gulā īnsignis erat; convīvia eius plūrimā pecūniā reī pūblicae stābant. ventrem habuit obēsum et faciem vīnō rutilātam. rērum mīlitārium perītus nōn erat; ab aliīs mīlitibus
5	dēlēctus, ab aliīs dēiectus est. Rōmae sē cēlāre cōnātus agnitus est et ā cīvibus crūdēlissimē occīsus; corpus eius in flūmen Tiberim tractum est. post Vitellium prīnceps ā mīlitibus factus est T. Flāvius Vespasiānus. is cum fīliō suō Titō
10	Iūdaeōrum, quī līberī esse volēbant, rebelliōnem asperrimē opprimēbat; cuius bellī cūrā fīliō trāditā, ipse prīmō Alexandriam, deinde Rōmam vēnit; multōs per annōs rem pūblicam bene gubernāvit. is iam itineribus per plūrimās reī
15	pūblicae partēs factīs et rērum mīlitārium et rērum cīvīlium perītus erat; cum iuvenis esset, secundae legiōnis Augustae, quae cum aliīs Britanniam invāsit, dux erat. prīnceps erat prūdēns et iūstus et facētus.

gula, -ae, f. = throat, (here) = gluttony
īnsignis, -e (+ abl.) = famous for
convīvium, -iī, n. = party
stāre (+ dat. + abl.) (here) = to cost
venter, ventris, m. = stomach
obēsus, -a, -um = fat
faciēs, -ēī, f. (here) = face
rutilō, -āre, -āvī, -ātum = I redden
mīlitāris, -e = military
perītus, -a, -um (+ gen.) = experienced i
dēligō, -ere, dēlēgī, dēlēctum =
    I choose
dēiciō, -ere, dēiēcī, dēiectum = I throw
    down
cēlō, -āre, -āvī, -ātum = I hide (trans.)
agnōscō, -ere, agnōvī, agnitum =
    I recognise
trahō, -ere, trāxī, tractum = I drag
līber, lībera, līberum = free
rebelliō, -ōnis, f. = revolt
asper, aspera, asperum = harsh
opprimō, -ere, oppressī, oppressum =
    I put down
cūra, -ae, f. = care, (here) = conduct
prīmō = at first
gubernō, -āre, -āvī, -ātum = I govern
cīvīlis, -e = civil
legiō, legiōnis, f. = a legion
invādō, -ere, invāsī, invāsum = I invade
prūdēns, prudentis = prudent
iūstus, -a, -um = just
facētus, -a, -um = witty, humorous
    (unlike the English 'facetious', this
    word is complimentary in Latin.)

Notes:

(i) Tiberim (line 7). This is the accusative of Tiberis, -is, m. = the river Tiber.

(ii) Iūdaeī, -ōrum (line 10) = the Jewish people. They were part of the Roman Empire, and revolted from it in 66 AD. The revolt was put down with terrible severity. I find it sad to think of Vespasian in this context, since, on the whole, he does not seem to have been a cruel man. As for Titus, I can't help thinking that if he had not died so soon, he might have ended up far less benevolent.

(iii) secundae legiōnis Augustae (line 17). This legion was called 'Augusta'.

(a) In line 3, to which declension does faciēs belong? What is its ablative singular? (It is very rare in the plural).
(b) aliīs (line 4); what is the accusative singular neuter of this word?
(c) In line 6, though cōnātus and agnitus are both past participles, what is the essential difference between them? Explain your answer.
(d) In line 7, what is the relationship between Tiberim and flūmen?
(e) In line 9, we call Vespasiānus Vespasian in English. What was his praenōmen in full?
(f) In lines 11-12, what is the construction of cūrā...trāditā? Translate these words literally.
(g) Mention and translate literally any other example of this construction in the passage.
(h) plūrimās (line 14); of what adjective is plūrimus, -a, -um the superlative?
(i) In line 16, what does cum mean here?
(j) List all the possible meanings of the word cum.

Exercise 10.4

Using the vocabulary given below, translate into Latin:

(i) All the leaders of the brave soldiers have been praised by the new queen.

all = omnis, -e	leader = dux, ducis, c.
brave = fortis, -e	soldier = mīles, mīlitis, c.
I praise = laudō, -āre, -āvī, -ātum	new = novus, -a, -um
queen = rēgīna, -ae, f.	

(ii) The cruel citizens were punishing the sad farmers in the great city.

cruel = crūdēlis, -e	citizen = cīvis, cīvis, c.
I punish = pūniō, -īre, -īvī, -ītum	sad = trīstis, -e
farmer = agricola, -ae, m.	great = magnus, -a, -um
city = urbs, urbis, f.	

Exercise 10.5

Study the following passage (do not write a translation) and answer the questions below in English. Complete sentences are not required.

Vespasian and Titus

1 Vespasiānō prīncipe, <u>amphitheātrum</u> Flāvium,
<u>aedificium</u> ingentissimum, in quō multī hominēs
et multa animālia per multōs annōs crūdēlissimē
necābantur, <u>cōnstrūctum</u> est; huius <u>aedificiī</u>
5 etiam nunc magna pars <u>exstat</u>. Vespasiānus,
decimō <u>prīncipātūs</u> suī annō, ut sē <u>dignum</u>
fuisse <u>prīncipātū</u> ostenderet, stāns mortuus est;
nam prīncipem morī <u>dēbēre</u> dīcēbat stantem. is,
prīmā <u>morbī</u> <u>accessiōne</u>, 'ut putǒ,' dīxit, 'deus
10 <u>fīō</u>.' post Vespasiānum, fīlius eius Titus prīnceps
erat; is Berenīcēn, rēgis Iūdaeae fīliam, maximē
amāverat; quam sēcum Rōmae habitantem
<u>dūcere</u> volēbat; sed eam, patre iubente, <u>invītus</u>
<u>invītam</u>, <u>ut</u> scrīpsit Suētōnius, <u>dīmīsit</u>. quod patre
15 vīvō saepe crūdēlis erat, multī <u>nē</u> prīnceps factus
etiam crūdēlior <u>esset</u> timēbant; sed prīnceps
<u>benevolus</u> erat; ōlim, cum tōtum diem nēminī
bene fēcisset, sē diem illum <u>perdidisse</u> dīxit.
subitō ūnum et quadrāgintā annōs <u>nātus</u>,
20 <u>morbum</u> passus, mortuus est. maximē ā
plūrimīs <u>lūgēbātur</u>.

amphitheātrum, -ī, n. = amphitheatre
aedificium, -iī, n. = building
cōnstruō, -ere, cōnstrūxī,
 cōnstrūctum = I build
exstō, -āre, no perfect or supine =
 I survive
prīncipātus, -ūs, m. = emperorship
dignus, -a, -um (+ abl.) = worthy of
dēbeō, -ēre, dēbuī, dēbitum =
 I must, I have to
morbus, -ī, m. = disease
accessiō, -ōnis, f. = onset
ut (+ indic.) = as
putǒ, -āre, -āvī, -ātum = I think
fīō, fierī, factus sum (irreg.) =
 I become
dūcō, -ere, dūxī, ductum (here) =
 I marry (of a man)
invītus, -a, -um = unwilling
dīmittō, -ere, dīmīsī, dīmissum =
 I send away
nē...esset = see below
benevolus, -a, -um = benevolent
perdō, -ere, perdidī, perditum =
 I lose
nātus, -a, -um + 'x' annōs = 'x' years
 old
morbus, -ī, m. = disease, illness
lūgeō, -ēre, lūxī, lūctum = I mourn

Notes:

(i) The Flavian amphitheatre referred to (line 1) was named the Colosseum in the Middle Ages.

(ii) The 'o' of putŏ (line 9) is regularly short.

(iii) 'deus fīō' (lines 9-10); when a 'good' emperor died, he was officially deified.

(iv) Titus (line 10) was emperor for two years only.

(v) Berenīcēn (line 11); this is the Greek accusative of the Greek name Berenīcē.

(vi) C. Suētōnius Tranquillus (line 14) (c.69-c.140 AD) wrote the lives of Julius Caesar and the emperors up to Domitian.

(vii) timeō nē (+ subj.) (lines 15-16) = 'I fear that...' (lit. 'lest')

(a) In lines 2-4, what used to happen in the Colosseum? Answer in full.
(b) In line 6, did Vespasian, like his three predecessors, rule for only a few months? Answer in full.
(c) In line 8, why did Vespasian die standing on his feet?
(d) stantem (line 8); what is achieved by placing this word at the end of the sentence?
(e) In lines 13-14, what is the effect of Suetonius' words invītus invītam?
(f) In lines 14-15, why did many fear that Titus would be a cruel emperor?
(g) In lines 16-18, were their fears justified? Give a reason for your answer.
(h) In line 19, was Titus' death expected? Which word gives you particular help in answering this question?

Exercise 10.6

Translate the following passage into good English:

Domitian

1　Domitiānus, quī post frātrem prīnceps factus est,
　　quamquam propter vultūs colōrem modestē
　　ērubēscere vidēbātur, rē vērā saevissimus
　　erat; is omnium prīncipum senātuī invīsissimus
5　erat; nam nōn sōlum suspīciōsus erat et
　　improbus, sed etiam rē pūblicā dīligentissimē ab
　　eō administrātā omnēs rēbus praefectī, quī vel
　　iniūstī vel rapācēs erant, pūniēbantur; quōrum
　　multī senātōrēs erant. secundum Suētōnium
10　neque iūstiōrēs umquam neque modestiōrēs
　　erant rēbus praefectī quam eī quōs praefēcit
　　Domitiānus. priōrēs prīncipēs sē ūnā cum senātū
　　rem pūblicam cūrāre dīcēbant; Domitiānus,
　　senātū plānē contemptō, sē sōlum omnēs
15　regere affirmābat et ab omnibus dominus et
　　deus vocārī voluit. ā mīlitibus sōlīs, quod
　　stīpendium eōrum auxit, amātus est.
　　adūlātiōnem contemnēbat, timēbat vēritātem;
　　paene omnibus diffīdēbat, paene omnēs ōderat.

vultus, -ūs, m. = face
color, colōris, m. = colour, complexion
modestus, -a, -um = modest, moderate
ērubēscō, -ere, ērubuī, no supine =
　　I blush
rē vērā = in truth
senātus, -ūs, m. = the Senate
invīsus, -a, -um (here) = hateful
suspīciōsus, -a, -um = suspicious (i.e.
　　of others)
improbus, -a, -um = wicked, cruel
dīligēns, dīligentis = diligent,
　　painstaking
administrō, -āre, -āvī, -ātum =
　　I administer, govern
praeficiō, -ere, praefēcī, praefectum
　　(+ acc. + dat.) = I put in charge of
vel...vel = either...or
iniūstus, -a, -um = unjust
rapāx, rapācis = extortionate
senātōr, senātōris, m. = senator
secundum (+ acc.) = according to
iūstus, -a, -um = just
umquam = ever
prior, priōris = former (goes like
　　melior)
ūnā = together
cūrō, -āre, -āvī, -ātum (here) = I
　　administer
plānē = utterly
contemnō, -ere, contempsī,
　　contemptum = I despise
affirmō, -āre, -āvī, -ātum = I declare
stīpendium, -iī, n. = pay
augeō, -ēre, auxī, auctum = I increase
adūlātiō, adūlātiōnis, f. = flattery
vēritās, vēritātis, f. (here) =
　　truthfulness
diffīdō, -ere (irreg.) (+ dat.) = I distrust
ōdī = I hate (see p.156)

Exercise 10.7

Study the following passage and answer the questions below in good English.
Complete sentences are not required.

Domitian and Nerva

1   Domitiānus saepissimē sōlus esse volēbat;
    muscās captāre solēbat; rogātus ōlim Vibius
    Crispus num comes cum prīncipe in conclāvī
    esset, nē muscam quidem cum eō esse
5   respondit. senātōribus magis magisque
    diffīdēbat; quōrum permultōs impūne occīdit;
    ubi tamen ā famulīs suīs timēbātur, ab eīs
    necātus est: dē hāc rē sīc scrīpsit Iuvenālis:

    sed periit postquam cerdōnibus esse timendus
10 coeperat; hoc nocuit Lamiārum caede madentī.*

    senātōrēs, cum Domitiānus mortuus esset,
    laetissimī, scalīs in Cūriam illātīs, imāginēs eius
    omnēs humī afflīxērunt; et porrō ubīque per
    omnem orbem terrārum memoriam eius dēlēre
15 cōnātī sunt; sed corpus Domitiānī ā nūtrīce
    Phyllide fūnerātum est. post Domitiānum
    prīnceps fuit M. Cocceius Nerva, senex mītis
    et lēnis; is fortiter eōs, quī Domitiānum
    necāverant, ā mīlitibus quī eōs occīdere
20 cōnstituerant dēfendere cōnātus est; sed frūstrā.
    Nerva post sēdecim mēnsēs mortuus est, sed
    ante mortem rem optimam fēcit: M. Ulpium
    Traiānum adoptāvit.

* Juvenal, Satire 4, 153-4

musca, -ae, f. = a fly
captō, -āre, -āvī, -ātum (here) = I catch
soleō, -ēre (irreg.) = I am accustomed
num (+ subj.) (here) = whether
conclāve, conclāvis, n. = a room
nē...quidem = not even
senātor, senātōris, m. = senator
magis = more
diffīdō, -ere (irreg.) (+ dat.) = I distrust
permultī, -ae, -a = very many
impūne = without being punished (adv.)
famulus, -ī, m. = servant
cerdō, cerdōnis, m. = craftsman,
   workman
timendus, -a, -um = frightening,
   dangerous
coepī, coepisse (defective) = I begin
   (see below)
noceō, -ēre, nocuī, nocitum (+ dat.) =
   I harm
caedēs, -is, f. (here) = blood
madeō, -ēre, maduī, no supine (here) =
   I flow
scāla, -ae, f. = ladder
Cūria, -ae, f. = the Senate House
īnferō, īnferre, intulī, illātum = I bring
   into
imāgō, imāginis, f. (here) = statue
humī = to or on the ground
afflīgō, -ere, afflīxī, afflīctum = I cast down
porrō = furthermore
ubīque = everywhere
orbis terrārum = the world (lit. circle of
   lands)
memoria, -ae, f. = memory
nūtrīx, nūtrīcis, f. = nurse
Phyllis, Phyllidis, f. = Phyllis
fūnerō, -āre, -āvī, -ātum (here) =
   I conduct the funeral of
mītis, -e, = mild
lēnis, -e, = lenient
mēnsis, -is, m. = month
adoptō, -āre, -āvī, -ātum = I adopt

Notes:

(i) scrīpsit Iuvenālis (line 8). D. Iūnius Iuvenālis, whom we call Juvenal, is the most famous Roman satirist. His dates are uncertain but were probably c.50-c.127 AD.

(ii) coepī (line 10) is another defective verb, going like ōdī (see page 156).

(iii) The Lamiae (line 10) were a distinguished senatorial family, whose fate mentioned here represents the fate of the Senate under Domitian. The subject of periit (line 9) is meant to be Domitian, who could wallow at will in the blood of the Lamiae (i.e. the Senate), but who came to grief when he became a source of fear to men of a far lower class (cerdōnēs).

(iv) M. Ulpius Traiānus (lines 22-23), whom we call Trajan, was given the name Optimus (= 'the Best') during his principate.

(a) In line 1, what is the dative singular of sōlus?
(b) In lines 4-5, what is the construction of nē muscam quidem...esse respondit?
(c) In line 6, to whom or what does quōrum refer?
(d) In line 7, explain the use of ā and ab here.
(e) In line 16, what is the case and gender of fūnerātum? And with what does it agree?
(f) In line 17, how does senex relate to Nerva?
(g) In line 19, what does ā mean here?
(h) In line 22, give M. in full. (Be careful here!)

Exercise 10.8

Using the vocabulary given below, translate into Latin:

(i) The tired old men have come by difficult journeys into the big town.

tired = fessus, -a, -um	old man = senex, senis, m.
I come = veniō, -īre, vēnī, ventum	difficult = difficilis, -e
journey = iter, itineris, n.	into = in (+ acc.)
big = magnus, -a, -um	town = oppidum, -ī, n.

(ii) The war was savage; the brave citizens were fighting on behalf of the king but they were conquered by the enemy.

war = bellum, -i, n.	was: use sum
savage = saevus, -a, -um	brave = fortis, -e
citizen = cīvis, -is, c.	I fight = pugnō, -āre, -āvī, -ātum
on behalf of = prō (+ abl.)	king = rēx, rēgis, m.
but = sed	I conquer = vincō, -ere, vīcī, victum
enemy = hostes, -ium, c.	

Latin Comedy

I thought it would be a good idea to end with the plot of a Latin Comedy. There are two famous writers of Latin Comedy, Plautus and Terence. Terence is the younger of the two. His Latin name is P. Terentius Āfer. He lived from 195? to 159 BC. He was of Libyan stock and was born in Carthage. He came to Rome as a slave of P. Terentius Lūcānus, a senator, who saw to his education, liberated him and furthered his career. In spite of his foreign birth, Terence wielded the Latin language with incomparable beauty; he was deeply aware of the workings of human nature. His portrayal of old men is a sheer delight, and, in spite of his vivid familiarity with the 'generation gap', we feel pretty sure that their sons will end up not so very different from their fathers. Yet none of Terence's characters is merely a stock character; you only have to put one of his plays on the stage to realise how special every single character is. Here is the story of one of his plays called 'Phormio'. The action takes place in the street in front of Demipho's and Chremes' houses. The Phormio is set in Athens and, like so many Latin Comedies, is based on a Greek original; yet its tone is unmistakably Roman.

Exercise 10.9

Study the following passage (do not write a translation) and answer the questions below in English. Complete sentences are not required.

Phormio: (i)

1   erant ōlim duo frātrēs, Dēmiphō et Chremēs;
     senēs erant; habitābant Athēnīs; domus
     Chremētis <u>iuxtā</u> domum Dēmiphōnis erat.
     <u>initiō</u> <u>fābulae</u> senēs domō aberant; Dēmiphō, ut
5   montēs pecūniae <u>acquīreret</u>, <u>abierat</u>; Chremēs
     uxōrem habuit Nausistratam; ea, mulier
     <u>sevērissima</u>, coniugem in īnsulam Lēmnum, in
     quā <u>praedia</u> habuit, ut ab eīs <u>mercēdem</u> <u>referret</u>,
     mīserat. absentibus senibus, Antiphō, fīlius
10   Dēmiphōnis, pulcherrimam <u>virginem</u> mātrem
     suam mortuam <u>lūgentem</u> forte vīdit, <u>adamāvit</u>,
     <u>dūxit</u>; <u>virgō</u> <u>pauperrima</u> erat, ūnam sōlam
     comitem habuit, <u>nūtrīcem</u> suam, <u>anum</u>. quid
     dīcet Dēmiphō, ubi redībit, dē <u>nūptiīs</u>? quid
15   faciet? id timentēs et Antiphō et Geta, servus,

iuxtā (+ acc.) = next to
initium, -iī, n. = the beginning
fābula, -ae, f. (here) = play
acquīrō, -ere, acquīsīvī, acquīsītum = I acquire
abeō, -īre, -iī, -itum = I go away
sevērus, -a, -um = severe
praedium, -iī, n. (here) = an estate
mercēs, mercēdis, f. (here) = rent
referō, referre, rettulī, relātum (here) = I bring back
virgō, virginis, f. = young woman
lūgeō, -ēre, lūxī, lūctum = I mourn
adamō, -āre, -āvī, -ātum (+ acc.) (here) = I fall in love with
dūcō, -ere, dūxī, ductum (here) = I marry (of a man)
pauperrimus, -a, -um = very poor
nūtrīx, nūtrīcis, f. = nurse
anus, -ūs, f. = old woman
nūptiae, -ārum, f. pl. = marriage

quī, absente patre, <u>monitor</u> erat Antiphōnis, hoc
<u>cōnsilium</u> ā Phormiōne <u>parasītō</u> datum secūtī
erant. dīxerat Phormiō sē amīcum fuisse patris
<u>virginis</u> et Antiphōnem <u>virginī</u> <u>proximum</u> <u>genere</u>
20 esse; <u>secundum</u> <u>lēgem</u> is quī <u>orbae</u> <u>proximus</u>
<u>genere</u> fuit eam <u>dūcere</u> <u>dēbuit</u>; sīc <u>effēcerat</u>
Phormiō ut Antiphō <u>virginem</u> <u>dūcere</u> coāctus
esse <u>vidērētur</u>. intereā Phaedria, Chremētis fīlius,
virginem <u>servam</u> maximē amat; sed dominus
25 <u>virginis</u> Phaedriae dīxit 'nisi crās mihi pecūniam
dabis quam <u>prō</u> eā <u>poscō</u>, mīlitī eam <u>vēndam</u>;
nam ille pecūniam quam poscō dabit. quid
facere potest Phaedria? miserrimus est; ipse
pecūniam nōn habet.

monitor, -ōris (+ gen.) = a person in
  charge
cōnsilium, -iī, n. (here) = advice
parasītus, -ī, m. = parasite
proximus, -a, -um = nearest
genus, generis, n. (here) = birth
secundum (+ acc.) = according to
lēx, lēgis, f. = law
orba, -ae, f. = (female) orphan
dēbeō, -ēre, dēbuī, dēbitum (+ infin.)
  = I have to
efficiō, -ere, effēcī, effectum (+ ut +
  subj.) = I bring it about that
vidērētur: the imperfect subjunctive of
  videor = I appear
serva, -ae, f. = (female) slave
nisi = unless
prō (+ abl.) (here) = in exchange for
poscō, -ere, poposcī, no supine
  (+ acc.) = I ask for
vēndō, -ere, vēndidī, vēnditum = I sell

Antiphō
tē dūcet.

Notes:

(i) Lēmnus, -ī, f. (line 7) = the island in the Aegean sea which we generally know by its Greek name Lemnos.

(ii) Geta (line 15), Phaedria (line 23): Many Roman men had names ending in '-a', which belong to the first declension.

(iii) Monitor (line 16); it was common practice for a senior slave to be responsible for the conduct of his master's son.

(iv) Being a parasite (line 17) was almost a profession in which one constantly increased the number of houses in which one could enjoy a free meal. This could be achieved in many ways, for example, by being useful to the master of the house or by knowing and keeping quiet about some of his less respectable secrets, or simply by being popular with the household.

Answer the following questions:

(a) In lines 4-5, why was Demipho away from home?

(b) In lines 6-9, why did Nausistrata send her husband to Lemnos?

(c) In line 12, what word in this line was most likely to be the cause of Demipho's foreseen disapproval of Antipho's marriage?

(d) In lines 15-16, who was Geta, and why did he regard Demipho's return with apprehension?

(e) proximum genere (line 19); can you think of a really good English translation of these two words?

(f) In lines 18-20, does there seem to be a weak point here in Phormio's plan? Answer in full.

(g) In lines 23-24, what relation was Phaedria to Antipho? There's an easy one at last!

(h) In lines 25-27, how would you describe the master of the girl whom Phaedria loved?

Exercise 10.10

Translate the following passage into good English:

Phormio (ii)

<table>
<tr><td>1</td><td>

ín scaenam currit Geta perterritus; rediit
Dēmiphō. Antiphō fortis esse cōnātur, sed
appropinquante patre fugit. Dēmiphō īrātissimus
est; virginem Antiphōnis cognātam esse negat.

</td><td>

scaena, -ae, f. = stage
virgō, virginis, f. = young woman
cognāta, -ae, f. = (female) relative
exprobrō, -āre, -āvī, -ātum (here) =
  I reproach

</td></tr>
<tr><td>5</td><td>

Getam exprobrat; cum Phormiōne ferōciter
altercātur; tandem trēs amīcōs advocat; rogat
eōs: 'possuntne filiī nūptiae rescindī?' dīcit
Cratīnus posse; Hēgiō negat posse; Critō rem
magnam esse dīcit! Dēmiphō reditum frātris suī

</td><td>

ferōx, -ōcis = fierce
altercor, -ārī, altercātus sum =
  I quarrel
advocō, -āre, -āvī, -ātum = I summon
  for advice
nūptiae, -ārum, f. pl. = marriage

</td></tr>
<tr><td>10</td><td>

Chremētis exspectāre cōnstituit; illīus cōnsilium
sequētur. eōdem diē redit Chremēs ā Lēmnō; is
iamdūdum in Lēmnō secundam uxōrem clam
Nausistratam dūxerat; et ea filiam pepererat;
nēmō Athēnīs praeter Dēmiphōnem hoc sciēbat;

</td><td>

rescindō, -ere, rescidī, rescissum
  (here) = I annul
reditus, -ūs, m. = return
cōnsilium, -iī, n. = advice
iamdūdum = long before
clam (+ acc.) = without the knowledge
  of

</td></tr>
<tr><td>15</td><td>

et, nē quis alius scīret, senēs Antiphōnem filiam
Chremētis dūcere iam diū voluerant; sed nunc
Antiphō aliam uxōrem dūxit.

</td><td>

dūcō, -ere, dūxī, ductum (here) =
  I marry (of a man)
pariō, -ere, peperī, partum (+ acc.) =
  I give birth to
Athēnae, -ārum, f. pl. = Athens

</td></tr>
<tr><td></td><td>

Geta nunc senibus dīxit sē Phormiōnī persuāsisse
ut, datā pecūniā, virginem ipse dūceret;

</td><td>

praeter (+ acc.) (here) = except
sciō, scīre, scīvī, scītum = I know

</td></tr>
<tr><td>20</td><td>

Dēmiphō, cum Getā, ad Phormiōnem, ut eī
pecūniam daret, abiit. manet sōlus in scaenā
Chremēs. domō Dēmiphōnis ēgreditur anus,
flēns; dē nūptiīs loquitur dominae suae virginis et
Antiphōnis; patrem iuvenis īrātissimum esse dīcit;

</td><td>

ne quis = lest anyone
abeo, -īre, -iī, -itum = I go away
anus, -ūs, f. = old woman
fleō, -ēre, -ēvī, -ētum = I weep
attonitus, -a, -um = astonished
agnōscō, -ere, agnōvī, agnitum =
  I recognise

</td></tr>
<tr><td>25</td><td>

nōn videt Chremētem, sed ille attonitus eam
agnōscit. Sōphrona est, filiae eius nūtrīx; sed quid
illa Dēmiphōnis domī faciēbat? allocūtus eam,
filiam suam cum mātre et Sōphronā Athēnās
vēnisse cognōvit. dīxit anus sē cum virgine et

</td><td>

nūtrīx, nūtrīcis, f. = nurse
alloquor, -ī, allocūtus sum (+ acc.) =
  I address, speak to
cognōscō, -ere, cognōvī, cognitum =
  I find out

</td></tr>
<tr><td>30</td><td>

mātre Chremētem, quod diū ā Lēmnō āfuisset,
petīvisse; virginem, mātre mortuā, Antiphōnī, quī
eam adamāvisset, nūpsisse.

</td><td>

adamō, -āre, -āvī, -ātum (+ acc.) (here)
  = I fall in love with
nūbō, -ere, nūpsī, nūptum (+ dat). =
  I marry (of a woman)

</td></tr>
</table>

Exercise 10.11

Study the following passage and answer the questions below in English. Complete sentences are not required.

Phormio (iii)

1   dē morte uxōris nihil dīxit Chremēs <u>nisi</u> 'male factum'; dē <u>nūptiīs</u> fīliae et Antiphōnis laetissimus erat; cum Sōphronā, ut omnia <u>cognōsceret</u>, exiit; in <u>scaenam</u> veniunt Dēmiphō et Nausistrata, uxor

5   Chremētis; dum <u>colloquuntur, inruit</u> Chremēs, <u>adhūc</u> laetissimus; uxōrem suam nōn videt; ubi <u>argentum</u> Phormiōnī datum esse <u>cognōscit</u>, hoc eī nōn <u>placet. tantum nōn</u> rem omnem Dēmiphōnī nārrat, sed, uxōre subitō vīsā, nōn

10   potest; Dēmiphō eī <u>interrogātiōnēs ingerere</u> nōn <u>cessat; abit</u> tandem Nausistrata; rem omnem Dēmiphonī nārrat Chremēs; <u>abeunt</u> frātrēs; init Antiphō, quem sequitur Phormiō; <u>argentō</u>, quod dedit Dēmiphō Phormiōnī, <u>virgō,</u> quam amat

15   Phaedria, ā dominō suō <u>ēmpta</u>, Phaedriae data est; init Geta laetissimus; senēs <u>inaudīvit</u> dē fīliā Chremētis loquentēs. Antiphō <u>fortūnātissimus</u> est; uxōrem suam <u>retinēre</u> potest; omnia bene <u>ēvēnērunt</u>; sed senēs <u>argentum</u> quod Phormiōnī,

20   ut uxōrem Antiphōnis dūceret, dedērunt, <u>recipere</u> volunt; id tamen <u>nōn iam</u> habet Phormiō; senēs <u>inrīdet</u>; illī <u>iūs</u> eī <u>minantur</u>; <u>tantum nōn</u> pugnant; sed Phormiō vōce magnā Nausistratam vocat et senēs, quamquam eum <u>comprimere</u> cōnantur,

25   nōn possunt; dīcit Nausistratae Phormiō Chremētem secundam uxōrem habuisse; <u>saevit</u>

nisi (here) = except
nūptiae, -ārum, f. pl. = marriage
cognōscō, -ere, cognōvī, cognitum (+ acc.) = I find out about, learn
scaena, -ae, f. = stage
colloquor, -ī, collocūtus sum = I talk (together with someone)
inruō, -ere, inruī, no supine = I rush in
adhūc = still
argentum, -ī, n. = silver, hence money
placeō, -ēre, -uī, -itum (+ dat.) = I please
tantum nōn = almost, nearly
interrogātiō, interrogātiōnis, f. = a question
ingerō, -ere, ingessī, ingestum (+ acc. and dat.) = I heap up
cessō, -āre, -āvī, -ātum = I stop (intrans.)
abeō, -īre, -iī, -itum = I go away
virgō, virginis, f. = young woman
emō, -ere, ēmī, ēmptum = I buy
inaudiō, -īre, -īvī, -ītum = I hear (especially a secret)
fortūnātus, -a, -um = blessed
retineō, -ēre, retinuī, retentum (here) = I keep
ēveniō, -īre, ēvēnī, ēventum = turn out (of things, events; *not* of people)
recipiō, recipere, recēpī, receptum = I take back, get back
nōn iam = no longer
inrīdeō, -ēre, īnrīsī, īnrīsum = I mock, I make fun of
iūs, iūris, n. = the law
minor, -ārī, -ātus sum = I threaten (see below)
comprimō, -ere, compressī, compressum (here) = I restrain
saeviō, -īre, saeviī, saevītum = I rage

Nausistrata; dīcit Chremēs 'nullus sum'; filiī suī iūdiciō trāditus est. Phormiōnem ad cēnam vocat Nausistrata; intrō eunt omnēs. fīnīta est fābula.

30 hīs verbīs cantor spectātōrēs alloquitur: 'vōs valēte et plaudite.'

nūllus, -a, -um (goes like ūnus) = no (adj.) (see below)
iūdicium, -iī, n. = judgment
cēna, -ae, f. = dinner
intrō (here) = indoors (adverb)
finiō, -īre, -īvī, -ītum = I end (trans.)
fābula, -ae, f. (here) = play
cantor, -ōris, m. = singer (see below)
spectātor, -ōris, m. = spectator (see below)
alloquor, -ī, allocūtus sum (+ acc.) = I address, I speak to
valeō, -ēre, valuī, valitum = I am in good health, I am well (see below)
plaudō, -ere, plausī, plausum = I applaud

Notes:

(i)   male factum (lines 1-2) literally means 'done badly'; it is an expression of regret.

(ii)   minor (line 22) = 'I threaten' (+ acc. and dat.). I hope you find the following helpful:

In English: 'threatens me with death'.
In Latin: 'threatens death to me'.

(iii)   nūllus (line 27) = no (body): nūllus sum = 'I am nobody', i.e. 'I am done for'.

(iv)   cantor (line 30) (lit.) = 'singer'; (here) it is an actor representing the cast.

(v)   spectātōrēs (line 30); we would say 'audience'.

(vi)   valē (sing.) and valēte (pl.) (line 31) = 'be well', i.e. 'farewell'.

(vii)   plaudite (line 31); the audience are asked to applaud.

During most of the play, the two old men have been straining every nerve to undo that which we at first suspect, and finally know, to be the very thing they want. Such is life!

Answer the following questions:

(a)   fīliae (line 2); what is the dative plural of this word?
(b)   In line 3, explain the tense and mood of cognōsceret.
(c)   In lines 4-5, what is the construction of uxōre...vīsā? Translate these words first literally, and then into better English.
(d)   In lines 15-16, if, instead of 'she has been given', we had wanted to say 'she was being given', to what would we have had to change data est?
(e)   In line 17, what is the case of loquentēs? With what does it agree? Translate it.

(f) volunt (line 21); turn this word into the imperfect subjunctive.
(g) Chremētem...habuisse (line 26); what is the construction here? Translate these words.
(h) eunt (line 29); give the principal parts and meaning of this verb.

Exercise 10.12.

Using the vocabulary given below translate into Latin:

(i) The cruel soldiers were overcome by the brave citizens.

cruel = crūdēlis, -e   soldier = mīles, mīlitis, c.
I overcome = superō, -āre, -āvī, -ātum   brave = fortis, -e
citizen = cīvis, cīvis, c.

(ii) The famous son of the noble leader will lead the little sister of the proud brothers into the city.

famous = clārus, -a, -um   son = fīlius, -iī, m.
noble = nōbilis, -e   leader = dux, ducis, c.
I lead = dūcō, -ere, dūxī, ductum   little = parvus, -a, -um
sister = soror, -ōris, f.   proud = superbus, -a, -um
brother = frāter, frātris, m.   into = in (+ acc.)
city = urbs, urbis, f.

Crossword 2

1	2	3	4		5	6	7	8	9		10
11				■	12					■	
13		■	14	15			■	16		17	
18		19				■	20	■	21		
22			■		23		24				
	■		25		■		26				
■	27	■		■	28	29					■
30		31		32			■		■		■
33				■		34		■			35
36						■		■	37	38	
39			■		■	40		41			
42			43	■	44				■	45	
	■	46		47			■	48	49		
50											

Across

1. Which things having been done (6, 6)
11. Whence? (4)
12. He got the Golden Fleece (5)
13. Give! (in reverse) (2)
14. Now (4)
16. Two thirds of eternity (4)
18. To shave (trans.) (6)
21. Attached to pronouns = self (3)
22. Having used (masc. pl.) (3)
23. Out of the midst (but not quite) (2, 4)
25. In compounds = back (2)
26. Three times, 999 (3, 2)
28. Who would trust a law-suit in reverse? (7)
30. Raise your eyes! (7)
33. I'm eating you (3, 2)
34. A duck bereft of consonants (2)
36. It sits on a royal head (6)
37. She swims (3)
39. Turn around and nearly take off everything! (3)
40. She has just emerged from the sea (6)
42. A good old emperor doesn't quite make it (4)
44. Unless, except (4)
45. Four (2)
46. (Backwards) swim! O virtuous (boy) (3, 2)
48. By which of two? (4)
50. You're getting near (12)

Down

1.	Of which (women) (6)
2.	You see these when you are sailing (5)
3.	It (2)
4.	I'm sure this is how you always behave (4)
5.	Without (5)
6.	Do! This lengthens its vowel when followed by 11 across, in an appeal to an eloquent man (3)
7.	This coin is worth very little (2)
8.	A grindstone (3)
9.	They will tremble (backwards) (7)
10.	God rested on this special day (7)
15.	O teddy! (4)
17.	They should cure you (6)
19.	(Ye) gods (2)
20.	I survive (4)
24.	Behold an army in line of battle: but it's facing the wrong way! (5)
25.	After he was absolutely seized (5)
27.	The departure from Egypt (backwards) (6)
28.	99 (2)
29.	Asking a question? (2)
30.	She follows the first (7)
31.	Backwards through the masters (4, 3)
32.	Going (4)
34.	And here's the duck in all her glory! (4)
35.	Can you count your Great-great-great-grandfathers? (6)
37.	Not out, backwards! (2)
38.	A rainless land is this (backwards) (5)
40.	Four sevenths of a famous little mouse (4)
41.	What's going backwards? (4)
43.	He is a real man! (3)
44.	God of woods and shepherds (backwards) (3)
47.	A great work (abbr.) upside down (2)
49.	In order that (in reverse) (2)

The following words should be useful:

Army in line of battle = aciēs, -ēī, f.
Back (in compounds) = re- (e.g. redūcō = I lead back)
Bear = ursus, -ī, m.
Coin of low value = as, assis, m.
Crown = corōna, -ae, f.
Doctor = medicus, -ī, m.
Drenched = madidus, -a, -um; ūdus, -a, -um
Dry = siccus, -a, -um; āridus, -a, -um
Duck = anas, anatis, f.
Eloquent = fācundus, -a, -um; disertus, -a, -um
God of woods and shepherds = Pān
Great-great-great-grandfather = atavus, -ī, m.
Grindstone = cōs, cōtis, f.
Lawsuit = āctiō, -ōnis, f.
Look up, I = suspiciō, -ere, suspexī, suspectum

Master = erus, -ī, m.
Seize = rapiō, -ere, rapuī, raptum
Self (added to pronouns) = -met (e.g. egomet = I myself)
Shave (trans.) = rādō, -ere, rāsī, rāsum
Stand out, survive, I = exstō (and extō)
Swim, I = natō, -āre, -āvī, -ātum; nō, nāre, nāvī, nātum
Three times = ter
Tremble, I = tremō, -ere, tremuī
Unless, except = nisi
Use, I = ūtor, ūtī, ūsus sum (+ abl.)
Virtuous = bonus, -a, -um; pius, -a, -um
Whence? = unde?
Which of two? = uter, utra, utrum? (goes like ūnus)

So there we are; that's it. It really is goodbye this time. It's sad. However, I only hope that you have enjoyed wading through this lengthy work as much as I have enjoyed writing it.

Valē, et plaude!

Proper nouns and adjectives

The following occur in the passages:

Achillēs, Achillis, m. = Achilles (a Greek hero)

Acrisius, -iī, m. = Acrisius (father of Danae)

Aeētēs, -ae, m. = Aeetes (King of Colchis, father of Medea)

Aēnēās, -ae, m. (acc. Aeneān) = Aeneas (a Trojan prince who escaped from Troy to build a new Troy in Italy)

Aeolus, -ī, m. = Aeolus (god of the winds)

Aesōn, Aesonis, m. = Aeson (father of Jason)

Agamemnōn, -onis, m. = Agamemnon (chief king of the Greeks)

Agrippīna, -ae, f. = Agrippina (wife of the Emperor Claudius, mother of Nero)

Aiāx, -ācis, m. = Ajax (a Greek hero)

Andromeda, -ae, f. = Andromeda (a princess who was rescued by Perseus)

Apollō, Apollinis, m. = Apollo (god of light, prophecy, poetry and much else)

Argō, Argūs, f. = *Argo* (the ship built by Argus for Jason)

Argolis, Argolidis, f. = the Argolid (a region in the N.E. of the Peloponnese)

Argonautae, -ārum, m. pl. = the Argonauts (the crew of the *Argo*)

Ascanius, -iī, m. = Ascanius (son of Aeneas)

Athēnae, -ārum, f. pl. = Athens

Augustus, -ī, m. = Augustus (the first Roman Emperor)

Baucis, -idis, f. = Baucis (wife of Philemon)

Britannicus, -ī, m. = Britannicus (son of Claudius)

Caesar, Caesaris, m. (C. Iūlius Caesar) = Caesar (the most famous of Roman statesmen)

Calchās, -antis, m. = Calchas (prophet of the Greek army at Troy)

Caligula, -ae, m. = Caligula (a Roman Emperor)

Carthāgō, Carthāginis, f. = Carthage (a great city in north Africa)

Catŏ, -ōnis, m. = Cato (a famous Roman statesman)

Claudius, -iī, m. = Claudius (a Roman Emperor)

Colchis, -idis, f. = Colchis (a region east of the Black Sea)

Danaē, -ēs, f. (acc. Danaēn) = Danae (mother of Perseus)

Dīdō, Dīdūs (or Dīdōnis), f. = Dido (Queen of Carthage who loved Aeneas)

Domitiānus, -ī, m. = Domitian (a Roman Emperor)

Etruscus, -a, -um = Etruscan (of Etruria, a country in central Italy)

Eurīpidēs, -is, m. = Euripides (the youngest of the three great Athenian tragedians)

Flāvius, -a, -um = Flavian (of the Flavian family)

Galba, -ae, m. = Galba (a Roman Emperor)

Gorgō, Gorgonis, f. = the Gorgon (one of three terrible sisters; see Medūsa)

Graeae, -ārum, f. pl. = the Graeae (sisters of the Gorgons, grey-haired from birth)

Hector, -oris, m. = Hector (Priam's eldest son, leader of the Trojans)

Herculēs, -is, m. = Hercules (greatest of the Greek heroes)

Homērus, -ī, m. = Homer (author of the epic poems *The Iliad* and *The Odyssey*)

Iāsōn, -onis, m. = Jason (leader of the Argonauts)

Īlias, Īliadis, f. = the *Iliad* (the great epic poem by Homer)

Iōlcus, -ī, m. = Iolcus (a town in Thessaly)

Ītalia, -ae, f. = Italy

Iūdaeī, -ōrum, m. pl. = the Jewish people

Iūnō, -ōnis, f. = Juno (wife of Jupiter)

Iuppiter, Iovis, m. = Jupiter (king of the gods)

Iuvenālis, -is, m. (D. Iūnius Iuvenālis) = Juvenal (the most famous Roman satirist)

Lamiae, -ārum, m. pl. = a distinguished senatorial family

Lāvīnium, -iī, n. = Lavinium (a city in Italy founded by Aeneas)

Līvius, -iī, m. (T. Līvius) = Livy (the great Roman historian)

Mārs, Mārtis, m. = Mars (the god of war)

Mārtiālis, -is, m. (M. Valerius Mārtiālis) = Martial (author of fourteen books of epigrams)

Mēdēa, -ae, f. = Medea (who loved Jason)

Medūsa, -ae, f. = Medusa (the most terrible of the three Gorgons)

Mercurius, -iī, m. = Mercury (a god, the messenger of the gods)

Minerva, -ae, f. = Minerva (goddess of wisdom, the arts, the sciences and much else)

Neptūnus, -ī, m. = Neptune (the god of the sea)

Nerō, -ōnis, m. = Nero (a Roman Emperor)

Nerva, -ae, m. = Nerva (a Roman Emperor)

Nymphae Stygiae, -ārum, f. pl. = Nymphs of the River Styx, one of the rivers of the Underworld

Octāviānus, -ī, m. = Octavian (later the Emperor Augustus)

Odyssēa, -ae, f. = the *Odyssey* (the great epic poem by Homer)

Othō, -ōnis, m. = Otho (a Roman Emperor)

Patroclus, -ī, m. = Patroclus (friend of Achilles, killed by Hector at Troy)

Peliās, -ae, m. = Pelias (King of Iolcos, uncle of Jason)

Perseus, -eī, m. (acc. Persea) = Perseus (a Greek hero, slayer of the Gorgon Medusa)

Philēmōn, -onis, m. = Philemon (husband of Baucis)

Phyllis, Phyllidis, f. = Phyllis (nurse of Domitian)

Phrygia, -ae, f. = Phrygia (a country in Asia Minor)

Polydectēs, -ae, m. = Polydectes (King of Seriphus)

Priamus, -ī, m. = Priam (King of Troy)

Remus, -ī, m. = Remus (co-founder of Rome, brother of Romulus)

Rōma, -ae, f. = Rome

Rōmulus, -ī, m. = Romulus (co-founder of Rome, brother of Remus)

Seneca, -ae, m. (L. Annaeus Seneca) = Seneca (one of the most famous Roman authors)

Serīphus, -ī, f. = Seriphus (a small island in the Aegean sea)

Sinōn, Sinōnis, m. = Sinon (a Greek soldier at Troy)

Suētōnius, -iī, m. (C. Suētōnius Tranquillus) = Suetonius (biographer of the first twelve Caesars)

Tacitus, -ī, m. (Cornēlius Tacitus) = Tacitus (a great Roman historian)

Terentius, -iī, m. (P. Terentius Āfer) = Terence (a writer of Latin comedies)

Thessalia, -ae, f. = Thessaly (a large district in the north of Greece)

Thetis, -idis, f. (acc. Thetin) = Thetis (a sea goddess, the mother of Achilles)

Tiberis, -is, m. (acc. Tiberim, abl. Tiberī) = the river Tiber

Tiberius , -iī, m. = Tiberius (a Roman Emperor)

Titus, -ī, m. = Titus (a Roman Emperor)

Traiānus, -ī, m. = Trajan (a Roman Emperor, nicknamed Optimus: 'the Best')

Troia, -ae, f. = Troy

Troiānus, -a, -um = Trojan

Ulixēs, -is, m. = Ulysses (the Latin name for Odysseus, hero of the *Odyssey*)

Venus, Veneris, f. = Venus (the goddess of love)

Vergilius, -iī, m. (P. Vergilius Marō) = Virgil (the most famous of the Roman poets, author of the *Aeneid*)

Vespasiānus, -ī, m. = Vespasian (a Roman Emperor)

Vitellius, -iī, m. = Vitellius (a Roman Emperor)

Volcānus, -ī, m. = Vulcan (the god of fire, son of Jupiter and Juno)

Vocabulary: Latin-English

ā, ab (+ abl.) = by, from

absum, abesse, āfuī (goes like sum) = I am absent

accipiō, -ere, accēpī, acceptum = I receive

ad (+ acc.) = to, towards

adeō, -īre, adiī, aditum = I approach (lit. I go to) (goes like eō)

adsum, adesse, adfuī (goes like sum) = I am present

adveniō, -īre, advēnī, adventum = I arrive

aedificō, -āre, -āvī, -ātum = I build

ager, agrī, m. = field

agricola, -ae, m. = farmer

alius, alia, aliud = other

altus, -a, -um = deep, high

ambulō, -āre, -āvī, -ātum = I walk

amīcus, -ī, m. = friend

amō, amāre, amāvī, amātum = I love, like

ancilla, -ae, f. = maid-servant

animal, animālis, n. = animal

annus, -ī, m. = year

ante (+ acc.) = before (preposition)

anteā = beforehand (adverb)

antequam = before (conjunction)

appropinquō, -āre, -āvī, -ātum (+ dat. or ad + acc.) = I approach

aqua, -ae, f. = water

arma, -ōrum, n. pl. = weapons

audāx, audācis = bold

audiō, -īre, -īvī, -ītum = I hear, listen (to)

aurum, -ī, n. = gold

aut = or

autem = however, moreover (not written 1st word in clause or sentence)

auxilium, -iī, n. = help

bellum, -ī, n. = war

bene = well

bibō, -ere, bibī = I drink

bonus, -a, -um = good

caelum, -ī, n. = sky

cantō, -āre, -āvī, -ātum = I sing

capiō, -ere, cēpī, captum = I take, capture

cārus, -a, -um = dear

celer, celeris, celere = swift, quick

celeriter = quickly

centum = a hundred

cēterī, -ae, -a = other, remaining, the rest (of)

cibus, -ī, m. = food

circum (+ acc.) = around

cīvis, cīvis, c. = citizen

clāmō, -āre, -āvī, -ātum = I shout

clāmor, -ōris, m. = shout

clārus, -a, -um = famous, clear, bright

cōgō, -ere, coēgī, coāctum = I force

colligō, -ere, collēgī, collēctum = I collect

comes, comitis, c. = companion

coniūnx, coniugis, c. = husband/wife

cōnor, -ārī, -ātus sum = I try

cōnspiciō, -ere, cōnspexī, cōnspectum = I catch sight of

cōnstituō, -ere, cōnstituī, cōnstitūtum = I decide

cōnsūmō, -ere, cōnsūmpsī, cōnsūmptum = I eat, consume

contendō, -ere, contendī, contentum = I hurry, march

contrā (+ acc.) = against

conveniō, -īre, convēnī, conventum = I meet

cōpiae, -ārum, f. pl. = forces

corpus, -oris, n. = body

crās = tomorrow

crēdō, -ere, crēdidī, crēditum (+ dat.) = I believe

crūdēlis, -e = cruel

cum (+ abl.) = with, together with

cum (conjunction): + imp. subj. = while, since, although; + plup. subj. = when, after

cupiō, -ere, -īvī, -ītum = I want, wish, desire

cūr? = why?

currō, -ere, cucurrī, cursum = I run

custōdiō, -īre, -īvī, -ītum = I guard

custōs, custōdis, c. = guard

dē (+ abl.) = down from, concerning

dea, -ae, f. = goddess (dat. and abl. pl. = deābus)

decem = ten

decimus = tenth

dēfendō, -ere, dēfendī, dēfēnsum = I defend

deinde = then, next

dēleō, dēlēre, dēlēvī, dēlētum = I destroy

deus, deī, m. (irreg.) = god

dīcō, dīcere, dīxī, dictum = I say

diēs, -ēī, m. = day. (A special or appointed day is usually feminine.)

difficilis, -e = difficult

discēdō, -ere, discessī, discessum = I depart

diū (adverb) = for a long time

dō, dăre, dedī, dătum = I give

dominus, -ī, m. = master, lord

domus, -ūs, f. (irreg.) = house, home

dōnum, -ī, n. = gift

dormiō, -īre, -īvī, -ītum = I sleep

dūcō, -ere, dūxī, ductum = I lead

dum = while

duo, duae, duo = two

duodecim = twelve

duodēvīgintī = eighteen

dux, ducis, c. = leader

ē (+ abl.) (not before vowel or h) = out of

effugiō, -ere, effūgī = I escape

ego = I
ēgredior, ēgredī, ēgressus sum = I go out
eō, īre, iī (or īvī), itum (irreg.) = I go
equus, equī, m. = horse
errō, -āre, -āvī, -ātum = I wander
et = and
et...et = both...and
etiam = even, also
ex (+ abl.) = out of
exeō, exīre, exiī, exitum (goes like eō) = I go out
exercitus, -ūs, m. = army
exspectō, -āre, -āvī, -ātum = I wait for, expect
facilis, -e = easy
faciō, -ere, fēcī, factum = I do, make
fēlīx, fēlīcis = fortunate, lucky, happy
fēmina, -ae, f. = woman
ferō, ferre, tulī, lātum (irreg.) = I carry, bear, bring
fessus, -a, -um = tired
festīnō, -āre, -āvī, -ātum = I hurry
fidēs, -eī, f. = trust, faith, promise
fīlia, -ae, f. = daughter (dat. and abl. pl.: fīliābus)
fīlius, fīliī (voc. fīlī), m. = son
flūmen, flūminis, n. = river
forte = by chance
fortis, -e = brave, strong
fortiter = bravely
frāter, frātris, m. = brother
frūstrā = in vain
fugiō, -ere, fūgī, fugitum = I flee (from)
gēns, gentis, f. = race, family, clan, nation
gerō, -ere, gessī, gestum = I wage (a war), wear; sē
    gerere = to behave
gladius, gladiī, m. = sword
gradus, -ūs, m. = a step
Graecus, -a, -um = Greek
habeō, -ēre, -uī, -itum = I have
habitō, -āre, -āvī, -ātum (+ acc. or in + abl.) = I live,
    inhabit
hasta, -ae, f. = spear
herī = yesterday
hīc = here
hic, haec, hoc = this; he, she, it
hodiē = today
homō, hominis, c. = person, man
hōra, -ae, f. = hour
hortor, -ārī, -ātus sum = I encourage, urge
hostis, hostis, c. = enemy (usually used in plural)
iaciō, -ere, iēcī, iactum = I throw
iam = now, already
ibi = there
īdem, eadem, idem = the same
igitur = therefore (not generally written 1st word in
    clause or sentence)
ille, illa, illud = that; he, she, it
imperō, -āre, -āvī, -ātum (+ dat.) = I order, command
in (+ abl.) = in, on
in (+ acc.) = into, on to

incola, -ae, c. = inhabitant
ineō, inīre, iniī, initum (goes like eō) = I go into
ingēns, ingentis = huge
ingredior, ingredī, ingressus sum = I enter
īnsula, -ae, f. = island
inter (+ acc.) = between, among
intereā = meanwhile
interficiō, -ere, interfēcī, interfectum = I kill
intrō, -āre, -āvī, -ātum = I enter
inveniō, -īre, invēnī, inventum = I find, discover
ipse, ipsa, ipsum = self
īra, -ae, f. = anger
īrātus, -a, -um = angry
is, ea, id = that; he, she, it
itaque = therefore
iter, itineris, n. = journey
iterum = again
iubeō, -ēre, iussī, iussum = I order
iuvenis, iuvenis, c. = young person (generally, m. =
    young man)
iuvō, iuvāre, iūvī, iūtum = I help
labor, -ōris, m. = work, labour
labōrō, -āre, -āvī, -ātum = I work
laetus, -a, -um = happy
laudō, -āre, -āvī, -ātum = I praise
legō, -ere, lēgī, lēctum = I read, choose
lentē = slowly
liber, librī, m. = book
līberō, -āre, -āvī, -ātum = I free
locus, -ī, m. = place
longus, -a, -um = long
loquor, loquī, locūtus sum = I speak
lūdō, -ere, lūsī, lūsum = I play
lūx, lūcis, f. = light
magister, magistrī, m. = master, schoolmaster
magnopere = greatly
magnus, -a, -um = big, great
malus, -a, -um = bad
maneō, -ēre, mānsī, mānsum = I remain, stay
manus, -ūs, f. = hand
mare, maris, n. = sea
māter, mātris, f. = mother
medius, -a, -um = middle
melior, melius = better
meus, -a, -um (voc. masc. sing.: mī) = my
mīles, mīlitis, c. = soldier
mīlle = a thousand
miser, -era, -erum = wretched, unhappy
mittō, -ere, mīsī, missum = I send
moneō, -ēre, -uī, -itum = I warn, advise
mōns, montis, m. = mountain
mora, -ae, f. = delay
morior, morī, mortuus sum = I die
mors, mortis, f. = death
mortuus, -a, -um = dead
moveō, -ēre, mōvī, mōtum = I move (trans.)
mox = soon

mulier, mulieris, f. = woman
multus, -a, -um = much; pl. = many
mūrus, -ī, m. = wall
nam = for
nārrō, -āre, -āvī, -ātum = I tell
nauta, -ae, m. = sailor
nāvigō, -āre, -āvī, -ātum = I sail
nāvis, nāvis, f. (abl. sing.: nāvī or nāve) = ship
nē (+ subj.) = in order not to, not to, lest
-ne?: introduces a question
nec, neque = nor, neither, and…not
necō, necāre, necāvī, necātum = I kill
nēmō (irreg.), c. = no one
nihil = nothing
nōbilis, -e = noble
nōlī / nōlīte (+ infin.) = do not…!
nōlō, nōlle, nōluī (irreg.) = I do not want, wish; nōluī
    often = I refused
nōmen, nōminis, n. = name
nōn = not
nōnāgintā = ninety
nōnne?: introduces a question (expecting the answer
    'yes')
nōnus, -a, -um = ninth
nōs = we
noster, nostra, nostrum = our
nōtus, -a, -um = well-known
novem = nine
novus, -a, -um = new
nox, noctis, f. = night
num?: introduces a question (expecting the answer 'no')
numquam = never
nunc = now
nūntiō, -āre, -āvī, -ātum = I announce, report
nūntius, nūntiī, m. = messenger, message
occīdō, -ere, occīdī, occīsum = I kill
occupō, -āre, -āvī, -ātum = I seize, occupy
octāvus -a, -um = eighth
octō = eight
octōgintā = eighty
ōlim = once upon a time
omnis, -e = every, all
oppidum, -ī, n. = town
oppugnō, -āre, -āvī, -ātum = I attack (a place)
optimus, -a, -um = best
opus, operis, n. = work, task
ostendō, -ere, ostendī, ostentum / ostēnsum = I show
paene = almost
parēns, parentis, c. = parent
parō, -āre, -āvī, -ātum = I prepare
pars, partis, f. = part
parvus, -a, -um = small, little
pater, patris, m. = father
patior, patī, passus sum = I suffer, allow
patria, -ae, f. = country, fatherland
paucī, -ae, -a = few, a few
pecūnia, -ae, f. = money

peior, peius = worse
pellō, -ere, pepulī, pulsum = I drive
per (+ acc.) = through, along
pereō, -īre, periī, peritum (goes like eō) = I die
perīculum, -ī, n. = danger
persuādeō, -ēre, persuāsī, persuāsum (+ dat.) = I
    persuade
perterritus, -a, -um = terrified
pessimus, -a, -um = worst
petō, -ere, petīvī, petītum = I seek
plūrimus, -a, -um = most, very many
plūs, plūris, n. = more
plūrēs, plūrium (adj.) = more
poēta, -ae, m. = poet
pōnō, -ere, posuī, positum = I place
portō, -āre, -āvī, -ātum = I carry
portus, -ūs, m. = harbour
possum, posse, potuī (irreg.) = I am able, can
post (+ acc.) = after (preposition)
posteā = afterwards (adverb)
postquam = after (conjunction)
praemium, -iī, n. = reward
prīmus, -a, -um = first
prīnceps, prīncipis, m. = chief, prince, emperor
prō (+ abl.) = on behalf of, in place of, in front of,
    instead of
proelium, -iī, n. = battle
proficīscor, proficīscī, profectus sum = I set out (on a
    journey)
prōgredior, prōgredī, prōgressus sum = I advance
prope (+ acc.) = near
propter (+ acc.) = on account of
puella, -ae, f. = girl
puer, puerī, m. = boy
pugnō, -āre, -āvī, -ātum = I fight
pulcher, pulchra, pulchrum = beautiful
pūniō, -īre, -īvī, -ītum = I punish
quadrāgintā = forty
quam = than
quam celerrimē = as quickly as possible
quamquam = although, though
quārtus, -a, -um = fourth
quattuor = four
quattuordecim = fourteen
-que = and
quī, quae, quod = who, which
quid? = what?
quīndecim = fifteen
quīnquāgintā = fifty
quīnque = five
quīntus, -a, -um = fifth
quis? = who?
quod = because
quoque = also (comes after the word it is emphasising)
redeō, redīre, rediī, reditum (goes like eō) = I go back,
    return
redūcō, -ere, redūxī, reductum = I lead back

rēgīna, -ae, f. = queen

regō, -ere, rēxī, rēctum = I rule

relinquō, -ere, relīquī, relictum = I leave (trans.)

rēs, reī, f. = thing, matter, affair

    rēs pūblica, reī pūblicae, f. = the state, republic

respondeō, -ēre, respondī, respōnsum = I reply, answer

rēx, rēgis, m. = king

rīdeō, -ēre, rīsī, rīsum = I laugh, smile

rogō, -āre, -āvī, -ātum = I ask

Rōmānus, -a, -um = Roman

ruō, ruere, ruī, rutum = I rush, collapse

sacer, sacra, sacrum = sacred

saepe = often

saevus, -a, -um = savage

sagitta, -ae, f. = arrow

salūtō, -āre, -āvī, -ātum = I greet

sapiēns, sapientis = wise

scrībō, -ere, scrīpsī, scrīptum = I write

scūtum, -ī, n. = shield

sē = himself, herself, itself, themselves (reflexive pronoun)

secundus, -a, -um = second

sed = but

sēdecim = sixteen

semper = always

senex, senis, m. = old man

septem = seven

septendecim = seventeen

septimus, -a, -um = seventh

septuāgintā = seventy

sequor, sequī, secūtus sum = I follow

servō, -āre, -āvī, -ātum = I save

servus, -ī, m. = slave

sex = six

sexāgintā = sixty

sextus, -a, -um = sixth

sīc = thus

sine (+ abl.) = without

socius, -iī, m. = ally

sōlus, -a, -um (goes like ūnus) = alone

somnus, -ī, m. sleep

soror, -ōris, f. = sister

spectō, -āre, -āvī, -ātum = I watch

spēs, speī, f. = hope

statim = immediately

stō, stāre, stetī, stătum = I stand

sub (+ abl.) = under

subitō = suddenly

sum, esse, fuī (irreg.) = I am

super (+ acc.) = over

superbus, -a, -um = proud

superō, -āre, -āvī, -ātum = I overcome

suus, sua, suum = his (own), her (own), its (own) or their (own)

tamen = however (not generally written first word in clause or sentence)

tandem = at last

tēlum, -ī, n. = missile, weapon, spear

tempestās, tempestātis, f. = a storm

templum, -ī, n. = temple

teneō, -ēre, tenuī, tentum = I hold

terra, -ae, f. = land, earth

terreō, -ēre, -uī, -itum = I terrify, frighten

tertius, -a, -um = third

timeō, -ēre, -uī = I fear

tōtus, -a, -um (goes like ūnus) = whole

trādō, -ere, trādidī, trāditum = I hand over

trāns (+ acc.) = across

trānseō, -īre, -iī, -itum (goes like eō) = I go across

tredecim = thirteen

trēs, tria = three

trīgintā = thirty

trīstis, trīste = sad, gloomy

tū = you (singular)

tum = then (next), at that time

turba, -ae, f. = crowd

tūtus, -a, -um = safe

tuus, -a, -um = your (belonging to you (sing.))

ubi = when

ubi? = where?

unda, -ae, f. = wave

ūndecim = eleven

ūndēvīgintī = nineteen

ūnus, -a, -um (gen. sing.: ūnīus, dat. sing.: ūnī) = one, only one

urbs, urbis, f. = city

ut (+ subj.) = in order to, in order that, to

uxor, -ōris, f. = wife

validus, -a, -um = strong

veniō, -īre, vēnī, ventum = I come

ventus, -ī, m. = wind

verbum, -ī, n. = word

vester, vestra, vestrum = your (belonging to you (pl.))

via, -ae, f. = road, street, way

videō, -ēre, vīdī, vīsum = I see

vīgintī = twenty

vincō, -ere, vīcī, victum = I conquer

vīnum, -ī, n. = wine

vir, virī, m. = man (as opposed to woman)

virtūs, virtūtis, f. = courage

vīvus, -a, -um = alive

vocō, -āre, -āvī, -ātum = I call

volō, velle, voluī (irreg.) = I want, wish

vōs = you (plural)

vōx, vōcis, f. = voice

vulnerō, -āre, -āvī, -ātum = I wound

vulnus, vulneris, n. = wound

Vocabulary: English-Latin

Able, I am = possum, posse, potuī (irreg.)
About = dē (+ abl.)
Absent, I am = absum, abesse, āfuī (goes like sum)
Across = trāns (+ acc.)
Advance, I = prōgredior, prōgredī, prōgressus sum
Advise, I = moneō, -ēre, -uī, -itum
Affair, matter = rēs, reī, f.
After (conjunction) = postquam
After (preposition) = post (+ acc.)
Afterwards = posteā
Again = iterum
Against = contrā (+ acc.)
Alive = vīvus, -a, -um
All, every = omnis, -e
Allow, I = patior, patī, passus sum
Ally = socius, -iī, m.
Almost = paene
Alone = sōlus, -a, -um (goes like ūnus)
Along = per (+ acc.)
Already = iam
Also = etiam; quoque (comes after the word it is emphasising)
Although = quamquam
Always = semper
Am, I = sum, esse, fuī (irreg.)
Among = inter (+ acc.)
And = et; -que
Anger = īra, -ae, f.
Angry = īrātus, -a, -um
Animal = animal, animālis, n.
Announce, I = nūntiō, -āre, -āvī, -ātum
Approach, I = appropinquō, -āre, -āvī, -ātum (+ dat. or ad + acc.); adeō, -īre, adiī, aditum (compound of eō)
Army = exercitus, -ūs, m.
Around = circum (+ acc.)
Arrive, I = adveniō, -īre, advēnī, adventum (+ ad + acc.)
Arrow = sagitta, -ae, f.
Ask, I = rogō, -āre, -āvī, -ātum
At last = tandem
Attack (a town or city), I = oppugnō, -āre, -āvī, -ātum
Bad = malus, -a, -um
Badly = malĕ
Battle = proelium, -iī, n.
Bear, I = ferō, ferre, tulī, lātum (irreg.)
Beautiful = pulcher, pulchra, pulchrum
Because = quod, cum (+ plup. subj.)
Before, beforehand (adverb) = anteā
Before (conjunction) = antequam
Before (preposition) = ante (+ acc.)
Believe, I = crēdō, -ere, crēdidī, crēditum (+ dat.)
Best = optimus, -a, -um
Better = melior, melius

Between = inter (+ acc.)
Big = magnus, -a, -um
Body = corpus, -oris, n.
Bold = audāx, audācis
Book = liber, librī, m.
Both...and = et...et
Boy = puer, puerī, m.
Brave = fortis, -e
Bravely = fortiter
Bright = clārus, -a, -um
Bring, I = ferō, ferre, tulī, lātum (irreg.)
Brother = frāter, frātris, m.
Build, I = aedificō, -āre, -āvī, -ātum
But = sed
By chance = forte
By = ā, ab (+ abl.)
Call, I = vocō, -āre, -āvī, -ātum
Can, I = possum, posse, potuī (irreg.)
Capture, I = capiō, -ere, cēpī, captum
Carry, I = portō, -āre, -āvī, -ātum; ferō, ferre, tulī, lātum (irreg.)
Catch sight of, I = cōnspiciō, -ere, cōnspexī, cōnspectum
Chief = prīnceps, prīncipis, m.
Choose, I = legō, -ere, lēgī, lēctum
Citizen = cīvis, cīvis, c.
City = urbs, urbis, f.
Clan = gēns, gentis, f.
Clear = clārus, -a, -um
Collect, I = colligō, -ere, collēgī, collēctum
Come, I = veniō, -īre, vēnī, ventum
Command, I = imperō, -āre, -āvī, -ātum (+ dat.)
Companion = comes, comitis, c.
Conquer, I = vincō, -ere, vīcī, victum
Country (fatherland) = patria, -ae, f.
Courage = virtūs, virtūtis, f.
Crowd = turba, -ae, f.
Cruel = crūdēlis, -e
Cross, I = trānseō, -īre, -iī -itum (goes like eō)
Danger = perīculum, -ī, n.
Daughter = filia, -ae, f. (dat. and abl. pl.: filiābus)
Day = diēs, diēī, m. (A special or appointed day is usually feminine)
Dead = mortuus, -a, -um
Dear = cārus, -a, -um
Death = mors, mortis, f.
Decide, I = cōnstituō, -ere, cōnstituī, cōnstitūtum
Deep = altus, -a, -um
Defend, I = dēfendō, -ere, dēfendī, dēfēnsum
Delay = mōra, -ae, f.
Depart, I = discēdō, -ere, discessī, discessum
Desire, I = cupiō, -ere, -īvī, -ītum

Destroy, I = dēleō, dēlēre, dēlēvī, dēlētum

Die, I = morior, morī, mortuus sum; pereō, -īre, periī, peritum (goes like eō)

Difficult = difficilis, -e

Discover, I = inveniō, -īre, invēnī, inventum

Do not…! = nōlī / nōlīte (+ infin.)

Do, I = faciō, -ere, fēcī, factum

Down from = dē (+ abl.)

Drink, I = bibō, -ere, bibī

Drive, I = pellō, -ere, pepulī, pulsum

Earth = terra, -ae, f.

Easy = facilis, -e

Eat, I = cōnsūmō, -ere, cōnsūmpsī, cōnsūmptum

Eight = octō

Eighteen = duodēvīgintī

Eighth = octāvus, -a, -um

Eighty = octōgintā

Eleven = ūndecim

Emperor = prīnceps, prīncipis, m.

Encourage, I = hortor, -ārī, -ātus sum

Enemy = hostis, hostis, c. (usually used in plural)

Enter, I = intrō, -āre, -āvī, -ātum; ingredior, ingredī, ingressus sum; ineō, inīre, iniī, initum (goes like eō)

Escape, I = effugiō, -ere, effūgī (trans. and intrans.)

Even = etiam

Every = omnis, -e

Expect, I = exspectō, -āre, -āvī, -ātum

Faith = fidēs, -eī, f.

Family, clan = gēns, gentis, f.

Famous = clārus, -a, -um; nōtus, -a, -um

Farmer = agricola, -ae, m.

Father = pater, patris, m.

Fatherland = patria, -ae, f.

Fear, I = timeō, -ēre, -uī

Few = paucī, -ae, -a

Field = ager, agrī, m.

Fifteen = quīndecim

Fifth = quīntus, -a, -um

Fifty = quīnquāgintā

Fight, I = pugnō, -āre, -āvī, -ātum

Find, I = inveniō, -īre, invēnī, inventum

First = prīmus, -a, -um

Five = quīnque

Flee (from), I = fugiō, -ere, fūgī, fugitum (trans. and intrans.)

Follow, I = sequor, sequī, secūtus sum

Food = cibus, -ī, m.

For = nam

For a long time = diū (adverb)

Force, I = cōgō, -ere, coēgī, coāctum

Forces = cōpiae, -ārum, f. pl.

Fortunate = fēlīx, fēlīcis

Forty = quadrāgintā

Four = quattuor

Fourteen = quattuordecim

Fourth = quārtus, -a, -um

Free, I = līberō, -āre, -āvī, -ātum

Friend = amīcus, -ī, m.

Frighten, I = terreō, -ēre, -uī, -itum

From = ā, ab (+ abl.)

General = dux, ducis, c.

Gift = dōnum, -ī, n.

Girl = puella, -ae, f.

Give, I = dō, dāre, dedī, dătum

Gloomy = trīstis, -e

Go, I = eō, īre, iī (or īvī), itum (irreg.)

Go across, I = trānseō, -īre, -iī, -itum (goes like eō)

Go back, I = redeō, redīre, rediī, reditum (goes like eō)

Go forth, I = ēgredior, ēgredī, ēgressus sum

Go in, I = ineō, inīre, iniī, initum (goes like eō)

Go into, I = ingredior, ingredī, ingressus sum

Go out, I = exeō, exīre, exiī, exitum (goes like eō); ēgredior, ēgredī, ēgressus sum

God = deus, deī, m. (irreg.)

Goddess = dea, -ae, f. (dat. and abl. pl. = deābus)

Gold = aurum, -ī, n.

Good = bonus, -a, -um

Great = magnus, -a, -um

Greatly = magnopere

Greek = Graecus, -a, -um

Greet, I = salūtō, -āre, -āvī, -ātum

Guard, a = custōs, custōdis, c.

Guard, I = custōdiō, -īre, -īvī, -ītum

Hand = manus, -ūs, f.

Hand over, I = trādō, -ere, trādidī, trāditum

Happy = laetus, -a, -um

Harbour = portus, -ūs, m.

Have, I = habeō, -ēre, -uī, -itum

Hear, I = audiō, -īre, -īvī, -ītum

Help = auxilium, -iī, n.

Help, I = iuvō, iuvāre, iūvī, iūtum

Her (own) = suus, sua, suum

Here = hīc

Herself (reflexive) = sē

High = altus, -a, -um

Himself (reflexive) = sē

His (own) = suus, sua, suum

Hold, I = teneō, -ēre, tenuī, tentum

Home = domus, -ūs, f. (irreg.)

Hope = spēs, speī, f.

Horse = equus, equī, m.

Hour = hōra, -ae, f.

House, home = domus, -ūs, f. (irreg.)

However = tamen (not generally written first word in clause or sentence)

Huge = ingēns, ingentis

Hundred = centum

Hurry, I = festīnō, -āre, -āvī, -ātum; contendō, -ere, contendī, contentum

Husband = coniūnx, coniugis, m.

I = ego

Immediately = statim

In = in (+ abl.)

In front of = prō (+ abl.)

In order that = ut (+ subj.)
In order to = ut (+ subj.); in order not to = nē (+ subj.)
In vain = frūstrā
Inhabitant = incola, -ae, c.
Into = in (+ acc.)
Island = īnsula, -ae, f.
Its (own) = suus, sua, suum
Itself (reflexive) = sē
Journey = iter, itineris, n.
Kill, I = necō, necāre, necāvī, necātum; occīdō, -ere, occīdī, occīsum; interficiō, -ere, interfēcī, interfectum
King = rēx, rēgis, m.
Labour = labor, -ōris, m.
Land = terra, -ae, f.
Laugh, I = rīdeō, -ēre, rīsī, rīsum
Lead, I = dūcō, -ere, dūxī, ductum
Lead back, I = redūcō, -ere, redūxī, reductum
Leader = dux, ducis, c.
Leave (trans.), I = relinquō, -ere, relīquī, relictum
Light = lūx, lūcis, f.
Like, I = amō, amāre, amāvī, amātum
Listen (to), I = audiō, -īre,-īvī, -ītum
Live (inhabit), I = habitō, -āre, -āvī, -ātum (+ acc. or in + abl.)
Long = longus, -a, -um
Lord = dominus, -ī, m.
Love, I = amō, amāre, amāvī, amātum
Lucky = fēlīx, fēlīcis
Maid-servant = ancilla, -ae, f.
Make, I = faciō, -ere, fēcī, factum
Man (as opposed to woman) = vir, virī, m.
Man (person) = homō, hominis, c.
Many = multī, -ae, -a
March, I = contendō, -ere, contendī, contentum
Master (lord) = dominus, -ī, m.
Master (teacher) = magister, magistrī, m.
Matter, affair = rēs, reī, f.
Meanwhile = intereā
Meet, I = conveniō, -īre, convēnī, conventum
Message = nūntius, nūntiī, m.
Messenger = nūntius, nūntiī, m.
Middle = medius, -a, -um
Miserable = miser, -era, -erum
Missile, weapon, spear = tēlum, -ī, n.
Money = pecūnia, -ae, f.
Moreover = autem (not written 1st word in clause or sentence)
Mother = māter, mātris, f.
Mountain = mōns, montis, m.
Move (trans.), I = moveō, -ēre, mōvī, mōtum
Much = multus, -a, -um
My = meus, -a, -um (voc. masc. sing.: mī)
Name = nōmen, nōminis, n.
Near = prope (+ acc.)
Neither, and...not = nec, neque
Never = numquam
New = novus, -a, -um

Night = nox, noctis, f.
Nine = novem
Nineteen = ūndēvīgintī
Ninety = nōnāgintā
Ninth = nōnus, -a, -um
No one = nēmō (irreg.)
Noble = nōbilis, -e
Nor = nec, neque
Not = nōn
Nothing = nihil
Now = nunc; iam
Occupy, I = occupō, -āre, -āvī, -ātum
Often = saepe
Old man = senex, senis, m.
On = in (+ abl.)
On account of = propter (+ acc.)
On behalf of = prō (+ abl.)
On to = in (+ acc.)
Once upon a time = ōlim
One = ūnus, -a, -um (gen. sing.: ūnīus, dat. sing.: ūnī)
Only (adj.) = sōlus, -a, -um (goes like ūnus)
Or = aut
Order, I = iubeō, -ēre, iussī, iussum; imperō, -āre, -āvī, -ātum (+ dat.)
Other (different) = alius, alia, aliud
Other (remaining) = cēterī, -ae, -a
Our = noster, nostra, nostrum
Out of = ex, ē (+ abl.); ē not used before vowel or h
Over = super (+ acc.)
Overcome, I = superō, -āre, -āvī, -ātum
Parent = parēns, parentis, c.
Part = pars, partis, f.
Persuade, I = persuādeō, -ēre, persuāsī, persuāsum (+ dat.)
Place, a = locus, -ī, m.
Place, I = pōnō, -ere, posuī, positum
Play, I = lūdō, -ere, lūsī, lūsum
Poet = poēta, -ae, m.
Praise, I = laudō, -āre, -āvī, -ātum
Prepare, I = parō, -āre, -āvī, -ātum
Present, I am = adsum, adesse, adfuī (goes like sum)
Prince = prīnceps, prīncipis, m.
Promise = fidēs, -eī, f.
Proud = superbus, -a, -um
Punish, I = pūniō, -īre, -īvī, -ītum
Queen = rēgīna, -ae, f.
Quick = celer, celeris, celere
Quickly = celeriter
Race, family, clan = gēns, gentis, f.
Really (in questions): use num (when expected answer is 'no')
Read, I = legō, -ere, lēgī, lēctum
Receive, I = accipiō, -ere, accēpī, acceptum
Remain, I = maneō, -ēre, mānsī, mānsum
Reply, I = respondeō, -ēre, respondī, respōnsum
Report, I = nūntiō, -āre, -āvī, -ātum
Reward = praemium, -iī, n.

River = flūmen, flūminis, n.
Road = via, -ae, f.
Roman = Rōmānus, -a, -um
Rule, I = regō, -ere, rēxī, rēctum
Run, I = currō, -ere, cucurrī, cursum
Rush, I = ruō, ruere, ruī, rutum
Sacred = sacer, sacra, sacrum
Sad = trīstis, trīste
Safe = tūtus, -a, -um
Sail, I = nāvigō, -āre, -āvī, -ātum
Sailor = nauta, -ae, m.
Same = īdem, eadem, idem
Savage = saevus, -a, -um
Save, I = servō, -āre, -āvī, -ātum
Say, I = dīcō, dīcere, dīxī, dictum
Sea = mare, maris, n.
Second = secundus, -a, -um
See, I = videō, -ēre, vīdī, vīsum
Seek, I = petō, -ere, petīvī, petītum
Seize, I = occupō, -āre, -āvī, -ātum
Self = ipse, ipsa, ipsum
Send, I = mittō, -ere, mīsī, missum
Set out (on a journey), I = proficīscor, proficīscī,
    profectus sum
Seven = septem
Seventeen = septendecim
Seventh = septimus, -a, -um
Seventy = septuāgintā
Shield = scūtum, -ī, n.
Ship = nāvis, nāvis, f. (abl. sing.: nāvī or nāve)
Shout, a = clāmor, -ōris, m.
Shout, I = clāmō, -āre, -āvī, -ātum
Show, I = ostendō, -ere, ostendī, ostentum / ostēnsum
Sing, I = cantō, -āre, -āvī, -ātum
Sister = soror, -ōris, f.
Six = sex
Sixteen = sēdecim
Sixth = sextus, -a, -um
Sixty = sexāgintā
Sky = caelum, -ī, n.
Slave = servus, -ī, m.
Sleep = somnus, -ī, m.
Sleep, I = dormiō, -īre, -īvī, -ītum
Slowly = lentē
Small = parvus, -a, -um
Smile, I = rīdeō, -ēre, rīsī, rīsum
Soldier = mīles, mīlitis, c.
Son = filius, filiī (voc. filī), m.
Soon = mox
Speak, I = loquor, loquī, locūtus sum
Spear = hasta, -ae, f.
Stand, I = stō, stāre, stetī, stătum
State (country) = rēs pūblica, reī pūblicae, f.
Stay, I = maneō, -ēre, mānsī, mānsum
Step = gradus, -ūs, m.
Storm = tempestās, tempestātis, f.
Street = via, -ae, f.

Strong = validus, -a, -um
Suddenly = subitō
Suffer, I = patior, patī, passus sum
Surely… = nōnne? (introduces a question expecting the
    answer 'yes')
Surely…not = num? (introduces a question expecting
    the answer 'no')
Swift, quick = celer, celeris, celere
Sword = gladius, gladiī, m.
Take, capture, I = capiō, -ere, cēpī, captum
Task = opus, operis, n.
Teacher = magister, magistrī, m.
Tell, I = nārrō, -āre, -āvī, -ātum
Temple = templum, -ī, n.
Ten = decem
Tenth = decimus, -a, -um
Terrified = perterritus, -a, -um
Terrify, I = terreō, -ēre, -uī, -itum
Than = quam
That = ille, illa, illud; is, ea, id
Their (own) = suus, sua, suum
Themselves (reflexive) = sē
Then (at that time) = tum
Then (next) = deinde, tum
There = ibi
Therefore = itaque; igitur (not generally written 1st
    word in clause or sentence)
Thing = rēs, reī, f.
Third = tertius, -a, -um
Thirteen = tredecim
Thirty = trīgintā
This = hic, haec, hoc
Though (although) = quamquam
Thousand = mīlle
Three = trēs, tria
Through = per (+ acc.)
Throw, I = iaciō, -ere, iēcī, iactum
Thus = sīc
Tired = fessus, -a, -um
To (towards) = ad (+ acc.)
Today = hodiē
Tomorrow = crās
Towards = ad (+ acc.)
Town = oppidum, -ī, n.
Trust = fidēs, -eī, f.
Try, I = cōnor, -ārī, -ātus sum
Twelve = duodecim
Twenty = vīgintī
Two = duo, duae, duo
Under = sub (+ abl.)
Urge, I = hortor, -ārī, -ātus sum
Voice = vōx, vōcis, f.
Wage (a war), I = gerō, -ere, gessī, gestum
Wait for, I = exspectō, -āre, -āvī, -ātum
Walk, I = ambulō, -āre, -āvī, -ātum
Wall = mūrus, -ī, m.
Wander, I = errō, -āre, -āvī, -ātum

Want, I = cupiō, -ere, -īvī, -ītum; volō, velle, voluī (irreg.)
Want, I do not = nōlō, nōlle, nōluī (irreg.)
War = bellum, -ī, n.
Warn, I = moneō, -ēre, -uī, -itum
Watch, I = spectō, -āre, -āvī, -ātum
Water = aqua, -ae, f.
Wave = unda, -ae, f.
Way = via, -ae, f.
We = nōs
Weapons = arma, -ōrum, n. pl.
Wear, I = gerō, -ere, gessī, gestum
Well = bene
Well-known = nōtus, -a, -um
What? = quid?
When = ubi; cum (+ plup. subj.)
Where? = ubi?
While = dum; cum (+ imp. subj.)
Who, which = quī, quae, quod
Who? = quis?
Whole = tōtus, -a, -um (goes like ūnus)
Why? = cūr?
Wicked = malus, -a, -um
Wife = uxor, -ōris, f.; coniūnx, coniugis, f.
Wind = ventus, -ī, m.

Wine = vīnum, -ī, n.
Wise = sapiēns, sapientis
Wish, I = cupiō, -ere, -īvī, -ītum; volō, velle, voluī (irreg.)
Wish, I do not = nōlō, nōlle, nōluī (irreg.)
With (together with) = cum (+ abl.)
Without = sine (+ abl.)
Woman = fēmina, -ae, f.; mulier, mulieris, f.
Word = verbum, -ī, n.
Work = labor, -ōris, m.; opus, operis, n
Work, I = labōrō, -āre, -āvī, -ātum
Worse = peior, peius
Worst = pessimus, -a, -um
Wound, a = vulnus, vulneris, n.
Wound, I = vulnerō, -āre, -āvī, -ātum
Wretched = miser, -era, -erum
Write, I = scrībō, -ere, scrīpsī, scrīptum
Year = annus, -ī, m.
Yesterday = herī
You (plural) = vōs
You (sing.) = tū
Young man = iuvenis, iuvenis, m.
Your, belonging to you (pl.) = vester, vestra, vestrum
Your, belonging to you (sing.) = tuus, -a, -um
Youth, a = iuvenis, iuvenis, m.